AFRICA IN THE NEW MILLENNIUM

About this series

The books in this new series are an initiative by CODESRIA, the Council for the Development of Social Science Research in Africa, to encourage African scholarship relevant to the multiple intellectual, policy and practical problems and opportunities confronting the African continent in the twenty-first century.

Publishers: CODESRIA in association with Zed Books

Titles in the series

African Intellectuals: Rethinking Politics, Language, Gender and Development *edited by Thandika Mkandawire* (2005)

Africa and Development Challenges in the New Millennium: The NEPAD Debate *edited by J. O. Adesina, A. Olukoshi and Yao Graham* (2005)

Urban Africa: Changing Contours of Survival in the City *edited by A.M. Simone and A. Abouhani* (2005)

Liberal Democracy and Its Critics in Africa: Political Dysfunction and the Struggle for Social Progress *edited by Tukumbi Lumumba-Kasongo* (2005)

Negotiating Modernity: Africa's Ambivalent Experience *edited by Elísio Salvado Macamo* (2005)

Insiders and Outsiders: Citizenship and Xenophobia in Contemporary Southern Africa *Francis B. Nyamnjoh* (2006)

About CODESRIA

The Council for the Development of Social Science Research in Africa (CODESRIA) is an independent organization whose principal objectives are facilitating research, promoting research-based publishing and creating multiple forums geared towards the exchange of views and information among African researchers. It challenges the fragmentation of research through the creation of thematic research networks that cut across linguistic and regional boundaries.

CODESRIA publishes the quarterly journal *Africa Development*, the longest standing Africa-based social science journal; *Afrika Zamani*, a journal of history; the *African Sociological Review*; *African Journal of International Affairs* (AJIA); *Africa Review of Books*; and *Identity, Culture and Politics: An Afro-Asian Dialogue*. It co-publishes the *Journal of Higher Education in Africa* and *Africa Media Review*. Research results and other activities of the institution are disseminated through Working Papers, Monograph Series, CODESRIA Book Series, and the *CODESRIA Bulletin*.

Negotiating Modernity

Africa's Ambivalent Experience

---

edited by Elísio Salvado Macamo

CODESRIA BOOKS
Dakar

in association with

ZED BOOKS
London & New York

UNIVERSITY OF SOUTH AFRICA PRESS
Pretoria

Negotiating Modernity was first published in 2005
by Zed Books Ltd, 7 Cynthia Street, London N1 9JF, UK,
and Room 400, 175 Fifth Avenue, New York, NY 10010, USA
www.zedbooks.co.uk

and in South Africa by UNISA Press, PO Box 392, Pretoria RSA 0003
www.unisa.ac.za

in association with

CODESRIA, Avenue Cheikh Anta Diop,
X Canal IV, BP3304, Dakar, 18524 Senegal
www.codesria.org

CODESRIA would like to express its gratitude to the Swedish International
Development Cooperation Agency (SIDA/SAREC), the International
Development Research Centre (IDRC), Ford Foundation, MacArthur
Foundation, Carnegie Corporation, the Norwegian Ministry of Foreign Affairs,
the Danish Agency for International Development (DANIDA), the French
Ministry of Cooperation, the United Nations Development Programme
(UNDP), the Netherlands Ministry of Foreign Affairs, Rockefeller Foundation,
FINIDA, NORAD, CIDA, IIEP/ADEA, OECD, IFS, OXFAM America,
UN/UNICEF and the Government of Senegal for supporting its research,
training and publication programmes.

Designed and typeset in Monotype Bembo by illuminati, Grosmont
www.illuminatibooks.co.uk
Cover designed by Andrew Corbett
Printed and bound in the EU by Gutenberg Press, Malta

Distributed in the USA exclusively by Palgrave Macmillan,
a division of St Martin's Press, LLC, 175 Fifth Avenue, New York, NY 10010

A catalogue record for this book is available from the British Library
Library of Congress Cataloging-in-Publication Data available

CODESRIA ISBN 2 86978 147 4

ISBN 1 84277 616 9 (Hb)
ISBN 1 84277 617 7 (Pb)

Contents

PART II   ...to Globalization

Acknowledgements

I wish to thank Francis Nyamnjoh, Director of Publications at CODESRIA, for inviting me to edit this volume. I extend the thanks to his staff, particularly to Josiane Iyabo Chifaou for organizing the contacts with contributors. I am also grateful to Zed Books, particularly to Robert Molteno, and to Lucy Morton, for their diligence. Dieter Neubert, of the University of Bayreuth, gave me useful insights into how to structure the volume. I am very grateful to him and to his intellectual support over the past five years. I discussed various titles with Andrea Jöckel and I am very grateful to her for taking the time. My appreciation goes to the contributors for their prompt response at very short notice. My family has been an important source of support over the years. The authors and I take full responsibility for the contents of this volume.

INTRODUCTION

Negotiating Modernity: From Colonialism to Globalization

Elísio Macamo

There is something ambivalent about the experience of modernity in Africa. A sense of this ambivalence is captured by the predicament of African Christian converts reported by Alda Saúte in this volume. Indeed, Christianity was to a large extent an essential element of the colonial project. Africans were brought under colonial rule also on behalf of Christianity, as this religion was seen not only as representative of the kind of European civilization Africans were expected to adopt but also as the standard against which their humanity could be measured. In other words, not to be a Christian or failure to convert marked the difference between being European or not being European. As non-Christian, one became *hors de catégorie* and, as such, any violation of one's human dignity could become acceptable. Becoming a Christian, therefore, played into the hands of the colonial project. To put it differently, Africans who converted were in certain very important respects denying themselves and their culture. And yet Christianity was for most the beginning of their emancipation from the colonial project. Through its agency, again as shown by Alda Saúte, Africans were able to carve a space for themselves and find a language to articulate their unease not only with the system but also with their predicament.

Various chapters in this volume bring this ambivalence to the fore. Elísio Macamo, for instance, shows how the regulation of native labour by Portuguese colonial authorities in Mozambique was a way of denying modernity to Africans and how, through the agency of Christianity, the latter sought to recover a sense of self and community.

Armed with this sense, they were able to redefine their relationship both with the colonial authorities and with their own society. Teresa Cruz e Silva describes the impact of this conversion in a convincing manner in her book on the role of the Protestant Swiss Mission in Mozambique in the development of nationalism (2001). Cruz e Silva shows the extent to which specific elements of this Protestant Mission allowed African converts to restructure their social life and articulate their grievances against the Portuguese colonial state.

There have been many attempts by Africanist scholars to come to terms with colonialism and how it has shaped African social reality. These attempts can be situated on both sides of the concept of ambivalence. Indeed, while some have seen these attempts as a rejection of the modernity implied by colonialism, others have instead emphasized Africans' eagerness to join the promise of modernity entailed therein. The latter fall under the general category of modernization theories, which were particularly current in the period running from the early waves of independence in Africa all the way up to the 1970s. The former, in contrast, include a wide range of perspectives on the continent which stress Africans' ability to negotiate modernity on their own terms.

Modernization theories were generally upbeat about Africa's development. Much like Karl Marx's optimistic assessment of British colonialism in India (1978),[1] modernization theorists saw colonialism as a necessary stage in Africa's historical evolution. Their analytical framework gave pride of place to the tension between tradition and modernity. As far as the framework went, the challenge facing African societies consisted in overcoming tradition in order, thereby, to gain access to the benefits of modernity. Colonialism had introduced into Africa the value of wage labour, entrepreneurship, individualism and empathy (see Lerner 1964 for an early defence of this position). The absence of these values, in the view of modernization theorists, accounted for Africa's 'backwardness'. ⊥ Scotland

There are instances of colonial policy that represent this attitude very well. One such instance is described by Frederick Cooper, the American professor of African history, who in his book on decolonization analyses, among other things, the colonial preoccupation with the 'detribalized African' (1996: 168–70). As with almost everything else in colonial policy, this preoccupation was caught up in the contradictory nature of colonial intervention in African society. On the one hand, both French and British colonial establishments were in need of African labour sufficiently mobile, independent and autonomous to integrate into the world of capitalist labour markets. Yet they were wary of allowing Africans to lean too far out of the windows of their traditional society, not only because they would place demands on the system to treat them as citizens – and not as 'subjects', as Mamdani convincingly argues (1996) – but also because the idea of a primordial African society was functional to the reproduction needs of the colonial economic system.

Critiques of the kind of modernity purveyed by colonialism have tended to stress both African resistance to, as well as selective appropriation of, modernity. Jean and Joan Comaroff, for instance, have shown in their work that the seemingly irrational pattern of African social action over the past decades can be understood as a subtle critique of capitalism. In becoming deliberately unintelligible to the standard discourse of the social sciences, Africans have been resisting the conditions and terms of their integration into the world (Comaroff and Comaroff 1993; see also White 1993, 1995). A slightly different approach is taken by Jean-François Bayart (2000), who puts forward the idea that the encounter between Africans and Europeans has produced a specific logic within African social action. This logic is marked by a kind of instrumental action by Africans, which consists in seeking to take advantage of the chances and opportunities opened up by the continent's contacts with the rest of the world. He calls this 'extraversion', a concept which echoes some of the ideas suggested by the much older notion of 'rentier capitalism' as used by Marxist scholars in the past.

There is, therefore, an ambivalent moment in Africa's experience of modernity and colonialism. While in and by itself this finding does not present a radically new insight into Africa's constitution over the past decades, it does suggest an analytically useful angle from which to approach the continent from a social scientific perspective. Indeed, this ambivalence can be understood as a framework within which Africans negotiate their way into a world of their own making. In other words, Africans produce their own social reality in dialogue with modernity as they move from colonialism into a world defined by themselves and by what they do in their everyday life.

While colonialism provides the larger canvas against which the terms under which modernity is brought to Africans is viewed, it is modernity itself that Africans confront headlong. In this sense, therefore, it becomes extremely important to define the intimations of this modernity and the extent to which it plays a central role in the constitution of African social reality.

African Modernity

In social theory modernity is a hotly debated concept. Scholars differ widely as to whether it can be defined at all, and if so how, and which features should be considered. The more conservative attempts at a definition take an ethnocentric perspective and see modernity as a specific period in European history. It is believed to have ensued from the Enlightenment as the practical fulfilment of the emancipation of reason from the ties of medieval obscurantism and religious fanaticism. The ethnocentric element in this definition consists in the belief that there is something intrinsically European about the development of history connecting the Enlightenment back to the origins of Judeo-Christian and Hellenic culture. Hegel's philosophy of history (1959) is a case in point, particularly his much-quoted reluctance to contemplate the idea that the 'Spirit' may take hold of African imagination in its triumphal march through History.

One consequence of this idea of modernity was the insistence upon the view that modernity could only have occurred in Europe. A rather watered-down version of this is presented by Max Weber, the German sociologist, who locates the logic of capitalist development in European Protestantism (2002). While it might be arguable whether capitalism and modernity can be used interchangeably, the way Weber characterizes capitalism is consistent with the way in which modernity has tended to be described. Such features as a legal bureaucratic state, progressive entrepreneurship, belief in science as opposed to magic and religion, among others, are as typical of capitalism as they are of modernity. Weber, at any rate, did seem to use both concepts interchangeably, so much so that in his more pessimistic mood he believed them to be describing the process through which men were constructing their own subjection. He described modernity as an 'iron cage'. Theodor Adorno and Max Horkheimer's *Dialectic of Enlightenment* (1972) echoes some of these fears, particularly the introductory chapter equating the evolution of human history with Odysseus' travails.

Anthony Giddens, in *The Consequences of Modernity* (1990), makes a useful distinction between modernity and capitalism which, however, does not go far enough in differentiating the one from the other. In fact, what he sees as the aftermath of modernity – namely the use of symbolic tokens to express new social relationships and practices across time and space – is precisely what most would describe as the main features of capitalism, including Giddens himself (see Giddens 1979). Still, the distinction is useful because it takes us away from the sterile discussion about the origins of modernity, and rather draws our attention to how different societies come to terms with the passing of traditional society, or, at any rate, how different societies deal with the world as it is offered to them.

The more recent debates on modernity seem to be structured around these issues. They define modernity in terms of how different societies and cultures change as they come into contact with one another (see Lepenies 2003 for a useful introduction), with the spirit of capitalism and an ever-encroaching scientific rationality. In a special issue of *Daedalus*, the journal of the American Academy of Sciences (2000), there are several articles which come to the conclusion that it is more appropriate to think in terms of multiple modernities as against a single, Western and all-conquering singular modernity. Here modernity is understood as an immanent phenomenon that can be, and indeed is, shaped differently in specific contexts. In a way, then, what is important about modernity is not what it looks like, or should look like, but rather how it is differently experienced and the implications thereof to social theory.

In the same issue of *Daedalus* there is an approach to modernity by Björn Wittrock (2000) which offers useful insights into ways of accounting for the experience of modernity. Wittrock finds it less interesting to establish whether there is any European society that in its institutional patterns can be adequately described as modern (Wittrock 2000: 36), and rather more interesting to track down the basic cultural and institutional impulses that led to the formation of modernity. In his analytical quest he suggests that such impulses posited modernity as a series of promissory notes that challenged individuals and communities to reach out for culturally and histori- cally elaborated goals. In other words, Wittrock appears to assume that modernity can be understood as an immanent condition that structures social action in ways significantly different from previous epochs.

In his discussion of the notion of promissory notes, Wittrock iden- tifies a number of conditions which must be met for the institutional projects of modernity – for example, a democratic nation-state, a liberal market economy or a research-oriented university (Wittrock 2000: 36) – to be realized. It is beyond the scope of our discussion to present these conditions here. Suffice it to say that they refer to the implications which new assumptions about human beings, their rights and agency have upon social action and how thereby new affiliations, identities and institutional realities are constituted (Wittrock 2000: 37). As Wittrock puts it,

> modernity may be understood as culturally constituted and institutionally entrenched. Promissory notes may serve as generalized reference points in debates and political confrontations. However, these generalized reference points not only become focal points in ideational confrontations; they also provide structuring principles behind the formation of new institutions. (Wittrock 2000: 38)

I have argued elsewhere (Macamo 1999) that Africa is a modern construct. This claim is based on the premiss that the awareness of an African cultural identity that can lay claims to a single political and economic destiny was the result of a discursive and practical confrontation with existential conditions brought to the continent by its forced integration into European historicity. In other words, it was in the process of coming to terms with slavery and colonialism that a specific kind of African identity was constituted. This identity drew from the experience of slavery and colonialism to argue for the unity of race (see Appiah, 1992 for a critique of this), the common cultural roots that had brought about the suffering and the community of fate that followed from the realization of a common African destiny. Returned slaves from America were very instrumental in this, just as, later, pan-Africanist activists, nationalists and philosophers became as they wrestled with their own existential condition.

The argument was originally meant to counter some trends in African critiques of the European influence on the continent. These critiques appeared self-defeating in their outcomes. While they rightly pointed to the overbearing presence of Europe in the conditions of possibility of both an African reality and critique of European presence, they took their outrage too far by stripping Africans of any agency in the whole process. V.Y. Mudimbe's deservedly celebrated *The Invention of Africa* (1988) provides a good illustration of this. Much in line with Said's (1978) deconstruction of the 'Orient', Mudimbe argued that the European power of representation had led to the construction of a notion of Africa which did not necessarily represent reality on the ground. In fact, what individuals came to do and think actually perverted that reality as African social reality became a function of the European will to power. I understood Mudimbe to be suggesting that our idea of Africa was false because it was a European representation and, even more importantly, to be claiming that given the nature of power relations it might be difficult to recover genuinely African discourses about Africa. As he pointed out in an earlier work, paraphrasing Foucault's discussion of Hegel,

> So far as Africa is concerned, truly emancipating itself from the West means the ability to appreciate thoroughly how much it costs to detach itself from it; it means knowing the extent to which the West, perhaps in an insidious manner, came closer to us; it means knowing within the framework of that which allows us to think against the West what is still Western; and measuring how our revolt against it is perhaps a ruse which it poses against us and at the end of which it is awaiting us, still and distant.... The West which constricts us in this manner could suffocate us. Therefore, in Africa we must put to use a rigorous understanding of the present modalities of our integration into the myths of the West, but also explicit issues which might allow us to be openly critical towards this 'body'. (Mudimbe 1982: 12–13, trans. EM)

A commitment to history as the setting within which social reality is constituted stands in the way of an uncritical acceptance of Mudimbe's claims. To agree with him on this score would mean, in effect, denying Africans any original role in the constitution of their own social reality and, perhaps more crucially, promoting an essentialist view of reality. It appeared to me more useful to assume that real Africa was the very outcome of what people, both 'African'[2] and non-African, did within the endless flux of history. The argument to the effect that Africa is a modern construct was based on the study of the philosophical debate around the issue of whether there is an African philosophy. The study found out that the debate could only be understood within the framework of attempts by individuals to negotiate their way into a world made strange by the presence of strangers. To put it differently, the sociology of knowledge of the debate over the existence of an African philosophy suggested that the central issue therein was the definition of an African space and identity. This was done in dialogue – a dialogue at times violent – with colonialism, which had brought to Africa the promissory notes that Björn Wittrock identifies with the immanence of modernity.

In this sense, the debate owed as much to colonialism as to how Africans reacted to it. Starting with the returning slaves, who interpreted their predicament as God's 'providence' meant to make them the harbingers of the emancipation of their 'promised land', continuing with the Pan-Africanist demand for self-determination all the way through to *négritude*'s and ethnophilosophy's elaboration of an African essence, Africans were responding to the challenge of colonialism by reaching out to the promises which colonial practice denied them: human dignity, emancipation and progress.

The African experience of modernity is ambivalent precisely in this sense. Colonialism was the historical form through which modernity became a real social project on the African continent. Colonialism, however, was premissed on the denial of that same modernity to Africans. Since the onset of colonialism, African social experience has been structured by the ambivalence of promise and denial that is so constitutive of colonialism and, indeed, as we move into what some call a global era, of globalization. My claim is that for social theory to be relevant to Africa it must be able to offer concepts that can adequately describe and analyse this ambivalence.

Negotiating Modernity

One such concept is 'negotiation' which seeks to render African social experience historically coherent. The chapters that make up this volume bear witness to its descriptive and analytical potential. The presentation is structured in such a way as to establish a continuum between colonialism and globalization. The aim is to show on the basis of selected aspects of Africans' social experience over a period spanning a century, how individuals and communities within the continent have wrestled with the promise of modernity. The aspects addressed by the chapters include the role of the African diaspora in positing Africa as a *sui generis* category, conversion to Christianity by migrant labourers, the regulation of native labour in a colonial setting, African migration to the North, coping with war and natural disasters, land issues and the settlement of ensuing disputes, as well as the politics of protecting refugees.

The chapters are grouped into two parts which take into account the storyline of a continuous trajectory from colonialism to globalization. Those in the first part concentrate on African responses to slavery and colonialism. They tell the story of the kinds of promises Africans were able to make out from colonialism. The story begins with Jalani Niaah's account of the 'Back to Africa Movement' inspired by the work of Marcus Garvey. He starts by reminding Africa that if it chooses to forget its older Caribbean diaspora, the Back to Africa Movement of Jamaica will not forget it. The island people of Jamaica have emerged with a reputation as one of the 'loudest Pan African voices'. This, as Niaah shows in his contribution, is attributable to the work of persons such as Marcus Garvey, who was to ignite an awakening of African pride, especially in the Americas. Garvey's most lasting legacy, however, would take onto itself the characteristics of a new world religion, as his groundwork was ultimately to lead a marginal and downtrodden people to reverence the emergence of the Ethiopian emperor Haile Selassie as the harbinger of African redemption. These people now known to the world as the Rastafarians have been grossly misunderstood, especially as a contributing force to the liberation and redevelopment of Africa, as they hold their historical right of African ancestry as inviolable and consequently are often perceived as fanatical with regard to matters concerning the continent. After almost four hundred years in some instances, the children of Garvey are still presenting a potent critique of the Caribbean Columbian American project, especially the notion of acceptance of the ideals of modernity as fashioned by colonial and postcolonial North Atlantic agendas. The issues brought into focus by Niaah's chapter concern Africa's past and future – that is, the issue of leadership of a 'leaderless' population claiming Africa, Ethiopia and its sovereign emperor, Haile Selassie, as father of these 'conscious' scattered children and the iconic image of pan-Africanism. All of this is viewed as a part of the reclamation of African sensibilities and the refashioning of a 'collective esteem' as part and parcel of an active revising and revisioning of a progressive future for Africans, both at home and abroad.

A similar line of argument is pursued by Cassandra Veney in her chapter on the continuing links between the African-American diaspora and Africa. Veney argues that the original, historical diaspora in the USA retained linkages to the African continent despite the political, economic and social position that slavery and its legacy produced. Although this population was first enslaved, given a brief period to enjoy basic citizenship rights, disenfranchised, and won citizenship rights after many years of battling against lynching, beatings, poll taxes, and Jim Crow laws, the ties that linked them to Africa were not severed. Starting with a historical and contemporary overview of the linkages that the African diaspora in the USA maintained with Africa, Veney seeks to explain the role these linkages have and asks whether they could contribute towards solving Africa's brain drain problem. The historical overview is important because it illustrates that in the absence of political and citizenship rights, African Americans were in the forefront in fighting for these rights for Africans and in uncovering the hypocrisy of Europe's civilizing mission. With the improved political, educational, economic and social status of the African diaspora in the USA, its role in promoting African interests has expanded and improved. Finally, with modern communications and technology, the African-American community has global influence and visibility that benefit Africa. Veney's chapter illustrates the historical nature of social reality and shows the extent to which African social reality is constituted at the intersection of promise and denial.

Elísio Macamo takes up the problem of promise and denial. He draws attention to the central contradiction of colonialism and how, paradoxically, it opened up new possibilities for individual Africans. The regulation of native labour in colonial Mozambique was the privileged way Portuguese colonial policymakers chose to erect and establish their domination over African societies. The regulation of native labour was premissed on the twin ideas that, on the one hand, the proper fulfilment of the European civilizing mission depended upon a vigorous policy of making Africans work, and, on the other, that Africans needed Portuguese firm guidance into the world of wage labour. In effect, however, Portuguese tutelage claims over Africans effectively prevented Africans from fully integrating into the world of wage labour, amounting to a denial of the modernity promised by such a policy. Most of the chapter explores this contradiction and takes a brief look at its impact on politics in the postcolonial period.

Alda Saúte argues in the same vein. Her chapter examines the manifold ways that Mozambican migrant miners encountered and explored Christianity in all its complexity, interpreted it in their own cultural and historical contexts, and appropriated it as their own, forging in the process Christian congregations. By exploring the experiences of returning Mozambican miners from South Africa, Saúte contends that the Word of God, the Gospel and literacy in

Southern Mozambique, especially in the Maciene district, neither came from the sea with 'civilization' brought by big ships, nor was brought by European mission stations through catechists. Indeed, it was spread by returning Mozambican miner converts at their own initiative. By exploring the experiences of former miners in their relationship to the missionaries using both written sources as well as miners' own accounts, Saúte brings to light the ingenuity of Africans in dealing with what was new. Her study demonstrates that without training or commission by the missionaries, Mozambican miners were not only manifestly proclaiming Christianity and building Christian communities imbued with meaning within the context of their own values and experiences but also introducing literacy, multi-ethnic brotherhood, European notions of space and working days, clothing, agricultural instruments and new ways of building houses. They became, ironically, agents of a modernization denied to them by the colonial system. Their biggest impact, in this connection, was in the countryside.

The second group of chapters discuss aspects of the legacy of colonialism as they impinge on Africa's postcolonial situation. These include migration movements, natural and man-made disasters as well as land issues and refugees. While African social reality cannot be reduced to these phenomena, they do represent some of the major constraints individual Africans face as they structure their everyday lives. What gives them a new quality is the fact that they take place under the conditions of globalization. A number of scholars have expressed misgivings as to the usefulness of the notion of globalization (see, e.g., Cooper 2001). For our purposes in this volume it appears enough to subsume under globalization the current international political, economic and social environment as it impacts on Africa. Much like in the colonial period, Africans are constrained by external forces in the choices they make, the practical actions they take and the visions they have. They have to define a space and time of their own within the constraints placed on them by these forces.

It is within this framework that we can read Francis Njubi Nesbitt's chapter. It deals with the problems posed by mobility, especially of those who are highly qualified. Nesbitt argues that stakeholders such as governments, development agencies and universities need to come to terms with the reality of brain mobility in the era of globalization and learn how to harness the intellectual, material and financial capital of the African diaspora that is embedded in the North. He sees the challenge as being located in the move from brain drain to brain gain as these itinerant intellectuals seek the best resources and conditions for the reproduction of knowledge. This shift from drain to gain has ample precedence in the historical African diaspora which has long sought to influence US Africa policy. Nesbitt establishes a parallel with two historical case studies of African diaspora politics (abolitionism and the anti-apartheid movement) and one contemporary movement (reparations) and seeks to show how both the old and new African diasporas have successfully influenced bilateral and multilateral policies in the North. He argues that these historical precedents should serve as models for future efforts to represent Africa at the table of global trade and governance. His chapter ends with recommendations that governments, civic organizations and institutions of higher education should consider if they are interested in creating policy frameworks that make it easier for the diaspora to contribute to Africa's development.

Inês Raimundo builds on and contributes to the work on internal migration in Mozambique and raises issues which bear on relief and development work, two major external factors in the constitution of African social reality. Since the signing of the General Peace Agreement between FRELIMO and RENAMO in the early 1990s, migration has become a crucial factor in weighing options on the resettlement of former refugees. Raimundo points out that over the last decade it has become clear that it is not only refugees who seem to be resettling. Other segments of the population appear to be leaving their homesteads in rural areas for different reasons and converging on the cities. They are not beaconed by city lights as modernization theories used to argue, but rather they move from areas of low opportunity to the areas of high opportunity such as Maputo, the capital city of Mozambique. They take advantage of the spread of means of transportation to the most remote rural areas and, of course, of peace to become mobile, both internally and externally. Of direct relevance to our frame of analysis, Raimundo remarks that the increase in population mobility is not due solely to hazardous conditions and political reasons, but also to the degree of regional, national and international inequalities in economic opportunities. These have opened up opportunities for national and international movements and Africans are seizing them. In so doing Africans may even be pioneering an international trend, and thus anticipating what some have argued to be the final outcome of globalization processes, namely that we all acquire the status of migrants.

Samwel Okuro depicts various ambivalences that key agrarian players, particularly in Kombewa division of western Kenya, have faced as they continue to experiment with colonial institutions and values. Using land tribunals as an illustration, he seeks to bring to the fore the extent to which the postcolonial Kenyan government has struggled to negotiate and manage alien structures in land dispute resolution. Okuro notes that the precursor to all these was the British government's decision to turn Kenya, or the East African Protectorate, as it was then called, into a settlement colony. This necessitated the introduction of a land tenure system sympathetic to British settlers and modelled according to English Law. Okuro delves into this problematic in order to show how the postcolonial regime failed to break with the past. It is interesting to note that the types of land disputes experienced so far symbolize a clash between English law and the customary law. In attempting to negotiate the clash, the Kenyan government, with several setbacks, continues to establish policies, laws, and legal and/or paralegal systems for not only land ownership but also land dispute arbitration that can meet the test for legitimacy without losing control of the very process.

Finally, Ekuru Aukot discusses the legal and moral predicament of the African refugee issue in the era of globalization. He notes that the original notion of refugee protection, barely more than fifty years old, was idealistic. In time the much-celebrated history of law, policies and practice ceased to be in tune with contemporary changes, especially at the domestic level of most African nations and more profoundly in the new millennium. Consequently, the impact of global processes, particularly economic globalization, has changed the scenario. The refugee problem has become one aspect of a wider global process, resulting in complexities and dilemmas for developing countries which prevent them from pursuing an effective refugee protection. Ekuru Aukot emphasizes that refugee protection is a complex matter in the developing world and asks a series of questions, such as how the poor economies cope with refugee protection, whether globalization can be a remedy in itself and whether it can offer Africans ways of reforming the asylum regime. Aukot's analysis stresses the diminishing role of the traditional nation-state and considers how that greatly affects the protection of refugees and the enforcement of international refugee law and other legal instruments. The analysis raises a number of issues, chief among which is the question of whether refugee protection in Africa today can be realized under the conditions of globalization.

Conclusion

This volume brings together reflections on several aspects of African social reality which provide insights into the ambivalent experience of modernity in Africa. While the literature on modernity has tended to emphasize, on the one hand, modernity's alien nature in Africa and, on the other, the way in which Africans have resisted it, the volume seeks to show the extent to which this very tension has been constitutive of African social reality. In other words, modernity is understood as the basic impulse behind the constitution of African society over the past one hundred years. The issues that the contributions address in this connection are related to the ways in which, first, Africans negotiated the terms of this modernity during the colonial period and, second, how they are coming to terms with it in the postcolonial period. The chapters in the volume argue that the African experience of modernity is both unique and, at the same time, extremely relevant for social theory in general. It is not only important to describe this experience but also to acknowledge that such a description may provide African studies with valuable analytical insights into the constitution of African social reality.

Notes

1. See the two articles published in the *New York Daily Tribune*, 25 June and 8 August 1853.
2. I realize how problematic this adjective might be in the absence of a clarification of what is meant by the noun. In fact, I reserve it for those intellectuals from the continent who through their work and reflection participate in the definition of a local space that they label 'African'. An extreme version of this understanding of Africanness is constructivist in its elaboration and goes as far as to suggest that no one is born an African, as they become aware of belonging to a community of destiny.

References

Adorno, Theodor, and Max Horkheimer (1972) *Dialectic of Enlightenment*, London: Verso.

Appiah, K.A. (1992) *In My Father's House: Africa in the Philosophy of Culture*, London: Methuen.

Bayart, Jean-François (2000) 'Africa in the World: A History of Extraversion', in *African Affairs* 99: 217–67.

Behrend, H. (ed.) (1999) *Spirit Possession, Modernity and Power in Africa*, Oxford: James Currey.

Comaroff, J., and Comaroff, J. (eds) (1993) *Modernity and its Malcontents: Ritual and Power in Postcolonial Africa*, Chicago: Chicago University Press.

Cooper, Frederick (1996) *Decolonization and African Society: The Labour Question in French and British Africa*, Cambridge: Cambridge University Press.

Cooper, Frederick (2001) 'What is the Concept of Globalization Good For? An African Historian's Perspective', *African Affairs* 100: 189–213.

Cruz e Silva, Teresa (2001) *Protestant Churches and the Formation of Political Consciousness in Southern Mozambique (1930–1974)* Basle: Schlettwein.

Daedalus, (2000) 'Multiple Modernities', vol. 129, no. 1.

Giddens, Anthony (1979) *Capitalism and Modern Social Theory: An Analysis of the Writings of Marx, Durkheim and Max Weber*, Cambridge: Cambridge University Press.

Giddens, Anthony (1990) *The Consequences of Modernity*, Stanford: Stanford University Press.

Hegel, G.W.F. (1980) 'Introduction: Reason in History', *Lectures on the Philosophy of World History*, Cambridge: Cambridge University Press.

Lepenies, Wolf (ed.) (2003) *Entangled Histories and Negotiated Universals: Centers and Peripheries in a Changing World*, Frankfurt am Main: Campus Verlag.

Lerner, Daniel (1964) *The Passing of Traditional Society: Modernising the Middle East*, New York: Free Press of Glencoe.

Macamo, Elísio (1999) *Was ist Afrika? Zur Kultursoziologie eines modernen Konstrukts*, Berlin: Duncker & Humblot.

Mamdani, Mahmood (1996) *Citizen and Subject: Contemporary Africa and the Legacy of Late Colonialism*, Kampala: Fountain.

Marx, Karl (1978) 'On Imperialism in India', in Robert Tucker (ed.), *The Marx–Engels Reader*, New York: W.W. Norton, pp. 653–64.

Mudimbe, Valentin Y. (1982) *L'Odeur du Père: Essai sur les limites de la science et de la vie en Afrique Noire*, Paris: Présence Africaine.

• Mudimbe, V.Y. (1988) *The Invention of Africa: Gnosis, Philosophy and the Order of Knowledge*, London: James Currey.

Said, E.W. (1978): *Orientalism*, London: Routledge & Kegan Paul.

Weber, Max (1968): *Economy and Society: An Outline of Interpretive Sociology*, New York: Bedminster Press.

Weber, Max (2002) *The Protestant Ethic and the Spirit of Capitalism*, ed. Stephen Kalberg, Oxford: Blackwell.

White, Louise (1993) 'Vampire Priests of Central Africa: African Debates about Labor and Religion in Colonial Northern Zambia', *Comparative Studies in Society and History* 35: 746–72.

White, Louise (1995) 'Tsetse Visions: Narratives of Blood and Bugs in Colonial Northern Rhodesia, 1931–9', *Journal of African History* 36: 219–45.

Wittrock, B. (2000) 'Modernity: One, None, or Many? European Origins and Modernity as a Global Condition', *Daedalus*, vol. 129, no. 1: 31–60.

PART I

From Colonialism...

I

Absent Father(s), Garvey's Scattered Children and the Back to Africa Movement

Jalani A. Niaah

Returning to Ourselves:
Rastafari and the Project of Redemption

Tell the people to come home. Here their race originated and here it can be lifted to its highest plane of usefulness and honour. Assure them of the cordiality with which I invite them back to the homeland, particularly those qualified to help solve our big problem.

Message from His Highness Ras Tafari, 1922 Convention
(in Hill 1985: 1006)

In response to this message from Ethiopia many started to study the movements of the dynamic visionary prince, Ras Tafari. Amy Garvey was to publish the following year (1923) Marcus Garvey's rendition of a similar message, drawing on the biblical idea of Ethiopia stretching forth her hand:

Africa like a bereaved mother, holds out her hands to America, and implores you to send back her exiled children ... what a mystery, when the youthful patriarch, lost to his father, was sold into slavery.... Send them home instructed and civilized, imbued with the pure principles of Christianity. (Garvey 1986)

Whereas the idea of a return to Africa is not new, the approaches developed in the twentieth century are unique in their global reach and organizational logic. In particular, the approach of the Rastafarians stands out historically. His Imperial Majesty Haile Selassie in Ethiopia provided the first evidence of a *systematic embrace* by the African continent of members of the diaspora when, as Crown Prince, he sent a message to Africans in the West in 1922 instructing Marcus Garvey to tell the people to come 'Home to Africa' where they could serve their highest purpose. Garvey actively sought to advance this position in the West amid great adversity, as presented by the dominant white supremacists and an underdeveloped folk intellectual class. It was not until 1960, when Arthur Lewis became the first West Indian of African descent to hold the office of principal of the University College of the West Indies, that there was any evidence of West Indian academic interest in the issue of returning the captive children of Africa to Africa. Lewis wrote to the premier, Norman Manley, requesting urgent action on the part of the government to assist the Rastafari brethren in their struggle for human dignity and recognition. Thirty-eight years later, the vice-chancellor of the University of the West Indies, Rex Nettleford, in a keynote address to a conference celebrating the work of key Rastafarian elders, identified the Rastafarian movement as follows:

> Of all the people who have been fighting for Human Dignity, for Black Dignity, and justice to People of African ancestry the Rastafarians are the only ones who have made the kind of quantum leap that all civilization must make, in terms of determining its own God, its own image and this is a fantastic development and this of course is not usually understood. When we did the 'Report' in 1960, we were regarded as blasphemous. … They have lived to eat their words, thank God. (Nettleford 1999)

The culture of the movement has sustained millions who choose to identify with it. The words of Rastafari have literally created food for millions of people connected to the production and dissemination of the music of reggae. Human dignity, as expounded and articulated by international governments and non-governmental organizations, still eludes the majority of us African people. It is the Rastafarian movement that has pioneered its reinstatement. It is this contribution of the Rastafarians towards the securing of basic rights for Africans generally that Nettleford identifies as misunderstood. Mortimo Planno speaks of his basic human right to hold opinions by asserting that 'God allows us … to say all we do of Haile Selassie I.' Planno further provides a fitting context in which to engage with this new interpretation of God as a central part of the movement's claim, with his concept of 'a New Faculty of Interpretation':

Them say the pope, him infallible. We Rasta man say Haile Selassie is infallible – the pope is no King, this whole warfare is to protect the King – not to make Him checkmate that is our part of the whole [thing]. (Planno 1998)

Jamaican people often say that 'belief kill and belief cure'. At the heart of Planno's reasoning is the need to deconstruct this belief system now ingrained as a part of a Caribbean world-view. This world-view recognizes that people are socialized and governed so as to believe in Our Father, Our Lord Our God and Our King. The irony is, as Chevannes points out, that the activism around the preaching of God and his revelations could be viewed as madness, because people are socialized to believe that they cannot touch or feel God (Chevannes 2002). It is this belief system into which Planno immediately enters: that of the people and some of the accepted ideas by which they conduct their lives. He enters the realm of the mind when he presents this argument, his project being to overthrow slavish ideas. The presentation of *them* versus *we Rasta man* also is instructive as it helps to personalize the concept of the nature of our struggle as Africans in this warfare, which he identifies as perpetuated by the papacy in the Vatican. This belief system locates its ideas in its ability to see and discern for itself, and through this ability dismissing *them* and their belief in the infallible pope, while asserting that *we Rasta man* possess evidence of the promised Messiah in Emperor Haile Selassie I, the King of Kings. Planno provides a picturesque visual schema in which to understand the reality of the system under which Babylon holds its captives – the game of chess. With this metaphor, he illustrates the nature of the reality, the characters, the powers and principalities, role play and the experiences. Lastly he identifies *our* part in this game, that being 'to protect the King … not to make Him get checkmate'. The clear sentiment of Planno's thesis is that there is a system in place, an inevitable *them* against *we*. Haile Selassie is *we Rasta man*'s choice over the pope.

Rastafari has emerged as one of the most identifiable and highly visible characteristics of Jamaica and is seen as a mouthpiece of the African Liberation struggle in general. Horace Campbell (1994) identifies Rastafari as one of the most significant shapers of pan-African ideas. Despite its marginal status, Rastafari managed to sustain an evolving current of pan-African philosophy and praxis for much of the last century. In recent times a wealth of literature has developed seeking to track and record this world African resistance phenomenon. Many, including Ethiopians, find it difficult to understand the 'logic' of the Rastafari movement, especially as it defines 'our' roles, and in particular our 'place' in African society today. A key factor has been the failure to understand the logic of Rastafari philosophy centred on Ethiopia and its legendary priest king, manifested in the person of Emperor Haile Selassie I.

If the Bible is transposed onto existing reality, then it is apparent that the 'Rastafarian life' since heralding the King of Kings, has become a living testament to the prophecy of the coming of the Almighty Saviour God. To support this claim, elders such as Brother Planno, Bongo Watto Everald Brown, and Brother Shaggy – persons who use their lives to demonstrate the prophetic nature of experiencing the faith of Rastafari – become a necessary and compelling source for understanding some of the logic, perhaps even the inner logic, of the movement's Back to Africa aspiration. Their ideas and visions, represented through this movement, have assumed the character of a global institution for emancipation, developed by 'ordinary folk' to refashion the reality encountered in the world. This discourse is woven from the individual and collective testimonies of the Rastafari experience, through the facility of the Elders.

Exploration of Related Concepts

> How good and how pleasant it would be, before God and man,
>   yeah, to see the unification of all Africans yeah.
> As it's been said already, let it be done, yeah.
> We are the children of the Rasta man...
> we are the children of the higher man.
>
> Bob Marley, 'Africa Unite'

Patriarchs, or the founding elders of the movement, interpreting from Garvey's teachings on Africa, adopted the Amharic words *Ras Tafari* as new words for God. The following is an exploration of some terms as they relate to core ideas that have evolved in the movement.

Ras Tafari means 'head creator': 'head' defined as the position or locus of leadership, authority or honour – a person to whom others are subordinate, as to a leader or chief; 'creator' construed as the Almighty Father who brings all into being, the maker of the universe, God rendered as *Jah*. These two ideas embodied in the concept of Rastafari have come to be widely embraced globally as a foundation of the modern critique of colonialism and neocolonialism. This interpretation of the significance of the name Ras Tafari and its meaning is an important foundation – if not one of the core insights – of the Rastafarian faith, which holds the philosophy that word-sound is power. Emerging from the name Ras Tafari, a movement has emerged bearing this name. Rastafari identify this as fulfilment of the Revelation that states that God's name shall be in their foreheads (Rev. 22:4). To place an identity on the Rastafari movement, we once more look to Planno's experience where he talks of Rastafari as 'an organism'. It is, he says, 'a Movement not a "stayment"'.[1] He identifies the Rastafarian as the *Earth's Most Strangest Man*. With this description he aims to express a sense of the world he has seen professed and engaged in by those who identify themselves and are identified as Rastafarians. He further expounds:

> We are a visionary movement who believe in the religious aspect of His Majesty Haile Selassie being the returned Messiah. (The movement derives its name from Ras Tafari – Haile Selassie's name as a prince.) We got this belief from the direction of Marcus Garvey pointing the vision to us. (Planno 1979)

Peter Tosh defines Rastafari through some choice words: 'progress', 'love' and 'light' ('Honorary Citizen'). Crucial to the movement and those identified within it is a philosophy, a system of reasoning and understanding that Chevannes identifies as a gateway into critical thinking within the folk paradigm (Chevannes 2001b.). The Rastafari movement is therefore – for the purpose of this work – viewed as an 'African liberation' force, which emerged in Jamaica in 1928–32, concentrated around the leadership of Emperor Haile Selassie I. The movement comprises those 'ones' who hold claim to understand themselves as Ethiopians/Africans and strive to return to the African homeland. This is often, especially in the older literature, referred to as the Back to Africa Movement.[2]

The principle of repatriation within the cosmology of Rastafari covers a spectrum of ideas related to Back to Africa. It has taken on added significance and meaning especially since the granting of some land, Shashamanie, the proverbial Promised Land, by Emperor Haile Selassie as a reward to those who supported Ethiopia during the Italo-Ethiopian war of 1935–41. However, repatriation goes back to the earliest experience of African transplantation from the African continent – it is a part of Caribbean folk *marronage* philosophy. This is connected to an oral memory, African rooted, developed and espoused, by peoples who hold strong attachment to the land. Often the meaning of repatriation is interpreted to embody two elements, one spiritual, the other physical. What is underemphasized is that both have to operate in tandem and that the development of repatriation within Rastafari represents a strong actualization of that faith in the physical movement. The word 'repatriation' contains nuances of the idea of a 'return to the way of the father', which is perhaps the most familiar and therefore poignant reading of the concept. Such a reading affords us a deep insight into this way of the father.

The message sent by Haile Selassie to Marcus Garvey's 1922 convention aptly describes the essential thought surrounding the idea of repatriation. Haile Selassie immediately becomes in that gesture a fraternal anchor for Africans abroad. This invitation to the 'scattered Africans' was a huge point of engagement for populations that had been severed from their source for centuries. In the emerging social debate on 'decolonization', repatriation was seen by some as a repudiation of Jamaican statehood, which was then just coming into being. The prevailing attitude on the island can perhaps be best explained through Lindsay's *Myth* (1981), whereby the 'mother country' had so well constructed her 'institutions' as civilizing symbols that the colony's only ambition was to inherit the mantle and mandate of the alien mother. In this context neither Norman Manley nor Alexander Bustamante, the two mulattoes who were to lead and politicize the people's popular movements after the demise of Garvey, placed the issue of repatriation on the national agenda officially. Up to the present no government of Jamaica has done so. The state visit of Haile Selassie I to Jamaica in 1966 was therefore a powerful demonstration of the movement's visionary integrity and logic as it served to confirm the emperor's embrace of the brethren. Indeed the Rastafarian brethren contend that the '"polluticians" [politicians] are selling us out' for their own self-serving interests. Tekla Mekfet, a Rastafarian teacher, expounded on the concept of repatriation in an insightful way to the author of this chapter. Mekfet emphasized the meaning of repatriation as a 'Return to the *ways* of Father', pointing out that it is a consistent image and aspiration in history which is also evidenced in the Bible and interpretable in phenomena such as suicide among slaves during the colonial era. Between Lindsay and Mekfet there is a great void which needs attention. One might even say there is a breach which is in need of repair.[3] These white mother myths perpetuate the breach, thus preventing an understanding of this returning to the ways of the black father. The untended image is the implied orphan child, the colony/scattered African who can only be anchored externally, through its white European mother's myths or the hidden real but missing link of its black Ethiopian father.

The concept of 'teacher' is a reading of father offered as simple explanation for the key role played by the Rastafarian ideologues such as the early 'patriarchs' of the movement (Howell, Hinds, Hibbert and Dunkley). There are traces of the designation 'teacher' in the movement: Joseph Hibbert, for example, is still referred to by those who knew him as 'Teacher Hibbert'. This 'teacher' was invoked by the founding patriarch of the Rastafari movement, Leonard Howell, who described himself as 'Gangunguru Maragh', or teacher of famed wisdom, teacher of what is good (Hill 2001). The folk who followed him rendered this as 'the Gong' – as in to have awakening resonation.[4] Bob Marley, who emerged some forty years after the movement's formation, was to take on the title 'Tuff Gong' in continuation of this tradition of what one could call 'oral resonance'. He too could be viewed as a 'teacher' – perhaps one of the twentieth century's most outstanding teachers, teaching the illiterate millions of the liberation message. Marley's practice drew on a system of thinking and interpretation which was provided for him and others largely from the Rastafari movement, with Mortimo Planno and a few other key elder teachers constituting his closest circle.

What was the lesson taught by the elders? Planno, who has been connected with the university since its inception in 1948, describes himself as a 'Karmanic thinker'. He explains that he sat in council with Bob Marley 2000 years ago. The parallel with the image of Christ and the context of his experience in effecting the revolution from which Christianity emanated is conjured up in the imagination: Bob the son manifesting a work in honour of his spiritual father. It is this ability and even audacity possessed by the Rastafarian which was taught by the elders. It is the re-membering of the African Nation, the re-establishment of the familial network, that view of the most holy family in Africa, our father afore – Abba, who teaches all who may come how to live. 'Preaching' and teaching of the divinity of Haile Selassie are seen as embodiments of the core faith of this visionary movement. This is so because the emergence of this emperor is viewed as the fulfilment of the prophesies of repatriation/redemption. The two basic indicators (his divinity and Return to Africa) are important cornerstones of the movement's philosophy or attitude to life, the main ideas around which its teachers work. Key teachers are identified through their works, especially viewed through that of their students. The teachers are seen as repairers of the breach caused by 'head decay shun'. The Rastafarian teacher is therefore perceived as the transformer activist, creator, server/social saviour, constituting a revolutionary nexus in communities on a continuum of self-empowerment and change. The teacher is the creator of the revolution of culture, a basic ingredient in the methodology of mental liberation. Through them 'ones' are transformed back to 'themselves', based on the praxis of 'Reasoning' or informal gatherings for social and intellectual exercising. Reasoning is a means of viewing one's situation and examining reality and deciding on the way forward.

There is a commonly held view within the movement that 'each one teach one'. The teaching relates to the ability to inculcate within 'ones' a system of empowerment. Planno's residence in Trench Town, nicknamed the 'Fifth Street University', welcomed scholars and researchers from around the world. The environment provided a richness of critical thought for iconoclastic work and knowledge building. The Trench Town construction of a vision of African liberation is potentially of great benefit to African knowledge systems. Planno is thus regarded as not a mere teacher but rather an institution generating, disseminating and archiving knowledge and creating a space for the business of liberation − thinking.[5]

Folk ideas, like unsung heroes, are generally undervalued and quite often ignored by the official societies from which they emerge. Often sophisticated solutions are ignored because of their apparent simplicity. Even after a hundred years of pan-African activism there is still no 'acceptable' paradigm and vision of leadership within diasporan African discourses. Absent fathers, Garvey's Children and the Back to Africa Movement come to us as an interpretation, in a bid to review the idea, perhaps even the inner logic, of one of the African diaspora's most successful revolutionary practices. The interpretation speaks to an African reality that has been inverted and undervalued within the context of the Caribbean (Carry Beyond) as the male core of these societies has been configured and reconfigured in order to meet the challenges of the diaspora.

The father, absent and significantly disfigured by the experience of colonialism, is re-examined to determine how it is that he has survived between the forces of progressive resistance and those of systemic domination and destruction. The notion of the absent father, especially when considered in the context of Kingston's inner-city ghettoes, challenges the imagination, conjuring up ideas of Port Royal, reputedly the 'wickedest city on earth'. What does this say of the role and place of the Rastafarian movement within this space from which it has affected the world? In the context of the work of Ras Tafari, the idea of absent father(s) is most profitably understood as part of a historicizing of Caribbean people's thought within the paradigm of 'progressive resistance', congealing the story of capture in Africa. The idea is evident at three levels: the continental depletion of the male population (the male-to-female ratio of imported slaves was 2:1); the institutional (psychological) destruction of the male/father figure, as the white planters took the role of surrogate father(s); and, lastly, with respect to those in the Anglo-Caribbean, white sovereign Britain becoming the mother country. The post-independence ethos of father and family among African Jamaicans is increasingly defined in the urban margins by a high incidence of female dominance within the household.

Whilst the educated elites placed their faith in Western scholarship in the search for legitimacy, the intellectuals among the folk searched Africa. The assertion of an African identity was made and a civilized critique of colonialism was developed. Imperial support came through the unique African, Haile Selassie. The character of Ras Tafari, publicly crowned 'His Imperial Majesty Haile Selassie I, Emperor of All Ethiopia' on 2 November 1930, is one that has only been fully proclaimed by visionaries. Rastafarians in Jamaica see him and hail him as the godhead, the 'All Mighty Father Jah Rastafari'. This idea and its emergent ontological pathways have led to Mortimo Planno's (1996) view of the Rasta man, the Rastafarian, as 'the Earth Most Strangest Man'. Based on the faith held by members of the movement, Rastafari constitutes an important 'new faculty of interpretation', its genesis pre-dating World War II. The simple logic of this new way was also founded on the very idea of the Christian teachers who taught of the word becoming flesh. In Jamaica the words of Emperor Haile Selassie became a source of inspiration. By the 1950s a distinct national movement was discernible, attracting academic, legal and colonial scrutiny. By the late 1960s this movement had fine-tuned its approach, with the emergence of a music industry transmitting a philosophy which captured the ear-waves and spoke to youth worldwide, especially those who saw themselves as oppressed. In 1960 the University College of the West Indies (UCWI) undertook to survey the Rastafarian movement in Kingston to help to interpret the movement's ideas for the public and government. This was a time that saw various confrontations and hostile encounters between the supporters of the movement and the police. The emerging social problematic was one that saw the movement as a symbol of new enlightenment, a new resistance against systemic colonial repression aimed at keeping the loyal colonial subjects docile and compliant. The repression of the Rastafarian movement by the colonial authorities, along with domestic class prejudice, had rendered necessary the sensitive academic work that would be undertaken by UCWI. This, at least, was the perception of leading members of the movement − including Sam Brown, Mortimo Planno and Bongo Watto − who sent a letter to the principal, Arthur Lewis, inviting the University's help in articulating the movement's legitimate case. The brethren concluded that someone like Lewis, who had worked in Ghana, was experienced enough to mobilize the kind of intellectual commitment the movement's claim deserved. The wider society had failed to see the inner logic of the Rastafarian claims. Lewis pulled together an eclectic team, multidisciplinary in character, to survey and report its findings. These were then communicated to the government of the day for urgent action. At the recommendation of the university to the government of Jamaica, this produced two tours of Africa in order to explore the logistics of repatriation by way of a fact-finding mission to five countries. Why was it that the return of people to their homeland so inspired and invigorated people that a 'new Ethiopianism' emerged as a social movement?

This question is crucial for a true understanding of what the Rastafari movement represents to Jamaica. Chevannes posits the view that storytelling is what we do at the university while also saying that Rastafari is the memory of the Jamaican people (Chevannes, 2001a; 1999b). These two perspectives, when viewed in light of the work of Chevannes and other scholars (Nettleford et al., Campbell, Rodney, Yawney, etc.), place the Rastafarian movement at the centre of the project of the construction of diasporan history as it concerns African redemption. The stories of the Rastafarian movement hold cultural and historical value. In 'charting history' through the epistemological framework of the movement we are given the ability to see history as local webs with global networks of ideas, actors and events.

The problematic of dysfunctional families and the marginalization of the male father figure is a lingering presence in Jamaican society, and a lasting legacy of European colonialism. Chevannes maintains that the problem is one of our own doing when he reminds us that 'what we sow is what we reap'. He outlines the predicament of our society as follows:

> One of the charges leveled against Jamaican men is their sexual irrespon-sibility. Not only do they not stick to one partner, but they also run from commitment and from paternity. The number of single mothers is proof enough: the fathers have abandoned their responsibility. That is why, in this country, it is the women who father their children. The men who stick to one partner, who acknowledge paternity and live up to their responsibility as fathers are the few exceptions. (Chevannes, 1999)

Who are these few exceptions? This 'absent father' syndrome has deep socio-historical roots. The Rastafari movement has engaged with this situation faced by the African diasporan family in a critical and transformative way. It is argued that the Rastafarians are an exception to this general perception of the Jamaican male. In essence they provide a revolutionary cosmology inasmuch as the movement represents the fundamental position of a return of the father, through his physical presence and involvement in the sphere of socialization; as well as a return to the African homeland. This, it is argued, is the meaning of the embrace of the Ethiopian godhead, Haile Selassie I, as well as of the claims to repatriation the movement makes. Additionally, it is argued that in the construction of this cosmology the Rastafari brethren have claimed the common fatherhood of God and brotherhood of man, in the terms in which Marcus Garvey described the African as worshipping God through the spectacles of Ethiopia. But perhaps most importantly the movement expresses the idea of the dispersed African being; it is a modern version of the captive children of Israel spoken of by the Old Testament prophets who articulated the vision of the releasing of the captive children in Babylon and their return to the ways of righteousness. During the twentieth century the Rastafarians have applied the Bible's rhetoric literally in demanding that the North 'give up', and the 'South to keep not back', as the liberators work to bring the 'sons from far, and daughters from the ends of the earth'. This vision of a return to the land of the 'our' father required the awakening of the hearts of the fathers. It is Malachi who spoke of this return as the day of the lord, when the Great Redeemer would infuse the people. Malachi bore witness of the great redemption, stating: 'And he shall turn the heart of the fathers to the children, and the heart of the children to their fathers, lest I come and smite the earth with a curse' (Malachi 4:6). It is argued that an examination of articulations and ideas contributed by the Rastafari show that the movement represents a return of the scattered and estranged offspring of Africa to the way of the original foundation, the All Mighty Father Creator.

A Return to... Abba, Dada, Fada, Papa, Masa Gad

> failings in the past, present and future will be through our failures to know ourselves and realize the true functions of man on this mundane sphere. (HIM)

What is the 'true function of man on this mundane sphere'? In this tropical belt of the Western hemisphere, thinking on African diasporicity, its foundation and logic is not immediately translatable into grassroots empowerment and activism. Rodney's *The Groundings with My Brothers* is perhaps one of the few exceptions. Study of the historical development of the Rastafari movement provides useful insight into the evolution of a collective cultural vision of the phenomenon of diasporicity. It contains a view of redemption, and how it is that this project can be achieved based on the history and culture of the Africans who were scattered. And so Marcus Garvey's mobilization of the scattered Africans' consciousness was but only one important starting point for work that is still in progress. The Rastafari movement marked a new direction for the ideas of Garvey, in so far as it involved immediate engagement of the system through its preaching of a 'mental disengagement' from the oppressive administration and an embrace of the kind favour of the African Redeemer King. This was the achievement of Howell at Pinnacle. The Rastafari movement's message of liberation quickly caught on, with each of its converts feeling empowered to reason and preach about their position in society. Never before had the ideas of a return to Africa held such a supreme place in popular folk consciousness. The idea of a return to Africa was viewed by the Colonial Office as potentially subversive. It is this concept of returning to Africa that the traditional academics have failed to engage sufficiently.

'Marcus Garvey wi fada... help wi find fi wi Africa'

Garvey, while commenting on the retrograde individuals he encountered, described the context of the diasporan African as one where it was 'impossible to find a real man' (Garvey 1986: 24–5). With the exception of Marcus Garvey's work, there is little evidence to suggest that Jamaican scholars understand the inner logic concerning the project of African redemption. Garvey is often interpreted as a John the Baptist character. In the face of the colonial empire and in the United States he anchored his project and embarked on the rebuilding of the African nation and spirit through the Universal Negro Improvement Agency. Garvey asked crucial questions, such as: how has man changed since creation? Garvey's critique of the 'negro', the 'Black American', provided a point of introspection for those questioning their position in the world. He provided a foundation, and the early publication of his *Philosophy and Opinions* (1986) provided a core document. It was a liberation text even for his growing worldwide web of awakened Africans.

In the virtual absence of other early Jamaican scholarship, and the relative silence of the educated elite concerning the rehabilitation of the enslaved African, it falls to the so-called 'illiterate', to the 'organic intellectuals', the African diasporan folk, who have angst themselves, to chart a course for the 're-humanizing' of Marcus Garvey's children. One is left to find non-scribal sources for an account of the experience of that large section of the Jamaican Caribbean population who are marginalized in the academic literature and dismissed as Afrocentric fanatics, escapists and lunatics by their society. In this approach, what immediately becomes apparent is that the source of folk scholarship is the culture within which it springs up. In the realms of thinking on liberation, for example, music has been one of the most vocal and sustainable discourses. It could be argued that Marcus Garvey was resurrected through the music of Rastafari, in particular that of Burning Spear.

This notion of the resurrection of Garvey leads us to the issue of the African presence and the role of Rastafari, to the movement's ideas for administering 'thoughtful leadership' to the Jamaican People regarding the vision of Africa. Planno (1996) once more provides us with the light with which we may begin to discern the logic of the movement's approach to redemption. He reminds us that the memories of slavery live on in the blood even of the unborn children. The psychology of a society built on slavery has little concern for the harmony and balance in creation. Within the Jamaican family, historically the fathers disappeared, since children belonged to the owners of estates and were given these planters' surnames. In essence they were given a new *history*. The absence of the biological father is further known to the society through the testimonies of some 50 to 70 per cent of the population in Jamaica born to single mothers, many of whom lack the support of the male parent.

This absent father has thus evolved through the interplay of culture, history, violence, and 'polite violence',[6] creating a Jamaican male who is rendered officially marginal in the environment in which children are raised. Men are perceived as absent from society due to their invisibility in domestic, day-to-day issues. The male figure often seems to be looking for work, a place to live, food; often he is a migrant from the country into the city in search of opportunity, often opting to migrate (to North America and Europe) in search of a way of sustaining himself and his family. Illegal activity is often the choice made in search of betterment. The transience of the male life (affected by the high rate of murder in the cities) produces further complications. These are discussed by Planno, who uses the analogy of Miss Rainbow to describe a woman who loses all the men she encounters, and is left with a brood of children (begotten by these absent men) with a spectrum of surnames such as Brown, Green, Gray, Black, etc. In this society based on the overarching 'Christian' teachings under colonial rule, such a woman and her family would be engaged in a constant struggle for survival. Society would also judge her as indecent, on account of her repeated misfortune with male partners.

In their rejection of Babylon, Rastafari rejected the brutal logic of gun culture, violence and death in favour of the image of a new man. To this extent exponents of the movement made the first comprehensive attempt to arrest the situation among the African dispersed family. This came by way of its construction of a community with an inner logic based on returning the presence of the Father to that unit. This was achieved at the spiritual, domestic and community levels based on a synthesis of cultural knowledge. Nettleford notes that at the time of the *Report on the Ras Tafari Movement*, when the camps were visited, the women were absent and the men were present with the children. It is in these camps, strewn from Rock Fort in eastern Kingston to Trench Town in western Kingston, that the Rastafarian brethren and their families developed a system of critical thinking for survival. The music industry was a gentler but perhaps a more potent way by which men could fight the battle for mental liberation, and it was a fight that children could participate in without fear of danger. A man such as Bob Marley from quite early was able to bring his children into the training camp at 56 Hope Road and they emerged with a tremendous capacity to carry on their father's work.

Grafting History: A New Faculty of Interpretation

Garvey estimated that in fifty years, undisturbed or unmolested, 'our comeliness will outshine the age of Solomon'. Since the movement's emergence, its development might be viewed as claiming and asserting its demand for this undisturbed or 'gestational independence' that Marcus seems to recognize as necessary. The leadership ideas of Rastafari suggest to researchers that there are links with traditional and current African Presences, combined with information brought from the experience of multiculturalism in the Caribbean. These experiences took on a radical difference with the rising visibility of Ethiopia after the coronation. When examining the critical ideas that moulded the movement's cultural identity the noticeable periods are as follows.

Pan-Africanism, characterized by the teaching of Africa in the Pan-African mode of Garvey, which generated a positive picture of Africa to take root in the consciousness of the folk. *Athlianism*, with the Holy Piby as its new gospel, emerged in this period (1913–32). *Modern Ethiopianism* emerged with the ascension of Haile Selassie to the throne. Its development intensified during the Italo-Ethiopian war, which saw Africans globally coming together to defend Ethiopia and her ancient historical past in the 1930–40s. This translated into *Ethiopian Volunteerism* in Jamaica and North America and the action politics of engagement of society, seeing in Jamaica the growth of anti-colonial sentiments, with riots replicated throughout the colonial world. This period saw the promulgation of the new truth about Rastafari, and the new faith in his name (1940–54). The social welfare concerns that developed in the environment of the movement's urban poverty (1955–66) resulted in the development of bases and common areas for meeting. The *Ras Tafari Movement* Association, Planno's 'Local 37', is identified with this phase. The growth of organized activity under the auspices of the Ethiopian World Federation is one of the chief characteristics of this period. Common survival strategies were a characteristic of this time, in a way which unified many in the urban areas in centres of Rastafari teaching. Music production, the visits of Haile Selassie to the west, and to Jamaica in particular, were highlights. By the 1970s the idea of the Rastafarians (characterized by the Dread phase) had become routinized, they launched their music on the world as the ambassadors of Rastafari. For many outside, Rastafari was the symbol of Jamaica. The maturity of the movement in the 1980s came with an understanding of the 'Universal Liberation' and evidence of continuous work, facilitated by extensive travel (near and far by the reggae messenger of Jah) to the ends of the earth.

A Cultural Studies Approach

After more than seventy years, what Chevannes describes as a 'Caribbean worldview' clearly exists within the Rastafari tradition. The extensive experience of the movement (history, philosophy, literature, politics, sociology), all of which have received some measure of scrutiny within the framework of those disciplines, has yet to be put together as a paradigm for integrated research. Cultural studies provides us with an eclectic and essential tool with which to view this project.

Multi-disciplinary research brings the inner logic of the worldview together, thus allowing for a clearer and wider interpretation through the broadening of the texts. Viewing more, and viewing more sensitively, are part of the requirement for projects in cultural studies, and in this Caribbean space they could also be said to be the basis of the project of returning to ourselves. This culture, when viewed by its own creators and practitioners, becomes part of a project of *self-articulation*.

The ideational and philosophical high points of the movement's history as a mode of perceiving the emergence of such an 'organism' of liberation in the face of extreme struggle, persecution and op-

pression are of key concern. Such events as the coronation of the
emperor of Ethiopia 1930, the Italo-Ethiopian war of 1935–41, the
riots in Jamaica in 1938; the political activism in the lead-up to
the Second World War and especially its peace settlement (which
set the new tone of international relations); the granting of adult
suffrage in Jamaica in 1944 and the Universal Declaration on Human
Rights in 1948; Haile Selassie's movements towards the West in the
decade of the 1950s; the decades of the 1950s to 1970s – these and
other events reveal a connected thread, or a 'wave-like motion', of
ideas and related events. Viewed at the level of the 'glocal', that is
to say the local and global operating in tandem, these occurrences
display patterns of *spiritual bonds*.[7] To the extent that the Ethiopian
Emperor Haile Selassie's work was so successfully projected that
Jamaicans hailed him as God, his contribution to the project of the
're-membering' of self', and of the Ethiopian–African empire, was
considerable. Given the contributions made by Rastafari to discourses
on the liberation of African people and the perception of Jamaica as
home to this mass religion against oppression, it is not far-fetched
to construe Jamaica as a Mecca of Pan-Africanism with the Ras
Tafari faith the leading sustainable populous (mass) movement. It is
in this regard that Sir Arthur Lewis's pronouncement that 'we are all
Rastas' (Nettleford, 1999) makes sense. Those inhabiting this space
are connected to everyone else through the crucible of a common
European colonialism, which Nettleford invokes as the melody of
Europe with the rhythm of Africa (Nettleford, 1972). Rastafari has
been acknowledged as a vocal African diasporan voice in the war
of words for the liberation of apartheid South Africa, against nuclear
war, in the rejection of crime and violence. But the Rastafarians,
more than others, have actively engaged the system from the margin.
They represent through 'wordsound' the feelings, the memories, the
pain, the homelessness, the poverty, and estrangement because of
'this faith'.

Music as a Medium

Music is a significant medium. Its text provides crucial evidence
that can be used to identify the movement's ideas. Planno provides
an interesting view of the medium of music:

we decided now to use the POP MUSIC ... to take out the E in the POPE and call it POP, and use the POP MUSIC to influence the youth. And if one really looks at the world today you'll see that apart from the seven hundred million Roman Catholics the church boast about, there are more than seven hundred million youth attracted to pop music. (Planno 1979).

Bob Marley is a textbook case of the construction of a philosophical weapon through the medium of music. His sentiments of peace and love, as well as his advocacy of human rights and liberty, are unparalleled in our modern epoch. His works such as *Confrontation*, *Uprising*, and *Survival* contain theses on Rastafarian philosophy, and work generally with liturgical significance. The clarity of his oratory has gained almost cult status, rendering his image an icon of Rastafari representation. The historical anthems 'Redemption Song' and 'Africa Unite' are unambiguous messages of African experience and hope. Marley envisioned the return of Africans to the native land as 'Exodus', and the testament is of particular importance to this thesis. Marley's work resounded with the truth about the conditions faced by Africans the world over. Marley's lyrics are of such insights: 'Them belly full but we hungry, a hungry man is an angry man ... a pot a cook but the food no 'nuff.' The 'them' versus 'we' dichotomy plays out still as a core feature of the struggle faced within the system. His brethren note that Bob Marley had no idea that there were 'concrete jungles' all over the world, and that his themes spoke for humanity. It is clear that in Jamaica there was a large group who were responsible for and dependent on Bob Marley for their survival. Chris Blackwell, Bob Marley's manager/producer, estimates that Marley's personal financial responsibilities may have extended to some four thousand persons affiliated to his courtyard. To this extent Bob Marley's 56 Hope Road residence marked the outward growth and expansion of his original home base at 5th Street, Trench Town, which had provided an open learning atmosphere. Marley's relocation to Hope Road was testimony to the movement's journey. He was the people's mouthpiece and breadwinner, and they were in turn his source of insight and understanding.

The use of songs as a succinct expression of the philosophy of liberation by the movement started early. Reggae is an outgrowth of that practice of reasoning, along with other urban community innovations. These form a commonly available lyrical text made even more highly accessible through media as well as the informal trading of records abroad among dispersed Jamaicans. In more recent years radio stations such as Irie FM and Roots FM have formed important vehicles for ideas coming out of the folk culture and in particular the culture of reggae music. When music is viewed in the historical context of the dancehall as a Jamaican institution for cultural training with an increasing amplification, Rastafari music (particularly reggae) can be seen as a major contributing source for the discourse. Since 1990, artists such as Capleton, Buju Banton, Garnet Silk, Luciano, Anthony B and Sizzla have emerged to carry on the tradition of iconic teacher, musician and leader. Prior to this time, leaders such as Count Ossie, Prince Emmanuel Charles Edward, Bongo Watto, Sam Brown, Mortimo Planno and then Bob Marley were among the best-known examples of the Rastafarian teacher–leader.

The Rastafari approach may be viewed as a new method for looking at the social dynamics and power negotiations taking place. This new anchor can be identified as developing from a 'carry beyond' (Caribbean) faculty of interpreters constructing a praxis of cultural studies from an African Ethiopian-centred point of view. Within this are the seeds of a counter-hegemonic world religion, a foundation for Caribbean tradition as well as for the development of a Caribbean cultural studies programme, by virtue of its purpose and approach. One could argue that this Caribbean Cultural Studies programme was concretized in the form of a 1960 report, *Report on the Ras Tafari Movement in Kingston, Jamaica* (Smith et al. 1988). The literature to date largely situates the Rastafari movement as an expression of underclass millenarian expedient response to oppression. Little attempt has been made to recognize the movement formally as a body of cultural theorizing, as a topic worthy of scholarly endeavour, as a social science or even as a social art of the African spirit. What Nettleford describes as the 'inner logic' of a people's way of being is still to be adequately explored in scholarship (Nettleford 1999). The *Report on the Ras Tafari Movement* is the one notable exception. That study brought together a multidisciplinary team of researchers consisting of a historian, an anthropologist and a social scientist to engage in a truly unique project of socially interventionist research.[8] The movement contends that the scrutiny of researchers has been the source of national profit, tourist fascination and economic reward for many, in particular the University of the West Indies.

'The movement of Jah People...
back to my father's land'

'Emperor Haile Selassie is my Father' is proclaimed by a majority in the Rastafarian faith. Consequently it provides us with a useful point of engagement with the vision of the father as a Jamaican embracing an Ethiopian tradition with regard to the Emperor (Abba Jannoi). It urges us to understand what is meant by the term 'father' and to discern its fullest meaning. Is the father that force which glues and functionally links individuals to society? To what extent are fathers *the* determinant of the family's life chances and 'way of being'? Within the Rastafarian movement the example of the father, and of the family in general, shows itself to be a socio-historical mode of organization. This family has a prescribed role and works according to a set of expectations, which quite often are officially organized around the father. This 'patriarch' is the figure around which horizontal and vertical relations are built. His role is perhaps first and foremost a spiritual one, which translates into varying physical manifestations.

In Jamaica and much of the Caribbean, children may or may not bear their father's name; he may or he may not provide for them; and he may or may not relate to their mother. His options regarding commitment to his offspring are different to those of women. There is increasingly the issue of manifest anger, which many males express with society for providing little opportunity for their economic and social sustenance; this tends to encourage greater dysfunction in families and in the children. The issues of male nurture, fathering and the father's influence – the absence or invisibility of the paternal source – are usually ascribed to the notion of sexually irresponsible men. In contrast to the archetypal Jamaican male, Rastafari has brought increasing stability to the society. It has done so through an omnipresent testimony of music and community hands-on involvement in counselling and guiding the youth, and in particular the men.

King Ras Tafari, through an embrace of the African diaspora, and through a guiding philosophy centred on the ideas of progress, has provided a way of life to repair the breach inflicted on the African family. This is the testimony of the movement. Through its acceptance of the paternity of the dispersed children, and the responsibility of leadership of self as a counter-force to the slave master, Rastafari presents an operational critique to avert a continuum of genocide of the species. For all those who were oppressed and heavily burdened, a place was prepared. Some of the earliest social activism for social improvement and justice in general was carried out by the movement. These issues as they relate to civil liberties and freedoms later became described as human rights. Rastafari provided one of the earliest critiques of those practices of the Church that were antithetical to the gospel of love, and instead evaluated the Church as an oppressor; these practices included the shunning by society of children born out of wedlock, designating them 'bastards' who could not be baptised in regular church services. The abused, especially the marginalized male, found refuge in the open yard gatherings on the Dungle and, later, in Trench Town. The situation of the innocent children and their inheriting the social baggage of their parents, becoming the victims of prejudicial social mores – the requirement of legal marital status – were demonstrably resolved by brethren such as Howell, who is said to have attracted many single mothers, orphans and outcasts. He was able to reinstate these people by providing a solid model of 'father', but in the sense of a community father in the way of the 'shepherd's creed'. This 'creed' spoke of the community of infants, aged and the sick, and the need to care for them in the Rastafarian society. Nettleford's observation of fathers seated reasoning with children while mothers were out working is a potent critique of Western gender roles and accompanying stereotypes concerning the male provider. These social reinterpretations were an early feature of what has been labelled by some as a patriarchal and conservative movement.

Who is the Rasta Man?

A methodology, what Brodber (1996) calls 're-engineering Black space', has been perfected by the movement. Characteristic of this has been a drive for literacy, the early publication of the liberation discourses and of Jamaican literatures (Garvey 1986; A. Rogers 2000), an outstanding feature of which have been the claims made about Ethiopia. Marcus Garvey's reminder that we will worship through the spectacles of Ethiopia was a clear and timely message. The Gong, Leonard Howell, teacher of famed wisdom (Gangunguru Maragh), was to capitalize on these principles, weaving them into the movement.

By 1950 he had created a 'Black space' to instil conscience into the world, teaching the message from Ras Tafari, 'Tell[ing] the people to come home' to Africa. He turned the embrace of repatriation into a religion, with the ideal of a return to the 'Way of the Father'. By so doing he established a cure, a panacea for 'mental slavery', emancipating ourselves, because 'none but ourselves can free our minds'. The method employed consisted of the affirmative confidence in oneself and one's own abilities – a return to our senses.

The movement has also provided a brotherhood and family, established by its Patriarchs, especially Howell, seeking to develop an African-centred consciousness among the illiterate Jamaican masses. It has preached communalism and cooperative economics as a key contribution to resisting systemic oppression. Essentially the patriarchs adopted a commonsense approach, engaging all the senses. This included new presentations of self, dreadlocks as a profound symbol, coupled with the embrace of ganja as sacrament. Reggae was seen as the foundation sound of spirit music in tune with the heartbeat, word-sound power as a touchable practice and tangible philosophy, to redeem the estranged children. All these features brought a simple logic to resistance, a new feeling, which the system of Babylon viewed as greatly subversive due to its active disengagement from the 'system' represented by the British mother.

A New World African

Rastafari and reggae music (with Bob Marley as its vanguard) have been crucial agents in charting the course of African liberation. The ways of the father had been suppressed. The movement represents a resurrection and a return to the Way of the All Mighty Father Creator. In reality the Ethiopian Abba, the father, has stretched forth his hands to embrace the diasporan, in particular those with the memory of their original homeland and those capable of helping solve Africa's problems. The Rastafarians from far off in the 'carry beyond' lands have embraced Ethiopia/Africa. This has placed Africa at the centre, replacing the white mother country, white civilization, and essentially replacing the white god. These developments represent a spiritual and physical re-pa-tri-a-tion or a reconnecting, back to the source, back to Africa, to its inner logic and reality.

In conclusion: the movement is often misunderstood and nega-tively interpreted. It represents in fact one of the earliest and most successful diasporan marginal and mass-appeal fraternities or faculties for the interpretation of the peoples' liberation praxis. As such, it has pioneered a way to emerge within Pan-Africanism, with Africa at its core representing the re-empowerment of the idea of the Africa Nation, or, in Planno's words, a 'new faculty of interpretation'.

Notes

1. Mortimo Planno, field notes. This movement should be distinguished from the Rastafari Movement Association, a specific organization established in the 1960s.

2. The coming of the new era in Ethiopianism brought about by Haile Selassie's emergence is marked by the adoption of *new culture* – language, philosophy, food, lifestyle – while holding still to the central idea of manifesting the redemption or return to Africa, Zion.

3. The notion of repatriation as the repairing of the breach, of stolen nationality, land and heritage, was introduced by Bobo Trevor Stewart of Ethiopia Africa Black International Congress, substantiating this through reference to the United Nations Charter, Articles 1 and 15. Beckles, Black History Month lecture, 'The Theory of Repatriation', February 2002, Library of Spoken Word, Radio Education Unit, Mona, University of the West Indies.

4. This is also the accepted designation of Christ. See John 3:2; Matthew 8. Planno describes the gong as a sound resounding through the earth.

5. Outside of that first encounter between the university and Planno's circle in the work on the report on the Rastafarian movement in Kingston, Walter Rodney, Kamau Brathwaite, Professor Heyman, Carol Yawney, Rupert Lewis, Erna Brodber and others all benefited from the insights brought by Brother Planno at his 5th Street base. Heyman in particular identifies Planno as a teacher of teachers.

6. See Mortimo Planno's lecture, 'Polite Violence', Faculty of Social Sciences Folk Filosofi, 1998 (Library of Spoken Word, Radio Education Unit, Mona, University of the West Indies, Planno collection), for an exploration of the issue of violence and 'polite violence' on the Movement.

7. The author is grateful to Mr Arthur Newland and Rev. Steven Jennings for discussions on the idea of culture as 'spiritual bonds', wavelike and 'glocal'. These discussions where facilitated by the Institute of Caribbean Studies' colloquium in Cultural Studies.

8. Augier, 'The Norman Manley Initiative Revisited', Library of Spoken Word, Radio Education Unit, Mona, University of the West Indies, 1999.

References

The Bible (1987) Authorized Version, Bible Societies of the West Indies.

Blackwell, C. (1992) *Time Will Tell* (video), Island Visual Arts.

Brodber, Erna (1996) 'Re-engineering Black Space', Plenary presentation, Conference on Caribbean Culture, University of the West Indies, Mona Campus.

Campbell, Horace (1994) *Rasta and Resistance: from Marcus Garvey to Walter Rodney*, Trenton, NJ: Africa World Press.

Chevannes, Barry (1999a) *What We Sow is What We Reap: Problems in the Cultivation of Male Identity in Jamaica*, Kingston: Grace Kennedy Foundation.

Chevannes, Barry (1999b) 'Black Friday Commemoration of Coral Gardens Massacre', transcript by Michael Kuelker.

Chevannes, Barry (2001a) *Ambiguity and the Search for Knowledge: An Open-ended Adventure of Imagination*, University of the West Indies, the University Printery.

Chevannes, Barry (2001b) 'Rastafari and the Critical Tradition, Society for Caribbean Research', VIIth Interdisciplinary Congress, University of Vienna.

Chevannes, Barry (2001c) *Black Op* (record), Imani Productions.

Chevannes, Barry (2002) 'Roaring Lion: The Rise of Rastafari', interview transcripts, Frontline Production.

Garvey, Amy (1986) *The Philosophy and Opinions of Marcus Garvey, or, Africa for the Africans*, Dover MA: Majority Press.

Hill, Robert (ed.) (1985) *The Marcus Garvey and Universal Negro Improvement Association Papers*, Vol. IV, 1 September 1921–2 September 1922, Berkeley: University of California Press.

Hill, Robert (2001) *Dread History: Leonard P. Howell and Millenarian Visions in the Early Rastafarian Religion*, Research Association School Times Publication.

Imperial Ethiopian Ministry of Information (1972) *Importance Utterances of H.I.M. Emperor Haile Selassie I, 1963–1972*, Addis Abba.

Government of Jamaica, (1961) *Mission to Africa: Report*, Kingston: Government of Jamaica Printery.

Lindsay, Louis (1981) *The Myth of a Civilizing Mission: British Colonialism and the Politics of Symbolic Manipulation*, Jamaica: Institute of Social and Economic Research, ISER, University of the West Indies.

Lorne, M. (1997) *The Third Testament, Haile Selassie I Speeches*, Kingston, Jamaica: Head.

Marley, Bob (1992) *Bob Marley: Songs of Freedom* (record).

Mekfet, T. (1999) Transcript of 'The Norman Manley Initiative Revisited', Institute of Caribbean Studies.

Nettleford, Rex (1972). *Identity Race and Protest in Jamaica*, New York: William Morrow.

Nettleford, Rex (1999) Keynote Address, 'From the Cross to the Throne: Rastafari in the New Millennium' (researcher's transcription), Conference University of the West Indies, Mona Campus, Library of Spoken Word, Radio Education Unit.

Nettleford, Rex (1997) 'Foreword', in Edith Clarke, *My Mother Who Fathered Me: A Study of the Families in Three Selected Communities of Jamaica*, Mona: University Press, University of the West Indies.

Planno Mortimo (1979) 'The Truth About the Rastafari Movement as Told by Brother Cummie', Interview by Tam Fiofori for *Spear*, Nigeria.

Planno Mortimo (1996) *The Earth Most Strangest Man: The Rastafarian*.

Planno Mortimo (1998) 'Bob Marley, Christ and Rastafari: the New Faculty of Interpretation', lecture, University of the West Indies, Mona Campus, May, Library of Spoken Word, Radio Education Unit.

Planno Mortimo. (n.d.). 'Miss Rainbow', unpublished short story.

Rodney, Walter (1990) *The Groundings with My Brothers*, Chicago, IL: Research Associate School Times Publications.

Rogers, Athlyi (2000) *The Holy Piby or the Black Man's Bible*, Headstart/Research Association School Times Publications.

Smith, M.G., Roy Augier and Rex Nettleford (1988) *Report on the Ras Tafari Movement in Kingston, Jamaica*, Kingston: ISER.

Stewart, Bobo Trevor (2002) 'The Theory and Principle of Reparation', lecture, University of the West Indies, Mona, Library of Spoken Word, Radio Education Unit.

Tosh, Peter (1997) *Honorary Citizen* (record).

2

The Ties that Bind:
Lessons from the Historical
African Diaspora

Cassandra R. Veney

The historical African diaspora in the United States is the result
of the European slave trade, which led to millions of people being
taken from the African continent. Their intelligence, skills, ideas and
innovations were lost to Africa for ever. This was the original African
brain drain. However, with their increased economic, political and
social power, the descendants of these slaves are now in a position
to contribute to Africa's brain gain. Analysis of, and solutions to, the
African brain drain often leave this population out of the picture,
with much of the emphasis and research concentrating on the
contemporary African diaspora. This may be the consequence of the
arguments that contend that this historic diaspora lost all connection
to Africa, including language, religious practice and family structure.
On the other hand, a vast body of literature supports the claim
that the institution of slavery and all of its horrors failed to sever
totally the social, cultural, economic and political linkages to Africa.
Another point is that the research often addresses African influences
on the African-American community and not African-American
influences on Africa.

This chapter argues that the original, historical diaspora in the US
has retained linkages to the African continent despite the political,
economic and social culture that slavery and its legacy have produced.
Although this population was first enslaved, given a brief period to
enjoy basic citizenship rights, disenfranchised, and regained citizenship rights after many years of battling lynchings, beatings, poll
taxes and Jim Crow laws, the ties that linked them to Africa were

not severed. The chapter provides a historical and contemporary overview of the linkages that the African diaspora in the US has maintained with Africa and explains what role these might have in helping to resolve Africa's brain drain. The historical overview is important because it illustrates that, lacking political and citizenship rights themselves, African Americans have been in the forefront in fighting for these rights for Africans. With the improved political, educational, economic and social status of the African diaspora in the USA, its role in promoting African interests has expanded and improved. Finally, with modern communications and technology, the African American community has a global influence and a visibility that benefit Africa.

Educational Linkages:
Historical Black Colleges and Universities

The African diaspora in the USA engaged in a protracted struggle to gain access to education. As part of the master plan to keep slaves in their subordinate position, most Southern states enacted slave codes that made it unlawful for anyone to teach slaves how to read and write. This served to keep them in a subordinate position in society. However, the quest for education did not begin only after emancipation in 1865; rather, there was a concerted effort on the part of slaves and free blacks to gain access to education during the antebellum period by establishing private schools that they organized and funded. Immediately following emancipation, colleges were established for blacks, mainly in the South.

Given the themes of freedom, liberation, education and development commonly embedded in the lives of Africans and African Americans, it is important to continue to seek and implement linkages that will benefit both populations. The success of such an endeavour lies in utilizing established educational institutions. In the case of African Americans, these are the 105 two- and four-year post-secondary historically black colleges and universities (HBCUs), which have promoted and will continue to forge linkages through student, faculty and staff exchanges and collaborations. HBCUs, however, have themselves suffered from a version of brain drain. In the wake of the civil rights movements, the passage of civil rights legislation, and the implementation of affirmative action, many African-American professors, other academic staff and students applied to and attended predominantly white colleges and universities. Subsequently, however, the rising incidence of overt racism and the backlash against affirmative action led to a reversal of this trend – at least in the case of African-American students.

Traditionally, African Americans who have taught at HBCUs have demonstrated an interest in Africa and have established academic linkages. For example, Howard University, Clark Atlanta University and Lincoln University have connections that date back to their founding by individuals who were interested in missionary work in Africa. Tuskegee University, under the leadership of Booker T. Washington in the late nineteenth century, sent agricultural experts to what is present-day Togo to examine how cotton production could be improved. A number of African leaders and other professionals obtained their undergraduate education at HBCUs: for example, Kwame Nkrumah, Nnamdi Azikiwe, C. Cecil Denis (Lincoln University, Pennsylvania), Angie Brooks (Howard University), and Ellen Mills Scarborough (Shaw University).[1] In addition, the major HBCU medical schools (Howard University and Meharry Medical Schools) were responsible for educating many African doctors in areas that were beneficial to the continent: 'tropical medicine, bacteriology, microbiology, animal experimentation, statistical epidemiology'. Furthermore, 'the training advanced the development of black American education and institutions'.[2] Adell Patton has provided the names of some of the African physicians trained at these two medical schools. Those who attended Howard University Medical School include: J.H. Roberts (Liberia), Malaku E. Bayan (Ethiopia), David E. Boye-Johnson (Sierra Leone), Aderohunmau O. Laja (Nigeria) and Badejo O. Adebonojo (Nigeria). Meharry Medical School graduated John H. Jones (Liberia), Daniel Sharpe Malekebu (Malawi), Hastings Kamuzu Banda (Malawi), Joseph Nagbe Togbe (Liberia) and Henry Nehemiah Cooper (Liberia).[3]

Although the number of African students studying in the USA has declined from its peak in the 1980s, many are still attending HBCUs, with Howard University taking the lead. For example, some 13 per cent of Howard's 10,500 students are from various African countries. HBCUs have played a significant role in educating many of Africa's doctors, educators, engineers, computer scientists and health-care professionals – all crucial fields for both African and African-American development. The role of HBCUs in providing educational opportunities to African students is one way in which the historical diaspora is linked to Africa. However, if the students decide to remain in the USA, HBCUs are merely contributing to the problem of the brain drain and not the solution.

There are a number of ways in which HBCUs can contribute to Africa's brain gain. Many engage in innovative community-based programmes that African students can participate in and incorporate relevant ideas into their professions regardless of whether they return home or not. Many of the programmes address problems and concerns surrounding inadequate housing, education and health-care facilities, as well as providing programmes for small businesses. For example, Morgan State University, Central State University, Wiley College, the University of Arkansas, Pine Blue, and Bennett College are all engaged in housing construction or housing rehabilitation programmes for their respective communities. The provision of decent housing is paramount to both communities' development. In addition, Alabama A&M University is involved in an extension programme that may be of relevance for Africa. Most extension programmes for Africa focus on rural areas; with the implementation of structural adjustment programmes (SAPs) these have fallen upon hard times. However, Alabama A&M's extension programme focuses on urban communities in need of assistance. It is designed to assist families by providing services in financial management, nutrition, childcare and parenting skills.[4] Statistics show that Africa is becoming increasingly urbanized and that both groups experience similar problems in urban areas. These types of programmes and services can be tailored to fit the needs of African universities, students, faculty and communities. Moreover, African and African-American students and faculty can be recruited to work in these programmes on the continent.

Many African faculty and students are finding it increasingly difficult to study and conduct research in United States due to financial constraints and stricter visa requirements following the 11 September 2001 terrorist attacks. If opportunities for physical exchanges become limited, distance education via the Internet may be a solution, although both HBCUs and African universities face hurdles in establishing online courses. Both experience financial difficulties in providing and upgrading technology for distance education. Because faculties at both are overworked and underpaid, universities must be in a position to provide them with an incentive to develop online courses, such as release time from teaching or money. A number of

HBCUs have established online courses, and some confer graduate and undergraduate degrees through distance education in areas that are beneficial to Africa's development; these include nursing, business, electrical engineering technology, elementary education, occupational safety and health.[5] Moreover, through distance education, linkages can go both ways, as more African universities are wired for the Internet and students at HBCUs can take courses from African faculty and interact with African students.

A number of faculty members at HBCUs engage in research that can serve to deepen educational linkages and contribute to brain gain. For example, Howard University is committed to health and manpower development projects in Malawi that involve the treatment of tropical diseases, microbiology and virology. The HBCU and Malawian faculties work together and exchange ideas on this and similar projects. Clafin College in Orangeburg, South Carolina, has academic links with Africa University in Muture, Zimbabwe.[6] In other words, faculty exchanges are crucial for collaborative projects that allow the groups exposure to each other's work. The teaching staff involved in exchanges are able to benefit both institutions by providing lectures, teaching courses, and mentoring students. The exchanges allow both groups to examine the various community projects under way and assess their usefulness. The end result will be a brain gain for both groups.

Political Linkages

The various political linkages that African Americans have established or attempted to establish with Africa since arriving in the USA have often been predicated on domestic political and economic developments – the codification of slavery into law, the imposition of slave codes, the implementation of the Fugitive Slave Act, the inability and unwillingness of the government to protect citizenship rights, and the end of Reconstruction. On the other hand, political linkages have also resulted from developments on the continent – the independence of Liberia, the colonization of Sierra Leone and the Congo, the rise of nationalism, the imposition of apartheid in South Africa, the push for decolonization, and the civil strife that followed independence. Even the great civil rights leader Dr Martin Luther King, Jr participated in Ghana's independence celebrations in 1957. Of course, 'the two most internationally visible personalities … have been King's lieutenants: Andrew Young and Jesse Jackson.'[7] Both Young and Jackson took a keen interest in the issues of white supremacy and apartheid in southern Africa and advocated independence and self-rule for the region. Young's appointment as US ambassador to the United Nations did not stop him from speaking out against the injustices of apartheid in South Africa and white-minority rule in what was then Rhodesia. In fact, according to Smith, 'Young clearly thought he had a special mandate to participate in shaping U.S. foreign policy toward Africa, especially southern Africa.'[8] Jackson followed this pattern of putting southern Africa and apartheid on the US foreign policy agenda when he ran for the presidency in 1984 and 1988. Karioko argues that 'in his quest for the presidency, Jackson applied the universal ethic enunciated by his mentor, Dr. Martin Luther King: that injustice anywhere is a threat to justice everywhere … Jackson made apartheid a presidential matter, an item on the U.S. national agenda.'[9]

Even when slavery and, later, separate-but-equal were the law of the land, some members of the historical African diaspora forged political links with Africa, although these were not always positive – the main examples are Liberia and Sierra Leone that need no elaboration here. However, many leading African-American 'intellectuals and others in different walks of life voiced their opposition to imperialism', which was evident during a 1893 meeting that discussed the historical diaspora's links with the continent. The most significant leaders of the day, Edward Blyden, Alexander Crummell, Jakub Pasha, Booker T. Washington and Bishop Henry M. Turner, were present.[10] Another illustration of their political commitment to Africa was their opposition to the exploitation and mistreatment of Africans in the Belgian Congo. Booker T. Washington, George Washington Williams and other African-American leaders were 'horrified by Leopold I's ecological and economic rape of territory'.[11] Although Washington and others did not call for the independence of the territory, this action demonstrated that African Americans were concerned about Africa and European imperialism even when their domestic situation might indicate otherwise. Simply put, it would have been understandable if their political advocacy had concentrated on domestic issues such as lynching, Jim Crow segregation, political intimidation and violence, and the lack of economic and educational opportunities.

Yet another more positive example was the African–American response to the Italian invasion and occupation of Ethiopia of 1935–36. Several African–American newspapers wrote articles and editorials that demonstrated African Americans had political interests in Africa at a time when most of them could not vote. Still, some volunteered to 'fight for Ethiopia' while others engaged in 'fundraising and establishing Ethiopian aid organizations'.[12] And perhaps in response to the heightened interest in Africa following the invasion, the Council on African Affairs was organized in 1937. Its members comprised that day's leading African–American intellectuals: W.E.B. Du Bois, Adam Clayton Powell, Ralph Bunche, Paul Robeson, and the first African–American president of Howard University, Mordecai Johnson.[13]

Several other organizations that paved the way for the contemporary African–American advocacy groups should be noted: the American Society of African Culture (AMSAC), the American Negro Leadership Conference, and the World Congress of Black Writers and Artists. Again, the members and participants in these organizations read like a *Who's Who* in black America at that time: Richard Wright, Horace Mann Bond, Robert Carter, St. Clair Drake, and Saunders Redding. These organizations were concerned about decolonization efforts in Africa, democracy in Africa, and establishing and maintaining links to Africa. Kilson makes the argument that the AMSAC laid the foundation for the creation of two African–American organizations that worked on behalf of African issues: Operation Crossroads Africa and Africare.[14] Both organizations were created to play a role in brain gain and not brain drain. Operation Crossroads sends students to work in rural areas in Africa on various community development projects.

An African–American former Peace Corps official, C. Payne Lucas, founded Africare to provide assistance to African countries suffering from drought and other environmental problems. It is important to note that Lucas's goal was to get the African–American churches involved in the organization's relief efforts, which was a good strategy for several reasons. First, the African–American church has and continues to be the backbone of the community in terms of political leadership, mobilization and fundraising. Second, if the African–American church is mobilized, then so is the whole community, because a fair cross-section of the community's population is involved in the church. Other organizations may only have students, intellectuals, professionals or workers as their members.

Although the majority of the members of the historic African diaspora in the USA did not enjoy citizenship rights in terms of voting and political representation until 1965 with the passage of the Voting Rights Act, it still lobbied for African causes. It can be argued that it was not until the post-civil rights era that African Americans were in a position to lobby effectively for African interests. The educational, political, economic and social rights granted to them under civil rights legislation allowed them to pursue domestic as well as foreign policy interests, and Africa is at the centre of their foreign policy agenda. As Representative Donald Payne (Democrat, NJ) stated: 'to us – African Americans – we think Africa is in our strategic national interest ... Jewish voters care about Israel ... Greek-Americans about their issues. We are now doing that as well.'[15] It is important to have African Americans elected to Congress who are interesting in lobbying for Africa, but their membership on committees and subcommittees that deal with Africa is just as crucial for shaping a foreign policy agenda that will benefit Africa. Moreover, it is not membership alone that will advance the African agenda. African Americans must chair those bodies. For example, shortly after the Congressional Black Caucus (CBC) was formed, the late Congressman Charles Diggs became chairman of the House Subcommittee on African Affairs. In this position, he was able to push for the abolition of white minority rule in southern Africa by making sure that legislation was addressed and voted out of the committee. The fate of most legislation lies in the hands of the committee and subcommittee chairpersons because before any piece of legislation goes to the full House for a vote, it must pass the subcommittee or committee, and it is the leader of the committee who determines if a vote will take place. If chairpersons want to kill a bill, they simply refuse to call a vote and the bill dies a slow death in committee.

TransAfrica, formed in 1977, has been the premier African-American advocacy group for Africa, but it is important to note that the Council for African Affairs was the first advocacy group for Africa–US foreign policy.[16] TransAfrica's former executive director, Randall Robinson, was a tireless advocate of the abolition of apartheid in South Africa, the end of colonial rule in Zimbabwe and Namibia, the end of military rule in Nigeria, and the recognition by the international community of the genocide in Rwanda. The organization's involvement and contributions to the abolition of apartheid cannot be disputed, although it did not win all of its battles. The organization conducted numerous demonstrations against apartheid at the South African Embassy in Washington DC, along with sit-ins and hunger strikes, and provided testimony to Congress concerning the political, economic and social hardships endured by Africans under the harsh system of apartheid. TransAfrica took the lead in demanding that the US government impose economic sanctions, which were eventually enacted in 1986 following a presidential veto.

The CBC serves as the most prominent group for Africa for several reasons. First, its members hold elected offices which mean that their foremost loyalty and responsibility are to their constituents. Most of them are elected from districts with sizeable African-American and African immigrant populations, which are often interested in African issues. Because they serve in Congress, their national leadership responsibilities allow them to put Africa on the national agenda, which they have attempted to do since the 1970s when a sizeable number of African Americans were elected to Congress.[17] The numbers of African Americans elected to Congress were the result of several factors. First, there was the passage of the Voting Rights Act of 1965 (VRA), which prohibited the use of structural barriers such as poll taxes and literacy tests that often prevented African Americans from voting. Second, the VRA incorporated enforcement mechanisms. Federal examiners were sent to states that had a history of voting rights violations. Third, Supreme Court cases struck down the use of poll taxes in state elections and outlawed whites-only primaries and opened the voting arena for African Americans, along with the Twenty-fourth Amendment to the Constitution that outlawed the use of poll taxes in federal elections. The final factor was the 1982-amended VRA, which allowed for the creation of majority–minority congressional districts. All of these factors gave African Americans not only political rights but also the right to vote for and elect one of their own. Thus the CBC entered the picture. Although the CBC is underfunded and must meet the demands and needs of its domestic constituencies, it has been able to leverage political support or opposition for issues it contends are important to Africa and the USA. It often works in conjunction with other African-American organizations to achieve its goals.

The CBC and TransAfrica have continued to exert their influence on Africa–US relations, especially in terms of advocating human rights and democracy. During the conservative Reagan–Bush era of the 1980s, the CBC was instrumental in putting and keeping the issue of apartheid on the political agenda by rejecting Reagan's misguided constructive engagement strategy to end apartheid. The CBC advocated instead economic sanctions to hit the white minority government where it hurt, and through political and moral pressure it was able to pass legislation that called for economic sanctions against South Africa (the Anti-Apartheid Act of 1986). In more recent times, both organizations expressed their opposition to the Africa Growth and Opportunity Act (AGOA), which, according to its sponsors and supporters, is designed to create better trading conditions for Africa and the USA. However, Robinson and other members of the Caucus argued that the legislation will not benefit Africa because it stipulates a number of conditions that participating countries must meet, including complying with rules set out by the International Monetary Fund (IMF) and the World Trade Organization (WTO). According to some Caucus members and TransAfrica, the legislation is the manifestation of an American structural adjustment programme that will have a similar outcome to those imposed by the World Bank and the IMF. Finally, African-American political leaders and other concerned citizens contended that the legislation does not address human rights and the need for democratic rule in Africa. In the end, however, the CBC backed the legislation, and President Clinton used it and African Americans whom he had appointed to various positions to get the message out that the bill was good for Africa and had the support of Africans. Clinton established the Presidential Mission on Economic Cooperation to Africa. The mission, headed by Representative Charles Rangel, included other members of the CBC – William Jefferson, Carrie Meek, Sheila Jackson-Lee and Carolyn Kilpatrick; it travelled to six African countries in 1997 (Ethiopia, Eritrea, Uganda, Botswana, Mauritius, and Côte d'Ivoire).

The work of the late Reverend Leon Sullivan deserves attention at this point: his work was a combination of forging economic, political, cultural and educational ties to the continent, and alleviating the African brain drain. He was responsible for spearheading five African/African-American summits that addressed the issues of democracy, food security, debt relief, education and economic cooperation between Africans and African Americans. A significant contribution to the African brain gain is the Teachers for Africa Programme, developed by Sullivan with the assistance of Dr C.T. Wright of the International Foundation for Education and Self-Help

(IFESH). This initiative resulted in more than 700 teachers being sent to various African countries, including Ghana, Benin, Namibia and Nigeria. Another noteworthy programme sponsored by the two organizations that contributes to the brain gain is the Best and Brightest programme. This brings African bankers to the USA for additional training in order for them to obtain management and leadership positions when they return home.[18] Thus far, more than 4,000 bankers have been trained in the programme and returned home – an example of the role that the historical diaspora can play in curbing the African brain drain and contributing to Africa's development.

A fairly new organization in the post-civil rights era, the National Summit on Africa, needs to be included in the discussion on American-African linkages and the brain drain. This organization was founded in 1996 in response not only to post-civil rights political realities but to post-Cold War realities as well. With increased political and economic attention directed towards the former Soviet Union and eastern Europe, many feared that Africa would totally disappear from the foreign policy radar at a time when some argued that Africa was experiencing a renaissance. The goal of the National Summit is to educate all Americans on Africa, in terms of its history and linkages to the USA, and to explore ways in which the two can build partnerships around issues of concern (health, development, democracy, peace, security, etc.).[19]

The CBC, TransAfrica and other African-American organizations have continued to use their political leverage to lobby for African issues. They have voiced their concern and frustrations at the lack of attention given to civil wars in Liberia, Sierra Leone, Sudan, Burundi and the Democratic Republic of the Congo, along with other issues such as HIV/AIDS, drought and the overall poverty that too many Africans have to endure.

Economic Linkages and Brain Gain

Given the political and social situation of African Americans described earlier, it follows that their economic links to Africa in early years were virtually non-existent. Following the end of the Revolutionary War and with slavery firmly codified in the Constitution, many slaves and free people of African descent began to question their future in the USA, especially in terms of achieving full citizenship rights, economic and intellectual independence, and self-respect.[20] For some, emigration to Africa was the only solution, but there were economic considerations. Walker writes, 'opportunity for economic advancement was also important not only for émigrés, but also for those blacks in the United States who established enterprises that capitalized on Liberian exports. By the late 1850s a thriving commercial trade in palm oil, rice, camwood, and animal skins … and several settlers had amassed considerable wealth by this means.'[21] A leading proponent of emigration to Africa during the nineteenth century was Paul Cuffee, a free African who lived in Massachusetts. Cuffee acquired his wealth in the shipping industry and through the ownership of property and land. He could have remained satisfied with his freedom, property, and wealth, but he realized that he was not fully free. The future of 'free Africans' in the USA was precarious at best. He made two trips to Sierra Leone, one in 1811 to enquire about the feasibility of African emigration, and another in 1815, when he took thirty-eight free Africans with him. But he soon realized that a 'Back to Africa' movement would be very costly even for someone like himself who was independently wealthy and who was able to obtain financial backing from the British government.

Debates among the leaders prior to the Civil War (Frederick Douglass, Henry Highland Garnet, Martin Delany, Edward Blyden and Alexander Crummell) centred around finding a solution to the 'Negro presence in America'. Some believed that the end of slavery was a long way off. Others believed that free blacks were in danger of being recaptured and re-enslaved, and that emigration, not necessarily to Africa, was the only solution. Among the latter group was Joseph Brown Russwurm, who was one of the first people of African descent to graduate from college in the United States. He first contemplated migrating to Haiti but decided on Liberia in 1829, believing that 'full citizenship in the United States is utterly impossible in the nature of things, and those who want to pant for it must cast their eyes elsewhere'.[22] He firmly believed that African Americans could only have access to the much-needed means of production outside the USA, for example land in Liberia. Henry Highland Garnet, who headed the African Civilization Society, supported this line of thinking, along with Martin Delany and Edward Blyden. Delany developed the Niger Valley Exploring Party in 1858 and left for Liberia in 1859. They both believed that blacks from the United States could obtain economic independence in Africa by producing cotton and engaging in other economic activities.[23] National black emigration conventions were held in 1854, 1856 and 1858 to address the feasibility of emigration on a large scale. Shortly thereafter attention shifted to the Civil War and the political, economic and social rights that would be gained following a victory by the North.[24] However, the victory achieved by the Union troops did not bestow full citizenship rights upon people of African descent, and, again, another round of Back to Africa movements took place.

One of the most compelling factors that served as a catalyst for emigration was the lack of economic opportunities. For example, land for farming was much desired. It soon became evident that the promise of 'forty acres and a mule' to the freed slaves would not be forthcoming, and economic linkages with Africa were explored. For example, several blacks in South Carolina, with the assistance of Martin Delany, organized the Liberian Exodus Joint Stock Steamship Company in 1878 'to take back the culture, education, and religion acquired … in America until the blaze of the gospel truth should glitter over the whole broad African continent'.[25] The company purchased a ship (the *Azor*) and left for Liberia with 206 passengers. Although the organizers and participants held similar views as Christian missionaries, their goals and objectives included the economic empowerment that eluded blacks in the United States. Unfortunately, twenty-three of the passengers died before the ship reached Liberia. The company was not able to escape bankruptcy.[26]

Emigration clubs continued to emerge as the promises of Reconstruction went unfulfilled and political and economic disenfranchisement, along with threats, violence and intimidation, were the order of the day. Between 1878 and 1880, 126 blacks were resettled in Liberia from Phillips County, Arkansas. In Conway County, Arkansas, the Liberia Exodus Association, among many others formed in the state, was established in 1883 as thousands of blacks fled there from South Carolina in search of a better life.[27]

Economic opportunities were restricted for most African Americans. One sector where they found their niche was hair-care products, which were used to forge economic linkages with Africa. African-American women founded several of the companies. These women included Annie Turnbo-Malone, Madame C.J. Walker and Sarah Spencer Washington, who established companies in 1898,

1905 and 1920, respectively. Anthony Overton and Charles and Lilli Murray also forged economic linkages with Africa through their hair-care products company. This trend continued with companies such as Johnson Products, Soft Sheen, Carson Products and Pro-Line, until white companies began to buy them up, beginning in the 1980s.[28]

As W.E.B. Du Bois predicted, the problem of the twentieth century was the problem of the colour line. Therefore members of the historical diaspora continued to look towards Africa for economic, political and social salvation. These included attempts by Benjamin 'Pap' Singleton, who established the United Transatlantic Society in Kansas in 1885 after his venture to resettle former slaves in Kansas had failed. Another example is Alfred Charles Sam, who established the Akin Trading Company in Oklahoma during World War I.[29] He travelled around the country searching for investors for his company (he raised US$100,000) and forming emigration clubs 'to generate support for his plans'. These efforts culminated in the purchase of a ship, the *Liberia*). He transported sixty people to present-day Ghana, although most of them subsequently returned home.[30] Sam, on the other hand, remained in Africa until he died.

Marcus Garvey and his Universal Negro Improvement Association (UNIA) attempted to establish economic ties to Africa through Garvey's Black Star Steamship Line, but his plans never reached fruition. His vision of an African nation or homeland for all Africans in the historical diaspora was a continuation of the earlier themes of anti-colonialism, self-esteem and economic independence espoused by Cuffee, Douglass, Crummel, Washington and others. Garvey had grand plans for the historical African diaspora, which included an Empire of Africa headed by himself as the Provisional President, along with Dukes of Niger, Knights of the Nile, and Knights of the Distinguished Service Order of Ethiopia. Wilson, however, contended that the 're-Africanization fetish has been more ideologically flamboyant than institutionally or politically viable'.[31] Garvey's greatest successes were attributed to the numbers of people who joined his organization, and the establishment of restaurants, grocery stores, laundries, a hotel and a printing press. In addition, he managed to purchase three ships for the Black Star Line. For various reasons, all three ships were grounded. Although Garvey is one of the leading figures in the Back to Africa movement, he, unlike some of the lesser-known participants, never managed to set foot on African soil.

Thousands of blacks sold property and other belongings to pay for their passage and yet they too never reached Africa.

Again, with the passage of the VRA of 1965, its amendment in 1982, and the Civil Rights Act of 1964, educational, political and economic opportunities were expanded for the historical African diaspora, resulting in an expansion of the African-American middle and upper middle classes. As more and more African Americans went to colleges and universities (both HBCUs and predominantly white universities), opportunities in the public and private sectors became available, with a spillover effect on African linkages. The numbers of African Americans employed in federal government agencies that deal with African issues increased – the State Department; the Agency for International Development; and the Labour, Commerce, and Treasury Departments. The appointment of Andrew Young, US representative to the United Nations; the late Ronald Brown, secretary of the department of commerce; Alexis Herman, secretary of labour; Rosa White, assistant US trade representative for Africa; Susan Rice, assistant secretary of state for Africa; Colin Powell, head of the joint chiefs of staff and secretary of state; and Condoleezza Rice, national security adviser, all provide evidence of the effects of civil rights legislation.

This expansion of the new middle class coincided with an increase in interest in Africa that went beyond the wearing of *kente* and mud cloth. Many professionals and entrepreneurs wanted to establish economic linkages that would contribute to a brain gain for Africa, especially South Africa and Ghana. For example, approximately 1,000 African Americans were employed in more than '300 hundred companies and non-profits in South Africa in 1998, while others engage in freelance work or have set up their own businesses'.[32] One of those is Dennis L. Russell, a builder from San Diego, California. He is there to make money, but he is also interested in contributing to South Africa's development. As he says, 'sometimes you have to do things that put people to work'.[33] He is dedicated to training workers and future entrepreneurs. It is important to note that the American multinationals that returned to South Africa after the abolition of apartheid were interested in recruiting African Americans to senior-level management positions with the idea that they could secure a 'foothold in an emerging market in which competition is keen'.[34] Many of these African Americans have skills and training to contribute to the brain gain and many work in private and public sectors that are needed for the country's development – telecommunications, transportation, computers, health care, housing construction, financial management, banking law, and education. Another contributor to the brain gain is Donald King, an African-American architect from Seattle. He originally explored investment opportunities in South Africa, but has now set his sights on Ghana after travelling with other African Americans and Ghanaians there to explore business opportunities.[35] E.J. Simon of Minneapolis has parlayed his engineering expertise into a multimillion-dollar electricity development company in South Africa.

Although the emphasis of this chapter has been on the role of the historical diaspora in forging linkages, the contemporary diaspora cannot be overlooked, especially in terms of its economic significance in the form of remittances that fund education, finance small businesses, and cover health care and other needs. It has been estimated that 'Nigerians abroad send an estimated US$1.3 billion to relatives and friends at home. Sudanese do a whopping US$147 million and Malians US$103 million.'[36] When Africans have the opportunities to open and operate profitable businesses, send their children to school, obtain social services, they may remain on the continent and be able to participate in the brain gain instead of the brain drain. The economic role of the contemporary diaspora in the USA should not be overlooked. Cameroon–American Holdings, Inc., based in Houston, Texas, is the largest black-owned company in the country; its founder, chief executive officer and president, Kase Lawal, was born in Nigeria. The company specializes in oil and gas exploration and has business interests in Asia, Europe and Africa.[37] Others include the Ethiopian-born Noah Samara, who is founder and chief executive officer of an audio technology company; Rebecca Enonchong, born in Cameroon, who owns and operates a global information technology consulting company; and Chris Kirubi, Kenyan-born, who is the chairman of a property management, insurance and investment company. These individuals can be seen as examples of brain drain because they are in the USA and not in their respective home countries; yet they can also be viewed as a brain gain for Africa and African Americans. These companies provide employment and training opportunities for members of both groups in the USA. They allow both groups to obtain investment opportunities, and they invest their money, skills, training and expertise in Africans on the continent.[38]

With a yearly spending power of US$543 billion, cultural linkages to Africa can be expanded to economic linkages. This is just what the late Reverend Leon Sullivan tried to do by holding summits and conferences in various Africa countries. Both African and African-American leaders, government officials and business executives attended these meetings. Sullivan urged African Americans to 'build bridges to Africa' and to extend their skills, training and money to Africa because 'African-American businessmen might have more to do with shaping the future of Africa than anybody else'.[39]

Cultural Linkages and Brain Gain

This chapter does not argue that all of the African-American linkages to Africa have been positive, not least the cultural one. The African historical diaspora in the USA has been fed a steady diet of negative, derogatory and pejorative images of Africa and Africans since the arrival of the first Africans in Jamestown, Virginia, in 1619. The acceptance of such images and perceptions is illustrated in the colonization of Liberia and Sierra Leone, and in the work and attitudes of African Americans who were sent to Africa to work as missionaries. As stated earlier, Paul Cuffee believed that members of the historical African diaspora could achieve economic gains in Africa that were denied them in the USA. He also was a Quaker who believed they had a mission to evangelize, which is why he established the Friendly Society of Sierra Leone for the settlement of people of African descent and to enable them to engage in proselytizing. Others followed suit in the quest to spread the gospel, including William Crane, who established the Richmond African Baptist Missionary Society around 1815. In 1821, Lott Carey went to Liberia and in the following year established the First Baptist Church in Monrovia. He soon discovered that his duties would include more than spreading the gospel, as the settlement was threatened by attacks from indigenous groups, and suffered from lack of food, disease and death.

Many African-American settlers in Liberia and Sierra Leone believed they were culturally superior to Africans because they had arrived in Africa as free people, had a level of literacy, were able to own property, and moreover embraced Christian Western values. The settlers in the two colonies and the missionaries worked zealously to impart these 'superior' values to the Africans. They wholeheartedly believed that it was their mission to 'civilize' and to 'bring enlightenment' to Africans through Christianity and instilling in them the Protestant work ethic. In the process some indigenous cultural values and practices were opposed – mainly polygamy. Alexander Crummel and Martin Delany are two examples of this mind-set. However, many African-American missionaries were concerned about the welfare, education and economic needs of Africans. Ham described several settler women in Liberia who worked to secure jobs, skills, health care and education for both settler and African girls and women.[40] The interest in missionary work decreased for a period before and after the Civil War, but after the end of Reconstruction during the 1870s, when it became clear that racism and discrimination were the order of the day, a renewed interest in missionary work emerged.

The nineteenth and twentieth centuries were witness to many African-American cultural expressions, from literature during the Harlem Renaissance to gospel, blues, jazz, soul, and rap and hip-hop music, to the various forms of dress and hairstyles adopted by Africans that illustrate the existence of cultural links. Zine Magubane, for example, discusses the influence of the Fisk and Virginia Jubilee Singers on black South Africans' music after they toured the country in the late nineteenth century. She points out that '[it] is not surprising that soon after the Jubilee's arrival, African students who attended mission schools began to form similar musical ensembles.'[41] Today, there are many rap, hip-hop and jazz artists throughout the continent and African-American musical influence is evident. The emergence of hip-life music from high-life music in Ghana is just one example.

It is hoped that contemporary and future cultural linkages with Africa continue in a positive manner. One example is the increase in travel to Africa, especially by African-American church groups to Ghana and South Africa. African Americans make up by far the majority of American tourists to Ghana. For example, the congregations of the African Methodist Episcopal Churches were invited to participate in a special Black History Month Tour to Ghana. The trip included cross-cultural and educational components, with lectures on the history and culture of Ghana and African Americans. There were also tours planned for Benin, Senegal and other countries in West Africa. Another example is the trip to Ghana sponsored by the Full

Gospel AME Church in Temple Hills, Maryland. Members of this group visited the W.E.B. Du Bois Memorial Centre for Pan-African Culture, the Cape Coast and Elmina castles, and Kumasi.

African Americans and black South Africans enjoy a long history of both political and economic linkages, along with social, cultural and educational interchange. African-American visitors see the same important landmarks as everyone else, but their responses and reactions are different due to their connections to the country and to black South Africans that are largely based on the groups' shared histories of racial oppression, exploitation and domination. In addition, both groups are grappling with the problems, frustrations and prospects of living and prospering in a post-civil rights and post-apartheid era when the wider society has shifted its focus and attention to other issues; they must still tackle the basic issues of acquiring adequate employment, education, housing and health care. By wider society here, I mean whites who wield the political and economic power in the USA and whites who wield economic power in South Africa. Visits to former president Nelson Mandela's home, Steve Biko's grave, Robben Island, the Hector Peterson Memorial, and Soweto can be emotionally wrenching for these 'tourists' because the parallels between Jim Crow and apartheid and their lasting legacies are too glaring to ignore.

As already stated, not all African-American influences on Africa have been positive. Consider the influence of rap and hip-hop music and the videos that accompany them. There is no doubt that this genre of music has created a billion-dollar industry with global influence. Some would argue that rap and hip-hop are authentic expressions of African-American urban culture and that their importance cannot be denied. Others would argue that their messages of the 'gansta' life, violence and misogyny place them outside the realm of culture. Whatever position one takes, the fact is that this music has been around for twenty-five years and its appeal is not waning – it is found from 'New York to Nepal … and has become America's leading cultural export'.[42]

However, the question must be asked: what are African Americans exporting? Some of the lyrics (often composed of curse words) and videos portray African-American men as 'thugs' obsessed with acquiring the 'good life' by any illegal means necessary. The images of African-American women in these videos are not much better: usually scantily dressed and in search of a 'thug' who can provide them with money, clothes and a car, all known as 'bling-bling'. In exchange, they are willing to accept verbal and physical abuse, along with infidelity. There are, nonetheless, rap artists who prefer positive lyrics that address issues concerning the community; their videos portray African Americans and their community in a more realistic manner.

Conclusion

It would be incorrect to argue that the historical African diaspora in the USA lost its economic, cultural and political links to the African continent as the result of slavery. It would also be incorrect to argue that all people of African descent in the USA have at all times developed and maintained linkages to Africa. Their interest and participation in policy decisions, public debates, organizations, activities and programmes that concern Africa have ebbed and flowed over time depending on what was happening to them and what was happening on the continent and in the world at large. In other words, the linkages often depended on internal and external factors. Nevertheless, they existed and have been broadened and strengthened over time. As African Americans were finally able to exercise their political rights, they voted and elected African Americans not just to Congress but also to state legislatures, as mayors of large, urban cities, and to other state and local offices. All of these positions allow African Americans to have more influence on Africa–US foreign policy than in the past. With increased access to technology both African Americans and Africans should be able to forge and maintain these linkages more easily.

The political, educational, economic and cultural linkages, both historical and contemporary, cannot be ignored. And because these linkages exist, it is argued that they can be used to contribute to Africa's brain gain through educating Africans at HBCUs; engaging in exchange programmes and collaborative work; working in Africa, transferring skills, knowledge and expertise in fields needed for development; providing educational and cultural trips to Africa; spending money in Africa that can then be used for education and other useful purposes.

If slavery was unable to break the ties that bind the historical diaspora with Africa, it is unlikely that current and future events will do so. As long as these ties exist and the African-American community is able and willing to engage seriously in Africa with Africans on the continent and with the contemporary African diaspora, the end result should be a brain gain and not a brain drain.

Notes

This chapter first appeared in 'The African Brain Drain to the North: Pitfalls and Possibilities', special issue of *African Issues*, vol. 30, no. 1, 2003. It is reprinted here with permission.

1. Cynthia Frierson, 'Perceptions of African American Educators toward Historically Black Colleges and Universities', Committee on Under-representation in Education Abroad, www.jhpiego.jhu.edu/special/hbcu/tr521hb.htm, Accessed 30 May 2000.
2. Adell Patton, Jr, 'Howard University and Meharry Medical Schools in the Training of African Physicians 1868–1978', in Joseph E. Harris (ed.), *Global Dimensions of the African Diaspora*, 2nd edn, Washington DC: Howard University for Global Dimensions, 1993, pp. 109, 120.
3. Ibid., p. 117.
4. Frierson, 'Perceptions of African American Educators'.
5. Michael Arone, 'Historically Black Colleges Grapple with Online Education', *Chronicle of Higher Education*, vol. 48, no. 30, 5 April 2002: A27–8.
6. Linda Green, 'African Universities Link with Church Counterparts', United Methodist Church News Services, www.umc.org/headlines/AUAnniversary/church_links.htm; accessed 1 May 2003.
7. James N. Karioki, 'African Americans and World Peace', *Peace Review*, vol. 3, no. 2, 1991: 218.
8. Robert C. Smith, *We Have No Leaders: African Americans in the Post-Civil Rights Era*, Albany NY: State University of New York Press, 1996, p. 148.
9. Karioki, 'African Americans and World Peace': 221.
10. Toyin Falola, *Nationalism and African Intellectuals*, Rochester NY: Rochester University Press, 2001: 150.
11. Elliott Skinner, 'The National Summit on Africa Historical Framework Paper', Thematic Working Papers Series, June 1998, p. 2.
12. James Hunter Meriwether, 'The African Connection and the Struggle for Freedom: Africa's Role in African-American Life, 1936–1963', dissertation, University of California at Los Angeles, 1995, p. 48.
13. Martin Kilson, 'African Americans in Africa', *Dissent* 39, Summer 1992: 361–9.
14. Ibid.: 365.
15. Rebecca Cooper, 'Eye on Africa', *New York Times*, 19 January 1999, http://abcnews.go.com/sections/world/Daily News.

16. Alvin B. Tillery, Jr, 'Black Americans and the Creation of America's Africa Policies: The De-Racialization of Pan-African Politics', in Isidore Okpewho, Carole Boyce Davies and Ali A. Mazrui (eds), *The African Diaspora*, Bloomington/Indianapolis: Indiana University Press, 1999.

17. Smith, *We Have No Leaders*.

18. Susan Ellis, 'African-African American Summits Were Major Successes, New Organizers Says', US Department of State, 20 March 2002, http://usinfo.state.gov.regional/af/usafr/a203190.htm; accessed 11 June 2002.

19. The National Summit on Africa, 'Draft Policy Plan of Action', Document No. MW/81998/1, August 1998.

20. Falola, *Nationalism and African Intellectuals*, p. 146; John Hope Franklin and Alfred A. Moss, Jr, *From Slavery to Freedom*, 6th edn, New York: Alfred A. Knopf, 1988, p. 90.

21. Juliet E.K. Walker, 'Neocolonialism in the African Diaspora? Black American Business Competition in South Africa', in Alusine Jalloh and Toyin Falola (eds), *Black Business and Economic Power*, Rochester NY: University of Rochester Press, 2002, p. 546.

22. Lamin Sanneh, *Abolitionist Abroad*, Cambridge, MA: Harvard University Press, 1999, p. 221.

23. Ibid.

24. James P. Lubinskas, 'A Land of Their Own', *American Renaissance*, vol. 10, no. 4, April 1999, http://www.amren.com//994issue/994issue.html; accessed 13 October 2002.

25. Ken Curtis, Beth Jacobson, and Diana Severance, 'Black Americans Reach Ancestral Peoples in Africa', *Glimpses* 82, www.gospelcom.net/chi/Glimpsef/Glimpses/glmps082.shtml; accessed 12 October 2002.

26. Ibid.

27. Kenneth C. Barnes, 'The Back-to-Africa Movement in Faulkner County', Faulkner County Historical Society, 2001, www.faulknerhistory.com/articles/backtoafrica.htm; accessed 12 October 2002.

28. Walker, 'Neocolonialism in the African Diaspora?'

29. Ibid.

30. Lubinskas, 'A Land of Their Own'; Elliott P. Skinner, 'The Dialectic Between Diasporas and Homelands', in Harris (ed.), *Global Dimensions of the African Diaspora*, p. 18.

31. Kilson, 'African Americans in Africa', p. 362.

32. Suzanne Daley, 'US Blacks Find Chill in South Africa', *New York Times*, 7 April 1998, www.campbells.org/rant+rave/rtr; accessed 30 May 2002.

33. Frank McCoy, 'Tapping into Emerging Markets', *Black Enterprise*, May 1996: 80–82.

34. Cassandra Hayes, 'Can a New Frontier Boost Your Career?', *Black Enterprise*, May 1995: 71–4.

35. Jerry Large, 'America Could Benefit from Trade with Africa', *Seattle Times*, http://seattletimes.nwsource.com/news/lifesty; accessed 28 May 2002.

36. T. Henry, 'Investing in Africa', www.africana.comDailyArticles/index_20010502.htm, 5 February 2001.

37. Alan Hughes, 'A New Leader Emerges', *Black Enterprise*, June 2002: 127.

38. Steven Greenhouse, 'US Blacks Urged to Aid African Land', *New York Times*, 10 May 1995: A-3.

39. Curtis, Jacobson and Severance, 'Black Americans Reach Ancestral Peoples in Africa'.

40. Debra Newman Ham, 'The Role of African American Women in the Founding of Liberia', in Harris (ed.), *Global Dimensions of the African Diaspora,* pp. 369, 386.

41. Zine Magubane, 'The Influence of African-American Cultural Practices on South Africa, 1890–1990', in Paul Tiyambe Zeleza and Cassandra Rachel Veney (eds), *Leisure in Urban Africa*, Trenton, NJ: Africa World Press, 2003, p. 301.

42. Alan Hughes, 'Economy Hip-Hop', *Black Enterprise*, May 2002: 70.

3

Denying Modernity: The Regulation of Native Labour in Colonial Mozambique and Its Postcolonial Aftermath

Elísio Macamo

This chapter argues that colonialism, far from being the vehicle for the 'civilization' of Africa through the modernization of African 'traditional' society, was instead an important factor in denying modernity to Africa. Work and social order, it is argued, are best studied as a dialectical relationship. The analytical challenge is to explain how a specific set of conditions and factors led to a specific set of outcomes, rather than, as has often been the case, to attempt to account for large-scale changes in terms of a transition from tradition to modernity. This is an argument against notions such as Jean-François Bayart's 'extraversion' or, more recently, Patrick Chabal and Jean-Pascal Daloz's 'instrumentalization of disorder'.

Work can be defined as a social relation that is both the substance and the result of social action. In this sense the relationship between work and social order is best looked at as an attempt at ordering social relations on the basis of notions and practices of work. Seen from this perspective work appears as a privileged site for making out and describing how societies, individuals and, indeed, science are created. Just as it is plausible to argue, as some have indeed done (Ewald 1993; Conrad, Macamo and Zimmerman 2000), that the way in which labour relations were reorganized and the particular attention attached to work in European society towards the end of the nineteenth century had a profound impact on the nature of society, so one might claim, as a working hypothesis, that interventions in the sphere of work and work relations in the same period in Africa had a massive impact on the nature of social order. This is, indeed, the story of this chapter.

The story has several protagonists and a rich narrative without an end. It involves not only Africans but also two types of Europeans – Portuguese colonial administrators and Protestant Swiss missionaries. It is about how conflicting definitions and expectations of work produce a very particular type of social order, or, in the terms of Elias, it is a figuration that ends up not only defining work in a particular way but also shaping the protagonists themselves and writing their roles in the narrative in new ways. The plot is structured around three distinct interests. First, there were the colonial interests of the Portuguese, who invested their hopes of grandeur for Portugal in their ability to make Africans work. Second, there were the Swiss missionaries, who went to Africa in search of a 'New Jerusalem' and hoped to achieve this by converting Africans to their God through the inculcation of the Protestant work ethic. Finally, there were the Africans, who, far from being awakened from an eternal slumber without history, saw both the Portuguese and the Swiss missionaries as resources in the domestication of fate. These interests came together to form a context of what Shalini Randeria has described as entangled modernities that produced shared histories.

The Portuguese and the Golden Rule

In the late 1950s Portuguese settlers in Mozambique would tell the story of a letter written by a local administrative authority to another informing it that it was sending '50 voluntary workers duly handcuffed' (Castro 1980: 324). Since a law on native labour had been passed in 1898, making it illegal to force Africans to work against their will, Portuguese authorities in Mozambique prided themselves on the absence of forced labour in their colony. To be sure, this piece of legislation, like subsequent laws, was clear in prohibiting forced labour in Portuguese colonies. In practice, however, such laws were massively flouted – as the story of handcuffed voluntary workers suggests.

History books tend to claim that Mozambique, a southern African country on the Indian ocean, was a Portuguese colony for five centuries. It is an exaggerated claim, which neither the Portuguese nor the Mozambicans themselves seem interested to correct. It is likely that the former see in the claim a statement of their achievements, while the latter use it to give even greater coherence to their claims of nationhood. Whatever the case, the historical evidence indicates otherwise. While it is true that since the first Portuguese sailor set foot on the territory that would later be known as Mozambique various Portuguese rulers claimed possession of the territory by right of discovery, relations between the Portuguese and the native population were in practice limited to trade exchanges, shifting alliances and petty wars. Evidence suggests that local Portuguese garrisons usually had to pay tribute to local chieftains and warlords (see, for example, Rodney 1971).

The period from the end of the fifteenth century to the second half of the nineteenth century can hardly be described as one of Portuguese colonization of Mozambique. It was, on the one hand, the Berlin conference of 1885, which saw the partition of Africa among European colonial powers, and, on the other, renewed Portuguese attempts at establishing themselves in the territory that mark the beginning of colonialism. The partition of Africa, as well as the creation of a colonial state apparatus, formed the larger context in which this occurred. This watershed gave rise to a number of policy initiatives based on the regulation of native labour, and eventually contributed in a decisive way towards the successful establishment of the Portuguese colonial state not only in Mozambique but also in the remaining Portuguese colonies of Angola, Cape Verde, Guinea-Bissau and the islands of São Tomé and Príncipe.

The regulation of native labour produced not only the colonial state but also the colonial subjects themselves. It produced the colonial state in the sense that, over time, the institutional require-ments for the implementation of the regulations became consistent with the management of social relations within the framework of the Portuguese authorities' claims over their subject populations. In other words, the regulation of native labour became the raison d'être of the Portuguese colonial state; to this extent it was the main vehicle for the management of social relations. Over and above its defining role in the colonial state, the regulation of native labour constituted a massive intervention in the lives of Portuguese African subjects, to such an extent that it was instrumental in producing new types of individuals and identities more consistent with the central role that work came to occupy in the political economy of colonialism.

The Regulation of Native Labour

It is worthwhile taking a closer look at this regulation of native labour, as the conditions under which it came about tell eloquently of Portuguese motives and show the specific shape in which ideas and practices of work were forced upon Africans. As indicated, the watershed in the development of Portugal into a colonial power in Mozambique was the regulation of native labour. Throughout the nineteenth century Portugal had been under enormous political and economic pressure internationally to abolish slavery and forced labour in the territories under its purported control (see Hammond 1966; Duffy 1959). Let us consider a simple example. At one stage, Cadbury, the British chocolate company, faced with the threat of a consumer boycott in Britain, had to stop buying cocoa from the islands of São Tomé and Príncipe, where the Portuguese were known to use slave and forced labour from Mozambique and Angola in contravention of international labour laws. One of the Cadbury brothers undertook a trip to Portuguese possessions in Africa to ascertain the situation for himself (Duffy 1959: 161–3). No issue was more passionately debated in the Portuguese press and within administrative circles throughout the nineteenth century, or indeed during the entire colonial period, than Portuguese native labour policy in Africa.

Considering the pride with which the Portuguese defended their colonial policy as one based on spreading Christianity and European civilization, accusations of slavery and forced labour were a constant source of embarrassment. From the middle of the first half of the nineteenth century onwards, the Portuguese authorities adopted a dual strategy against international pressure. One line of reasoning sought to justify the use of slave and forced labour in Portuguese-controlled territories on the grounds that Portugal needed this type of labour in order to catch up with such countries as Britain, which had prospered on slavery (Andrade 1975). That is, calls for the abolition of slavery in Portuguese-controlled territories were seen as a form of unfair competition. The second line of reasoning was to prove more enduring. The Portuguese held that their colonial policy was not geared towards economic exploitation of the colonial possessions. Slavery and forced labour were mere instruments, so the argument went, of a civilizing project to initiate Africans into the rational and emancipatory habits of working hard for one's living (see Pitta e

Cunha 1961). Throughout the entire period of Portuguese regulation of native labour, the belief in the redemptive aim of forcing Africans to work was the one element that remained constant.

From 1820, the year in which a revolution toppled the monarchy and forced the introduction of the first written constitution, until 1910, when another revolution established a republic, Portuguese politics were characterized by a mildly liberal orientation. So far as colonial policy was concerned, this orientation found its expression in a series of laws that culminated in the formal abolition of slavery and forced labour in the year 1879. In Portuguese colonial historiography this period is known as the liberal and assimilationist stage, for during this time Portuguese overseas territories were officially designated as 'overseas provinces' and the law made no distinction between Europeans and Africans. In other words, the territories were not 'colonies' and Portuguese civil law applied to the Portuguese living there as well as to the Africans who had become Portuguese by virtue of Portugal's claims over their lands.

While not directly relevant to our theme, it is noteworthy that the so-called liberal period in Portuguese politics coincided with the independence of Brazil, in 1822, ironically in the year Portugal acquired its written constitution. Not surprisingly, this was considered a loss by many politically active Portuguese, some of whom, especially colonial officials, turned to Africa in search of what they called 'new Brazils'. To put it another way, to the extent that the liberal period coincided with the 'loss' of Brazil it also signalled the birth of a renewed Portuguese interest in Africa as a matter of national pride and sense of self. Indeed, against the charm offensive of assimilationist politicians, who by granting their African subjects the same status and rights as their own citizens in the metropole hoped to live up to what they believed to be Portugal's fate in the world, namely spreading Christianity and civilization, many politically active Portuguese, especially colonial officials, bore a grudge and believed the best way to reassert Portugal's standing in the world would be through a better economic exploitation of their overseas territories. This is certainly one reason among many why, in spite of a growing body of legislation making slavery and forced labour illegal, both thrived and continued to be a source of embarrassment for the country. (Freire de Andrade, a former governor of Portuguese Mozambique, overseas minister, foreign minister and permanent member of the Mandate Commission of the League of Nations, while denying the practice of slavery in Portuguese overseas territories, had to admit that this impression was caused by an embarrassingly high number of violations of relevant legislation (Freire de Andrade 1925: 15).

The stalemate lasted until just before the Berlin conference for the partition of Africa, when effective occupation was stated as a precondition for the recognition of a country's claim over African territory. In Portugal itself the tug-of-war between so-called liberals and conservatives over Portugal's standing in the world had slowly been building up. In the last three decades of the nineteenth century newspapers are replete with heated exchanges between proponents of these conflicting positions. One measure of this increased interest in the overseas territories was the foundation at around this time of several institutions such as the Geographical Society of Lisbon with the clear purpose of furthering knowledge of these lands for the sake of a better colonial policy. In a representation made by the Society's first secretary, Luciano Cordeiro, in 1880, the Society deplored the absence of a colonial policy and petitioned the government for more funds to carry out studies of Portugal's overseas territories which could serve as the basis for the formulation of the much needed colonial policy (Cordeiro 1980: 44–52).

In Mozambique, where Portuguese claims were still challenged by several local polities, particularly by the famous ruler of Gaza, Ngugunyan (Liesegang 1967; Rodney 1971), colonial officials had lost all illusions about the merits of an assimilationist policy and were actively canvassing their superiors in Lisbon for a different approach. The spokesman for these officials was António Enes, a man of letters who had come to fame in Lisbon through his newspaper criticisms of his own government's colonial policy. He was appointed Royal Commissioner to Mozambique in 1891, and soon after his appointment called and chaired a commission which was entrusted with the task of looking into the problem of native labour and drawing up proposals for its reform. Enes, along with a number of other colonial officials, had long been arguing against the way in which Portugal had abolished slavery. While declaring himself not to be in favour of slavery as such, he argued that Portugal could not do without native labour. In a manner reminiscent of what was the Portuguese standard argument against international pressure to abolish slavery, Enes insisted that work was the only tool the Portuguese had to carry out their civilizing mission in Africa. Labour power was, in his view, the only valuable resource the African native population had and, therefore, it was up to Portugal to use this resource in an intelligent way to fulfill its twin objectives of achieving glory and civilizing Africans (see Enes 1893). In an interesting passage of his famous report of 1893, Enes wrote:

> It is true that the generous soul of Wilberforce has not transmigrated into my body, but I don't believe that I have in my veins the blood of a slaver; I even feel an inner fondness for the Negro, this big child, instinctively bad like all children – may all mothers forgive me! – although docile and sincere. I do not consider him something to be exterminated because of the necessity for the expansion of the white race, although I may believe in natural inferiority. Still I do not understand by what moral or legal doctrine our metropolitan legislators can justify their scruples in not obliging the half-savage African, innocent or criminal, free or captive, to work for himself and his society, to be forced to work when he refuses to do so voluntarily. (cited in Duffy 1959: 238)

The law that emerged from the deliberations of the commission on native labour in 1899 bore both the mark of its chairman, António Enes, and that of the critics of liberal assimilationist politics. It was based on two central concerns, namely introducing the obligation to work on the part of the native and making the colonial state responsible for the well-being of the native. In the first instance the single most important innovation introduced by the Regulamento do Trabalho Indígena was the 'obligation to work', along the lines argued for by Enes. In other words, the relationship between the Portuguese colonial authorities and their African subjects was mediated by what the former saw as their duty towards the African, namely forcing him to earn his living from his own toil. As for assimilationism, the new law on native labour was premised on a distinction which legislators made between Europeans and Africans and what they perceived to be a legal framework more consistent with the civilizational stage of Africans. To put it differently, the law presumed the African not to be Portuguese until he had proven himself civilized through work.

The obligation to work

Let us take a closer look at this piece of legislation. The law comprised sixty-five paragraphs, reasserting the obligation to work on the part of the native population and calling for the institutions that would ensure its fulfilment. Having declared the labour of the native population as its main resource – decades later a French commentator remarked that making natives work was the golden rule of Portuguese colonial policy (Aurillac 1964: 243) – the law defined wage labour as work which all male natives between the ages of 14 and 60 had to be engaged in. Women were excluded from this definition, although in the absence of a male breadwinner they might be – and indeed were – forced to work for the state in order to meet their tax payment duty. Wage labour was described as employment on a Portuguese settler's farm, migrant work through officially sanctioned channels, and cash-crop farming for export. Traditional political authorities, the disabled and those serving in the Portuguese army were completely exempted from the fulfilment of their obligation to work.

This definition of work by a process of elimination was quite a problematic one in several respects, chief among which was the assumption that people who were not engaged in wage labour were idle. Indeed, colonial officials at the time saw the introduction of the obligation to work as part of a moral crusade against male Africans thought to be living off their female relatives. It had come to the attention of several observers that most agricultural work was done by women. Henri-Alexandre Junod, a Swiss missionary who wrote an influential two-volume monograph on the Tsonga of Southern Mozambique, estimated male contribution to agricultural work to have been three months of the year on average (Junod 1913). Portuguese colonial officials assumed, therefore, that male Africans spent the rest of their time idling. In 1907 Freire de Andrade, then Portuguese governor of Mozambique, said:

> Inasmuch as any form of imposition of work, or, for that matter, any measures tending to induce the native to work, can always be dubbed slavery, I would like to know what is meant nowadays by the term.... Slavery or forced labour are words that sound terrible to the ears of our century and perhaps this is why they are used to menace those who wish to take the black man from the idle state so dear to him.... I do not desire slavery in any form or aspect, but I do want the duty of labour, imposed by that great law of nature that is embodied in our status, and I do not think the black should escape it through the leniency of the law and through the practice of that veritable slavery he imposes upon the woman. (cited in Hammond 1966: 324)

Defining work as wage labour was, in this sense, probably also a way of liberating female Africans from their slave status in traditional domestic arrangements.

Marvin Harris, an American anthropologist who conducted a study of the causes of male labour emigration in Southern Mozambique in the 1950s, reached different conclusions to those drawn by the Portuguese, however (Harris 1959). Harris was struck by the fact that in spite of dismal working conditions in South Africa as well as long stretches of time away from their homes and families, many male Thonga poured into South Africa in search of employment. Harris, citing official Portuguese sources, estimated that between 1902 and 1940 a total of 81,166 Mozambique natives died in South African mines; this figure does not include those who died elsewhere as a result of diseases contracted in the mines; furthermore, it has to be seen against the background of a migration rate of up to 100,000 a year (Harris 1959: 52; see also Saldanha 1931 for more details on the hazardous nature of work in South African mines).

In the opinion of Harris two factors seemed to explain the high rates of emigration among the native population. One was internal to the social and political structure of the Thonga and had to do with the laws of inheritance that favoured the eldest son from the first wife. Along with trade and employment in European settlements migrant labour offered all those who did not inherit from their fathers a vehicle for social mobility. The second factor, however, had to do with the sexual division of labour, itself, as the South African historian, Patrick Harries, who has written a history of Mozambican labour migration, would corroborate, highly influenced by the local environment. Southern Mozambique was not blessed with enough farmland to support intensive forms of agriculture. Agricultural activity was concentrated, therefore, on very restricted areas where women were able to carry out a form of subsistence agriculture that did not seem to require much input from men (Harris 1959: 57–9). Patrick Harries adds to this political factors such as the fact that the whole region was ruled by Ngungunyan, the ruler of Gaza, who conscripted males into his army and whose regiments lived mainly from looting (Harries 1994; see also Vilhena 1996).

For Marvin Harris, therefore, the sexual division of labour made migrant labour an attractive proposition to local males, who more-over could acquire riches that would enable them to climb up the social ladder. Their long periods away from home did not disturb their families' chances of survival, since the little farming that their wives were able to do was enough to feed them. The decisive factor, however, was the introduction of the obligation to work, since by defining work as wage labour the law assumed the existence of several employment alternatives where there were in fact only two, namely either working for Portuguese settlers or migrating. Most Africans preferred migrant labour to employment on Portuguese farms because pay and conditions in South Africa were, despite everything, much better.

Harris counters the argument often made by Portuguese colonial officials to the effect that migrant labour had become a sign of manhood among the Tsonga of Southern Mozambique with the argument that it was actually spread as much by recruiters as by the recruits themselves. In fact, he interprets the preference expressed by young women for migrant workers as deriving from the fact that those who had worked at the mines had showed their superiority over those 'too stupid, frightened, or lazy to avoid government impressment' (Harris 1959: 60). Thus, the justification for the introduction of the obligation to work on the grounds that it contributed towards the relief of women was misleading. In fact, and again following Marvin Harris, since pay both in South Africa and on Portuguese farms in Mozambique was premised on the belief that African families could meet all their subsistence needs from farming, the obligation to work burdened women even more, as their husbands were not paid family wages (see also Schaedel 1984; First 1983).

No explicit reference has yet been made to the importance of migrant labour to the formulation of Portuguese labour policy. The regulation of native labour was to a large extent a pragmatic response to the emigration of labour. For generations, male Africans from Mozambique had been migrant labour, first in search of employment on South African sugar plantations and later, with the discovery of diamonds in Kimberley, intent on working in the mines. The role of migrant labour in the industrialization of South Africa has been discussed extensively in the literature, particularly within anthropology, notably the Manchester Marxist school, which has tended to emphasize the process of proletarianization that the phenomenon unleashed.

So far as Mozambique is concerned, Patrick Harries's work has been the most comprehensive (Harries 1994). He has looked not only at the process of proletarianization but also at forms of cultural expression that resulted from it. His most important contribution to the subject, however, is to have shown to what extent migrant labour flowed logically from a combination of cultural, environmental and political factors to establish itself as a central element in the political economy of Mozambique. Indeed, when the Portuguese were drawing up the law that regulated native labour, one of their hopes was also to tap into this golden seam. Up until then emigration outside of the country had been unregulated, and private recruiters, both South African and Portuguese, earned a living as intermediaries between employers in South Africa and Africans looking for work. One measure of the importance of migrant labour to the economy of Mozambique in those days was the observation made by a British consul who was astonished by the trade-induced prosperity of Lourenço Marques, the main urban centre then, in the absence of any visible cultivation. A local trader told him that 'the produce of this district is English gold. The native pays for everything here in hard cash' (cited in Harries 1959: 103–4). The story goes on, with the British consul remarking 'This is true … the natural produce of the district is almost nil; its wealth consists in the savings of the natives from their earnings in one of our South African colonies. Sterling is the local currency' (cited in Harries 1994: 104).

The law on native labour set out the conditions under which labour from Mozambique could be recruited and, not surprisingly, placed the interests of the workers under the tutelage of Portuguese authorities. In other words, labour emigration that had been going on for generations was transformed into an act of condescension by the Portuguese authorities, who, of course, expected to be rewarded accordingly. Recruiting agents had to pay fees to the Portuguese authorities for every labour contract; moreover, agreements were entered with the South African employers and authorities for migrant labourers to be paid part of their salary (50 per cent) on their return home. This helped ensure the liquidity of the Portuguese administration and also spending at home. Later, as a study carried out by a Portuguese economic historian shows, Portuguese and South African authorities reached an agreement for payment of part of the salary of migrant workers to be made in gold, which the Portuguese could freely sell on the world market. The proceeds from this system, which was known as 'deferred payment', were used by the colonial administration to pay its debts to Portugal (Leite 1990).

The Portuguese administration not only profited from licensing recruitment activities. By defining work as wage labour, the introduction of the obligation to work established a different kind of relationship between native workers and the authorities. This was based on their obligation as Portuguese subjects to pay taxes. In fact, the requirement to pay taxes was the way in which the obligation to work was translated in practice. Only through wage labour could people pay their taxes. Consequently, those who were not engaged in wage labour were not able to discharge their duties as citizens and could, under the provisions of the law, be forced to compensate the state by being forced to do public works. And this is indeed what happened. There are many independent reports (Ross 1925) which are unanimous in showing how the authorities used the failure of Africans to pay taxes as an important justification for forcing people to do public works. Private and official recruiters organized raids into the most remote areas of the country to conscript 'idle' natives – that is, people who did not pay taxes – for government work or sale to private employers. Usually, those compelled to work were not paid a salary, since this was seen by the authorities as compensation for the failure to pay taxes (Castro 1980: 326).

In sum, then, the Regulamento do Trabalho Indígena defined work as wage labour, and in so doing was both responding to a perceived need to turn African labour into the backbone of the economic exploitation of the colony and establishing the framework for the institutionalization of colonial rule. Work, as it came to be defined and practised, became the means through which Portuguese claims over Mozambique were given substance and legitimacy. The substance derived from the way in which the management of labour became the raison d'être of colonial rule. Throughout Portuguese colonial rule, Mozambique was nothing more than a labour reserve for neighbouring countries, and Portuguese claims over the country relied almost entirely on the ability of its colonial administration to control the movement of labour. At the same time, however, the belief in the civilizing effects of the obligation to work was the main argument for Portuguese colonial rule. Brito Camacho, a Portuguese governor of Mozambique in the 1920s, argued for instance that civilization was about creating new needs and the means of meeting them. Only the creation of such needs would make the African see the value of work and make it easier for Portugal to take greater advantage of the native's labour (Camacho 1926, 212).

The regulation of labour and the notion of tutelage

The Regulamento do Trabalho Indígena had another important aspect. If the obligation to work constituted an important element in the new law, the departure from earlier assimilationist policies was notable. Indeed, the solution to the problem of native labour seemed to require an entirely different approach in the eyes of the commission. In contrast to earlier Portuguese legislation, the new law did not assume the equality of all Portuguese before the law. While accepting that Africans from the overseas territories were just as much Portuguese as those of European descent, the commissioners argued that this should not necessarily translate into all-out equality. The law, they argued, had to acknowledge that Africans were much lower in the scale of civilization and could not be expected to understand and live according to the higher standards enshrined in European law. For their own good and for the sake of an effective colonial policy the law should provide for a different set of rules according to which Africans could be governed until such a time as they were able to assimilate properly. In other words, the fact that Portugal's colonial policy did not discriminate with regard to race did not imply that people declared to be Portuguese were de facto Portuguese. Assimilation was a process, a long one, that would require Africans to understand European norms and values before they could be considered assimilated (see Aurillac 1964; Munido 1949; Silva Cunha 1952; Moreira 1961).

To this end the law called for work to be done on the study of native customs and mores, which would be the basis for drawing up legislation that would govern native life. The magic word in this enterprise was the notion of 'tutelage' which Portuguese authorities claimed over Africans. Put differently, the Portuguese authorities placed all natives under their tutelage, by which they meant that the former could represent the latter in all matters. In the labour contracts between natives and employers, for example, the former were represented by the authorities upon whom the law had placed this responsibility, since Africans were not yet ready to understand such matters.

It took some time for the notion of tutelage to acquire a legal basis in Portuguese legislation. Only in 1914 was a corresponding law passed, which not only placed Africans under the tutelage of the state but also provided for a civil and penal code that set different legal norms and standards for Africans. Of particular interest to us, however, is the role played by work in this legislation. As a matter of fact, while acknowledging the importance of traditional African legal sanctions – so long as they did not conflict with European norms – the native civil and penal code provided for work for the state as the right punishment for criminal offences. The rationale for this was provided by Enes, who, in his famous report on his administration in Mozambique, had argued that mere imprisonment was not punishment enough, for, lazy as they were, the natives would see life at the expense of the state as a welcome relief from their much worse living conditions (Enes 1893: 70).

Portuguese colonial officials hailed this notion of tutelage as the distinctive mark of their country's specific form of colonization and contrasted it with French assimilationism and British indirect rule. They argued that, unlike both the French and the British, their colonial approach was a combination of assimilation and indirect rule, which not only lived up to the ideals of spreading Christianity and civilization that had always guided Portuguese colonial endeavours but also provided a much more solid basis for achieving these objectives. Portuguese colonial policy, so the argument went, took native culture seriously, and, much in the way the British policy of indirect rule allowed Africans to govern themselves according to norms they were familiar with, a separate legal code for natives ensured that this also was the case in Portuguese overseas territories. Unlike the British, however, and more like the French, the Portuguese policy was assimilationist to the extent that it held the door open for natives to rise up to the European level of civilization. It differed from the French in the sense that it made no tabula rasa of local culture (see Moreira 1961). The idea was that Africans could move from their native status to one which the Portuguese called 'assimilated'. Although this policy was hailed by colonial officials as a major development in terms of colonial policy, in practice it did not amount to much, as relatively few Africans managed to achieve the status of an 'assimilated' (see Aurillac 1964: 255–6). The requirements were not easy. One had to be able to speak, read and write Portuguese, be a Christian, have abandoned native customs such as polygamy and witchcraft, eat at the table and speak Portuguese with one's children. Eduardo Mondlane, a Mozambican sociologist and anthropologist, who fought for the independence of Mozambique from Portugal, would write, in the 1960s, of the Portuguese assimilationist policy that it only accepted the African as a person if the African renounced himself (Mondlane 1995: 48–9).

The logic of the notion of tutelage was deeply ingrained in the decision to use work as the main tool for the economic exploitation of the colonies. In this respect one may be tempted to see an elective affinity between this overriding economic concern and the ideological construct of a primordial native culture. Martin Schaedel, a German historian, who has written an otherwise convincing history of native labour in Portuguese colonies, slides into this conspiratorial form of argument (Schaedel 1984). Indeed, he sees a direct link between the control of labour, on the one hand, and the projection of an ideal traditional way of life, on the other, the purpose of which, in his view, is to transfer the reproduction costs of the labour force on to the traditional African communities whence the workers come (Schaedel 1984: 15; see also Webster 1978; Vail and White 1980; Isaacman 1976). The same line of reasoning is favoured by Ruth First, a South African sociologist, who wrote extensively on rural labour migration in Southern Africa, and who in her appropriately titled book *The Mozambican Miner: Proletarian and Peasant* (1983) actually argued that it was in the interests of neither South African mining capital nor Portuguese colonial administration to see the labour migrant develop into a proletarian. Keeping him both proletarian and peasant was a way of ensuring his docility towards the effects of capitalism in the mines and billing his family for the reproduction of his labour.

This is a point of view that cannot be lightly brushed aside. The regulation of native labour did create a specific political economy of colonialism, which in the particular case of Mozambique gave a new meaning to the obligation to work and the notion of tutelage. Both the colonial administration and mining capital were dependent, for several reasons, on migrant labour. And just as in other parts of colonial Africa, where in the 1930s and 1940s the so-called problem of the native became a source of worry for colonial officials, who felt that natives who spent too much time away from their homes lost the moral guidance that tribal life afforded them (see Cooper 1996), the design of a special legal code for Africans may have come to be seen as a welcome antidote. The more stable the traditional environment, the more surplus value, to stick to Marxist terminology, could be extracted from native labour.

Nonetheless, one should not forget that Portuguese colonial interests were not restricted to exporting labour. In fact the purported primary objective of reforming the laws governing the use of native labour was to make it available to Portugal itself in the colony. In other words, the idea was to use native labour in Mozambique itself and export the surplus. Governor after governor, settler after settler, repeated the litany about how much labour migration was damaging Portugal's own interests (Saldanha 1931; Camacho 1926; de Albuquerque 1934; Araújo 1920). Colonial officials licensed local recruiters to conscript native labour for local demand and often added fiscal incentives to that effect.

Moreover, with the advent of the corporate state, which saw António de Oliveira Salazar come to power in the early 1930s, Portugal attempted to exert more economic control over the colonies (Lopes Galvão 1925). There was a modicum of investment in the colonies, especially in Mozambique, which became one of the leading industrial countries in Africa, and this required a flexible and unfettered labour force (Schoeller 1992; see also Wuyts 1989). Such requirements conflicted with the conspiracy theory of the political economy of labour migration. While this in itself may not be enough to question the plausibility of this conspiracy theory, it at least suggests a much more complex picture.

To be sure, the sociological analysis of the role of the regulation of native labour and its role in making the colonial state possible craves such complexity, as it allows for a richer appreciation of the complex relationship between work and social order. Indeed, the regulation of native labour had four important elements, which should be considered more closely. First, it had an impact on individuals, particularly their self-perception. Second, to draw on Foucault's notion of governmentality (1991), society became an artefact of the regulation of labour without thereby being an illusion. Third, it was the basis upon which the state was created. Finally, it contributed in more ways that one to produce certain types of knowledge (for a clearer conceptual statement of the problem, see Conrad, Macamo and Zimmerman 2000).

The Impact of the Regulation of Native Labour

The impact of the regulation of native labour on the individual was threefold. To begin with it created an institutional framework within which work became the defining moment of an individual's status.

We have seen how the Regulamento do Trabalho Indígena defined work as wage employment. To the extent that this represented a departure from the normative context within which purposeful action had been interpreted, wage employment lifted those engaged in it out of their traditional context and gave a new meaning to their sense of self. In other words, wage labour created individuals out of undifferentiated social contexts and placed them before the need to find a personality within the new context. Second, however, wage labour not only became ascriptive of status; it also bound single individuals to an entity larger than their own families, clans and ethnic groups. The requirement to pay taxes, in particular, established a relationship between the individual and the state. The overwhelming size of the state, magnified by the atomized sense of self that the individual acquired through his status as wage labourer, made it imperative for the individual consciously to create his own social environment. Finally, wage labour made personal biographies possible in the sense that individuals were able to pursue individual projects of self-fulfilment within the framework of the political economy of modern consumption. In sum, then, the regulation of native labour turned the individual into a site for conflicting claims of community and personhood to emerge, thereby bringing issues of social change under the conditions of modernity into bold relief.

Another important aspect of Portuguese work practices and notions was the way in which the regulation of native labour also contributed towards the invention of society in a particular way. Regulating native labour was not just about making natives work, but also about ordering social things in a very specific manner. The differentiation of individuals was one aspect, which questioned the nature of community and community claims on the individual. Another was how social relations were organized according to the demands and needs of the management of the new labour relations. Put differently, the social landscape of the country was transformed into a uniform mass of communities and individuals tied to one another by the obligation to work and such practical consequences of this fact as the payment of taxes and submission to Portuguese tutelage. I have argued elsewhere that Mozambique is a modern concept to the extent that its territorial, political and social coherence were brought about by the political economy of colonialism (Macamo 1998). Third, Portuguese claims over Mozambique were given substance, as we have already seen, by the practical needs of managing native labour. Colonial domination was based on the ability to manage native labour, and the institutions that came to form the backbone of the state were, in the main, almost exclusively related to disciplining and exploiting labour. It is tempting to venture the hypothesis that the nature of the colonial sense cannot be adequately understood without reference to the history of native labour. In a nutshell, the colonial state was a product of the regulation of native labour.

Finally, it is necessary to mention the effect that the regulation of labour had on knowledge production. Already during the long controversies over the best policy options for Portugal one strategy adopted by some was to favour a deeper understanding of the physical, cultural and socio-political environment of the overseas territories. The foundation of the Lisbon Geographical Society is a case in point. Furthermore, the critique of earlier assimilationist policies was based on the assumption that Africans were fundamentally different, which in practical terms meant that knowledge about them should be acquired. Elsewhere I argue precisely along these lines by noting that, whereas in Britain and France anthropological interest preceded colonialism, in the case of Portugal it was made necessary by the regulation of native labour. Having assumed the fundamentally different nature of Africans, Portuguese colonial officials needed a way of gathering knowledge about Africans which corresponded to what they perceived to be their civilizational status. Accordingly, they set about collecting information about the customs of the natives, and systematized and codified them into bodies of legal, social and political norms. On a much more practical level, however, colonial authorities took a keen interest in the well-being of their natives. This took the form of a concern with their health, particularly those working in South African mines, and also with their fertility, which the Portuguese felt to be too low. This concern took on several forms. Portuguese anthropologists used it as an argument to prove the relevance of their services to colonial policy (see Mendes Corrêa 1954). Colonial officials themselves were more concerned about low fertility rates among natives, as the reports written by Serrão de Azevedo, the medical doctor appointed by the Portuguese authorities to look after the natives in Johannesburg, amply demonstrate (see Saldanha 1931: 53). Serrão's successor, Pires de Carvalho, went so far as to remark: 'migration to the mines is weakening the native races not only as a result of the illnesses which they get there, but also due to the long periods of time men spend away from home which tends to steadily reduce the birth rate' (Saldanha 1931: 53). In sum, the regulation of native labour was an important factor in the production of knowledge of a certain kind, chief among which was an understanding of the different nature of Africans as well as the means through which they could be bred in a healthy way.

The Swiss and the 'New Jerusalem'

The story of the Swiss in Mozambique is one of the most interesting chapters in the history of the country. It is about a missionary community that sets out to found a New Jerusalem in Africa and in the course of its efforts is appropriated by the local population in the grips of rapid social change. One hundred years after the first Swiss missionaries set foot in Mozambique the African members of the Swiss missionary church, the Presbyterian Church of Mozambique, are among the most influential citizens in the social, economic and political sphere. It is tempting, given the deep Calvinist roots of the original mission, as well as its relentlessly Protestant theological practice in Mozambique, to assume with Max Weber an elective affinity between the higher standing of its African members and the Protestant ethic.

One of the most striking features of the success of this church is, ironically, its Protestantism. Being a Portuguese colony, Mozambique was, at least in theory, a Catholic country. Portuguese colonial policy was also influenced by the need to spread Christianity, particularly of the kind practised by the majority of the Portuguese themselves. To that effect Portugal and the Vatican signed a concordat in 1940 granting the latter privileged rights to bring missions to the natives. In practical terms this meant, for example, that the education of those considered native – not 'assimilated' – was wholly delegated to the Catholic Church, which was the colonial state's church. On several occasions in the course of its missionary work in Mozambique the Swiss mission had to struggle against obstacles placed by the Portuguese authorities, who resented its Protestant orientation as well as feared that it might educate the natives into rebellion (van Butselaar 1984; Gonçalves 1960).

The Swiss mission is very proud of its record and achievements in Mozambique. These, as modesty and piety oblige, are entirely ascribed to Providence (Biber 1987). (Jan van Butselaar called the history of the Swiss mission in Mozambique *la belle histoire* in remarks made at a conference on Protestantism in Portuguese-speaking countries, held in Lisbon, December 1997.) The agency of Africans themselves, particularly the way in which they seem to have transformed the mission into a local resource for coming to terms with social change, appears to be ignored. And yet precisely this aspect of the history of the Swiss mission seems central, especially in its relationship to the regulation of native labour. This already suggests an analytical approach to the problem of understanding the impact of the outcomes, and the context within which the Swiss mission was able to produce them. Two aspects seem central to this endeavour: the conditions under which Africans came into contact with the mission, and the strategy that the latter adopted in order to go about its missionary work.

A society in crisis

So far as the conditions are concerned it is essential to know that Swiss missionaries were not originally based in Mozambique. They came into contact with people from Mozambique, mainly migrant workers and refugees from the many wars wreaking havoc in South Africa, the country where they had been doing missionary work for some time. It was these refugees and migrant labourers who came up with the idea of going back to their ancestral homes to spread the kind of Christianity preached by the Swiss.

Initially, these African Christians were imbued with a religious fervour that saw them leading awakening movements that sought to create new forms of community life out of the anomic conditions into which life in rural and urban areas had degenerated in the closing decades of the nineteenth century. They were known as *ceux de la prière* (van Butselaar 1984: 188), a tribute to their religious fervour, but already a recognition of a budding sense of community. The social composition of this community is of utmost importance for an understanding of its nature.

As already indicated, refugees and migrant labourers formed the bulk of the movement. Although sources are silent on what led people into Christianity, it is fair to assume in the case of refugees, who had been forced to flee their places of origin, that they may have found in it something which would allow them to create a sense of identity that was much more than just place of origin and culture.

One of the early African missionaries, who settled in Mozambique, seems to have been motivated by a personal desire for material fulfilment, but also by the hope of winning the allegiance of those he saw as his brethren on the basis of a new community of faith. Although Christianity was very important to him he laid emphasis on acquiring the skills that the mission could make available to them (Mapope 1925). (In the early days of the establishment of the mission a controversy erupted between so-called African evangelists and European missionaries over the demands of the former for better, if not comparable, material conditions as Europeans. Even as early as then, African Christians seem to have not been motivated solely by religious concerns. They were concerned about their material well-being and the demands they made for equal pay are evidence of this, as van Butselaar describes (1984: 78–92).

The same applies to migrant labourers, whose new material status made their integration into their traditional communities quite problematic. The community of Christians was an alluring alternative for those who, like them, felt constrained by their original community. This, to be sure, was not a rejection of tradition, as one might be tempted to assume, but rather an answer to a real problem of orientation in a rapidly changing world. Most of my interview partners in a small study I conducted on the influence of the Swiss mission on the work ethic in Southern Mozambique emphasized this aspect (the interviews were conducted in August 1997). Two teachers, who at the time of the interviews were well over 90 years old, and two migrant labourers in their seventies pointed out to me that what they found most attractive about the Swiss mission was the possibility of pursuing a career and marrying into a stable and morally upright community. A story reported by a missionary in 1913 is illustrative of some of the difficulties faced by Africans in their efforts at emancipation. M.H. Guye tells of an African by the name of Byamombo who had joined the church along with his family. Byamombo was dying of a tuberculosis acquired in South African mines and was worried that upon his death his family might dispossess his wife or even force her to marry his 'heathen' brother following traditional custom. The Swiss mission tried to prevent this and went to the Portuguese authorities for assistance but they refused to help on the grounds that Portuguese law respected native institutions and could not interfere in the case. What saved Nkothasi, the dying Christian man's wife, was the discovery made by Swiss missionaries that their convert was actually an adopted son of his traditional African family, an argument which they used to convince the Portuguese to set limits to the validity of native law in that particular case (Guye 1916: 139).

If one adds to these motivations the ravages wrought by the implementation of the law on native labour, with its constraining effect on the kinds of activities that would fall under the legal definition of work, it is not hard to understand why the Swiss mission might have been seen by Africans as a refuge against the Portuguese, a place where they could live out their experience of modernity. Joining the church was not an act of rebellion against the Portuguese, but rather a rational calculation based on the experience of their arbitrariness and their native labour laws.

The missionary position

The missionary zeal with which the Swiss went into Mozambique in 1888 played directly into this rational calculation by Africans, albeit by accident rather than design. We have seen that one important motivation for missionary work outside of Europe was a longing for a return to what they perceived to be a true Christian community. The Dutch theologian and historian of the Swiss missionary church, van Butselaar, has suggested in quite plausible terms that political factors in Switzerland may have played a major role in stimulating this longing. Indeed, the persecution of the free church of Vaud looms large in this respect (see van Butselaar 1984 for the early history of the Swiss mission).

Whatever the reason, it is clear that a major factor behind the departure of the missionaries was a religious one. Most of these missionaries, as Patrick Harries has pointed out (1981), were both theologians and scientists. A particularly poignant example is Henri-Alexandre Junod, who established himself as an authority in several areas of scientific inquiry. Not only did he write the most complete and widely acclaimed monograph of the peoples of Southern Mozambique – one which became an important quarry for the construction of Frazer's evolutionary edifice (Junod 1913) – but he was also well known as an entomologist, as can be seen from the fact that many insects, plants and butterflies in Southern Africa were named after him, and moreover was well versed in the Tsonga language, for which he wrote an authoritative grammar.

The combination of science and theology was no coincidence. Much along the lines argued by Keith Thomas (1980), the Protestantism that Swiss missionaries championed led them to see no contradiction between religion and science. Indeed, in an attitude reminiscent of Thomas Aquinas, they saw it as their duty as Christians to read the book of nature. Scientific pursuit was a form of service to God, and this influenced much of their missionary work in Mozambique.

Unlike the Portuguese Catholic Church, which in the early years was more concerned with christening as many Africans as possible, the Swiss mission pursued a strict policy of only accepting into its fold those who appeared to have internalized its precepts. In practical terms this meant that the process of membership into the Swiss mission family took a long time to come to fruition, as the Swiss missionaries tried to ensure that those who claimed to have been converted had to show, through their way of life and how they managed their social relations, that they had indeed become Christians. This was not always an easy undertaking. Monnier (1995) examined the diaries of a missionary who served in Mozambique between 1888 and 1896. They contain graphic accounts of some of these difficulties. The missionary writes, for example, about an attempt he made to preach to a group of Africans on the subject of death:

> I make pressing appeals to them by comparing these two types of death in order to show the overwhelming difference between them. Two or three of them listen to me attentively and look like they are impressed. Mandhia also looks at me attentively, but all of a sudden a mischievous smile crosses his lips and he interrupts me: 'When you die will you give me that?' And he points at my jacket. (Monnier 1995: 59, trans. EM)

The missionaries were particularly adamant on the issue of witch-craft, on which they never compromised. While respecting magical practices as part of the cultural background of the peoples they were trying to convert to Christianity, and often admiring the ingenuity of some of its premisses (Junod 1913), they insisted on its rejection as a precondition for membership of the church. Not only did they rant against it; they also saw it as an expression of a rather erroneous way of seeing the world and, consequently, tried as much as possible to instil in their converts scientific habits of mind. A favoured strategy in this connection was the building of hospitals, vocational schools and the training of their converts in several relevant professions such as nursing, agricultural work and education.

During research on the influence of the Swiss mission on the work ethic in Southern Mozambique, a full one hundred years after the inception of the mission, I was struck by the fact that most members of the Presbyterian community seemed to believe in magic and witchcraft, in spite of the principled stance of the official leadership of the church and, what is more, contrary to years of Swiss missionary endeavour. Belief in magic and science simply coexisted, as was poignantly pointed out to me by a witch doctor I interviewed, who was an active and committed member of the church, and who wished the church and witch doctors would come together to fight superstition (interview, August 1998). Moreover, this apparent syncretism did not appear to affect the leading social position of members of this church in Mozambican society. In an earlier publication (Macamo 2000) I argued that this was so because the mission had been used by the local population as a resource in their attempt at coming to terms with rapid social change. However, this does not mean that people were hypocritical and cynical in their embrace of Christianity. Most are firm believers and see Christianity as their main source of identity. Nearly all my interview partners described themselves first as *vakristi* (Christian) before they mentioned their ethnic background. The strong Calvinist orientation of the Swiss missionaries provided a framework within which all those who had been unsettled by the experience of Portuguese colonial rule, with its emphasis on the regulation of native labour, could find firm ground upon which to pursue individual life projects and build new communities. Swiss missionary Protestantism did not bring any new ethic; rather, it provided an economic and social framework within which hard-working and pious Africans could find alternatives to the constraining environment of regulated native labour. The apparent success of the mission is thus in a certain way a tribute to the ability of Africans to find a sense of purpose under the most difficult circumstances.

It is in this sense, therefore, and to summarize, that one can see the Swiss mission as a local resource. As wage labour fostered the pursuit of individuality, the Swiss mission provided a normative framework within which individuals could work on their projects of personhood. In response to a new society created by the regulation of labour the Swiss mission established its community of faith not so much as an alternative society, but as one more adapted to the new circumstances. Within this new community based on faith individuals could escape the most blatant abuses inflicted by the colonial state, at the same time as they positioned themselves to make the best out of their situation. Finally, the mission allowed its members to produce alternative knowledge bases, as the flourishing literature in Tsonga about the Tsonga bears witness to (see Mucambe 1988; Mnisi 1975; Baloyi 1967; Rikhotso 1985; Shilubane 1958).

Africans, Social Change and the Denial of Modernity

We have so far concentrated on two of the protagonists in the story of the relationship between work and social order. We have looked at the conditions that led to the regulation of native labour by the Portuguese and how the latter went about it. We have also examined Swiss missionary endeavours in southern Mozambique, with particular emphasis on the motivations and the actual practices. These are Portuguese and Swiss narratives, which even in their own terms would remain incomplete without considering the role played by Africans in them. It is tempting to see the role of Africans in these narratives as a supporting one, made necessary by the fact that the stories play out in Africa. To a certain extent this is true. Nevertheless, it is equally true that a full understanding of the whole story is not possible without including a narrative that gives Africans a much more prominent role than the Portuguese and the Swiss were ever prepared to grant them.

Indeed, both Portuguese as well as the Swiss narratives only make sense because they are about Africans. Portuguese dreams of international glory and national identity were premised on what Africans could do for them. The same goes for the Swiss, whose longing for a 'New Jerusalem' and a world with fewer mysteries, depended on their ability to carry Africans along with them. It appears then that the question concerning the role of Africans in both enterprises refers to something much deeper than just its nature as a supporting act. It is in fact about how Africans themselves perceived their role in these different projects, indeed, if they saw them as distinct projects at all or whether they too, like the Portuguese and the Swiss, saw their own project and wrote everyone else's role into its narrative.

Hints of how Africans might have written other peoples' roles into their own narrative were given during the discussion of the Portuguese regulation of native labour and Swiss missionary work. So far as the former is concerned we noted that in certain respects the obligation to work played right into changes that had occurred in African society and had made migrant labour an interesting option for Africans. We indicated that Christianity came to be seen as a resource in Africans' attempts to cope with social change. It would be fair to suggest that while the Portuguese and the Swiss represented major constraints on the ability of Africans to construct their social reality, they were also part of the world that Africans lived in and tried to transform. The world of Africans had long ceased to be an introverted one. Any realistic account of the role played by Africans in their own narratives should be able to acknowledge external influences as part of their real world, and not as some momentary distraction from the blissful isolation of their cultural island. And it is precisely on this point that work becomes an interesting starting point to discuss issues of social change, for it is indeed with social change that we are dealing.

Learning about Africans' notions of work and society is far from straightforward. One is faced with the perennial problem of sources. The only reliable accounts we have of preindustrial forms of work in Mozambique are those written by European travellers and missionaries. While these texts may allow us to gain important insights into ancient ways of life and social organization, they do not convey unequivocally what Africans' notions of work were. They do not give us a description rich enough to allow us to paint alternative scenarios to today's notions and practices of work.

This is not to say that the past is uninteresting, of course. What appears particularly relevant in the African case is not what people thought about work and how they went about it, but rather how Africans came to terms with ostensibly new forms of work. It is in the analysis of the specific consequences of a particular way of organizing and managing work relations that one can perhaps draw conclusions of relevance to other societies. Indeed, the current concern with the so-called crisis of employment in industrialized countries of the North provides a suitable background against which the African experience with new notions and practices of work can be fruitfully analysed. Jürgen Kocka and Claus Offe (2000) have produced a clear statement of this problem in their volume on the history and future of work. Unlike in Europe, where the codification of work went hand in hand with the recognition that society had to change accordingly, the regulation of native labour in Mozambique was premised on the assumption that modern forms of work could be foisted upon Africans without a corresponding change in their social organization. In practice the regulation of native labour went hand in hand with an attempt to re-create forms of social organization that could not support the new social structure created by wage labour. Thus whereas in Europe the regulation of work towards the end of the nineteenth century was accompanied by the gradual establishment of a welfare state to mediate between labouring men and their society, in Africa it was assumed that traditional forms of solidarity and social cohesion should continue to mediate between labouring individuals and society.

There is a parallel here with some aspects of deregulation in the industrialized world, where both the state and employers disengage from their social responsibility towards workers while expecting them to continue making their labour power available. The regulation of native labour in Mozambique was a massive intervention in people's lives, in terms not only of the police and disciplining apparatus that was necessary to make it work but also of what it meant to individuals as such with regard to how they managed their lives. The regulation of native labour was also a 'promise' that held the prospect, on an individual level, of emancipation from certain forms of social control and personal fulfilment.

This promise was shattered by the assumption, soon transformed into actual policy, that Africans were different and required distinct social forms of organization. While wage labour defined them more closely in terms of the authority claims of the colonial state, the policy of separate development extricated the state from its responsibility towards them. The state absolved itself from its responsibilities by denying Africans the possibility of social change consistent with the extent of transformation wrought by the introduction of wage labour. The Portuguese insistence on the re-creation of an imagined African past not only denied Africans the possibility of social change; more importantly, it was a denial of their modernity. More than a function of the political economy of colonialism, the idea that Africans had to be elevated into civilization in a gradual manner expressed a European ambivalence towards the conditions under which Africans were to be brought into modernity. It has become fashionable in African studies to argue for Africans' agency by interpreting Africans' actions as a critique (Comaroff and Comaroff 1993; White 1993, 1995) or resistance to modernity (e.g. Behrend 1999). Less attention has been given to the other aspect of the problematic, namely the way specific policies actually denied modernity to Africans (see Macamo 1999). Portuguese labour policy was a compromise between a basic belief in the primitive nature of African society and the colonial state's needs in terms of wage labour.

Postcolonial African history has been characterized by Africans' attempts at recovering and reconstituting political spaces. This has been Africans' experience of modernity and social change. If there is a lesson to be learned from this form of anticipated modernity then it will likely be one that will not see the crisis of employment as a technical issue, one that can be solved by simply investing more in the creation of jobs or finding an optimal distribution of available ones, but rather as a political issue, namely how to preserve a political culture that will ensure that everyone is heard in the debate over the desirable type of society.

Bibliography

Alburquerque, Mouzinho de (1934 [1898]), *Moçambique*, Lisbon: Agência Geral do Ultrama.

Andrade, B. (1975) 'Ao fechar a última página da colonização portuguesa', in B. de Andrade et al. (eds), *Balanço da colonização portuguesa*, Lisbon: Iniciativas Editoriais.

Araújo, J.B.C. (1920) *Relatório do Governador*, Coimbra: Imprensa da Universidade.

Aurillac, Michel (1964) 'Les provinces portugaises d'outre-mer ou la "force des choses"', *Revue Juridique et Politique*, vol. 18, no. 1: 239–62.

Axelson, E. (1969) *Portuguese in South-East Africa 1600–1700*, Johannesburg: Witwatersrand University Press.

Baloyi, S. (1967) *Murhandziwani*, Johannesburg: Swiss Mission in South Africa.

Behrend, H. (ed.) (1999) *Spirit Possession, Modernity & Power in Africa*, Oxford: James Currey.

Berthoud, P. (1888) *La Mission Romande a la Baie de Delagoa*, Lausanne: Georges Bridel.

Biber, C. (1987) *Cent ans au Mozambique: le parcours d'une minorité*, Lausanne: Editions du Soc.

Camacho, B. (1926) *Moçambique: problemas coloniais*, Lisbon: Livraria Editora.

Castro, A. (1980) *O sistema colonial português em África (meados do século XX)*, Lisbon: Editorial Caminho.

Comaroff, J., and Comaroff, J. (eds) (1993) *Modernity and Its Malcontents: Ritual and Power in Postcolonial Africa*, Chicago: Chicago University Press.

Conrad, S., E. Macamo and B. Zimmermann (2000) 'Die Kodifizierung der Arbeit: Individuum, Gesellschaft, Nation', in J. Kocka and C. Offe (eds),

Geschichte und Zukunft der Arbeit, Frankfurt am Main: Campus Verlag.

Cooper, F. (1996) *Decolonization and African Society: The Labor Question in French and British Africa*, Cambridge: Cambridge University Press.

Cordeiro, L. (1980) *Questões Coloniais*, Lisbon: Editorial Vega.

Corrêa, António Augusto Mendes (1954) *Antropologia e história*, Oporto: Istituto de Antropologia do Porto.

Costa, G. (1899) *Gaza: 1897–1898*, Lisbon: M. Gomes.

Doyle, D. (1891) 'A Journey through Gazaland', *Journal of the Royal Geographical Society* 13, pp. 588–91.

Duffy, J. (1959) *Portuguese Africa*, Cambridge MA: Harvard University Press.

Durkheim, E. (1978) *De la division du travail social*, Paris, Presses Universitaires de France.

Enes, António (1893) *Moçambique*, Lisbon: Agência Geral das Colónias.

Erskine, St. V. (1875) 'Journey to Umzila's, South-East Africa, in 1871–1872', *Journal of the Royal Geographical Society* 45: 45–125.

Ewald, F. (1993) *Der Vorsorgestaat*, Frankfurt am Main: Suhrkamp Verlag.

First, R. (1983) *Black Gold: The Mozambican Miner, Proletarian and Peasant*, Hassocks: Harvester.

Foucault, M. (1991) 'Governmentality', in G. Burchell et al. (eds), *The Foucault Effect: Studies in Governmentality, with Two Lectures by and an Interview with Michel Foucault*, Chicago: Chicago University Press.

Freire de Andrade, A. (1925) 'Trabalho indígena e as colónias portuguesas', *Boletim da Agência Geral das Colónias* 3: 3–15.

Gonçalves, J.J. (1960) *Protestantismo em África*, vol. 1, Lisbon: Junta de Investigações Ultramarinas.

Guye, H. (1916) 'Lettre de M. H. Guye aux "Amies de la M.R. à Neuchatel"', *Bulletin de la Mission Romande*, vol. 28, no. 359: 66–70.

Hammond, R.J. (1966) *Portugal and Africa 1815–1910: A Study in Uneconomic Imperialism* Stanford: Stanford University Press.

Harries, P. (1981) 'The Anthropologist as Historian and Liberal: H.-A. Junod and the Thonga', *Journal of Southern African Studies*, vol. 88, no. 1: 37–50.

Harries, P. (1994) *Work, Culture and Identity: Migrant Labourers in Mozambique and South Africa, c. 1860–1910*, London: James Currey.

Harris, M. (1959) 'Labour Emigration among the Moçambique Thonga: Cultural and Political Factors', *Africa*, vol. 29, no. 1: 50–66.

Isaacman, A.F. (1976) *The Tradition of Resistance in Mozambique: Anti-colonial Activity in the Zambesi Valley 1850–1921*, London: Heinemann.

Junod, H.-A. (1913) *The Life of a South African Tribe Vol.1/2*, Neuchatel, Attinger Frères.

Junod, H.-A. (1924) 'Le mouvement de Mourimi: un réveil au sein de l'animisme thonga', *Journal de Psychologie Normale et Pathologique* 21: 865–82.

Junod, H.-A. (1931) 'Le Noir africain – comment faut-il le juger?', *Actualités Missionnaires* 9: 4–20.

Kocka, J., and Offe, C. (2000) *Geschichte und Zukunft der Arbeit*, Frankfurt am Main: Campus Verlag.

Kuper, A. (1976) 'Radcliffe-Brown, Junod and the Mother's Brother in South Africa', *Man* 11: 111–15.

Lavradio, M. (1936) *Portugal em África depois de 1851: Subsídios para a História*, Lisbon: Agência Geral das Colónias.

Leite, J.P. (1990) 'La reproduction du réseau impérial portugais: quelques précisions sur la formation du circuit d'or Mozambique/Portugal, 1959–1973', *Estudos de Economia*, vol. 10, no. 3: 365–401.

Liesegang, G. (1967) 'Beiträge zur Geschichte des Reiches der Gaza Nguni im südlichen Moçambique 1820–1895', dissertation, Universität zur Köln.

Lopes Galvão, J.A. (1925) 'O regime de mão de obra indígena em Moçambique', *Boletim da Agência Geral das Colónias* 3: 116–28.

Macamo, Elísio (1998) *A influência da religião na formação de identidades sociais no sul de Moçambique*, Maputo: Livraria Universitária.

Macamo, Elísio (1999) *Was ist Afrika? Zur Kultursoziologie eines modernen Konstrukts*, Berlin: Duncker & Humblot.

Macamo, Elísio (2000) 'Die Protestantische Ethik und die Geister Afrika', in U. Bauer et al., *Interkulturelle Beziehungen in Afrika*, Hamburg: Lit Verlag.

Mapope, C. (1925) 'Comment les peuples africains pourront-ils trouver le salut?', *Revue Missionnaire* 5: 1–4.

Mnisi, M.G. (1975) *Vukati a byi na N'wini*, Braamfontein: Sasavona.

Mondlane, E. (1995) *Lutar por Moçambique*, Maputo: Centro de Estudos Africanos.

Monnier, N. (1995) 'Stratégie Missionnaire et Tactiques d'appropriation indigénes: La Mission Romande au Mozambique 1888–1896', *Le Fait Missionnaire* 2 (supplement).

Moreira, A. (1961) *Política ultramarina*, Lisbon: Junta de Investigações do Ultramar.

Mucambe, E. (1988) *Landikezani*, Braamfontein: Sasavona.

Munido, F.F.O. (1949) 'La Orientacion etnologica en el proyecto definitivo de codigo penal para indigenas de Mozambique', *Cuadernos de Estudios Africanos* 6: 9–34.

Palmer R., and N. Parsons (eds) (1977) *The Roots of Rural Poverty in Central and Southern Africa*, Berkeley: University of California Press.

Pitta e Cunha, P. (1961) *Sobre os motivos económicos na colonização*, Revista da Faculdade de Direito da Universidade de Lisboa.

Rebello de Souza, B. (1969) *Um ano de governo 1968–1969*, Lourenço Marques: Centro de Informação e Turismo de Moçambique.

Rikhotso, F. (1985) *Tolo a nga ha vuyi*, Braamfontein: Sasavona.

Rita-Ferreira, A. (1960) 'Labour Emigration among the Moçambique Thonga: Comments on a Study by Marvin Harris', *Africa* 30: 141–52.

Rodney, W. (1971) 'The Year 1895 in Southern Mozambique: African Resistance to the Imposition of European Colonial Rule', *Journal of the Historical Society of Nigeria*, vol 5, no. 4: 509–36.

Ross, E.A. (1925) *Report on Employment of Native Labor in Portuguese Africa*, New York: Abbot Press.

Saldanha, E.A. (1931) *Moçambique perante Genebra*, Oporto: Tipografia Porto.

Schaedel, M. (1984) '*Eingeborenen-Arbeit*' – *Formen der Ausbeutung unter der portugiesischen Kolonialherrschaft in Mosambik*, Cologne: Pahl-Ruggenstein.

Schlaefli-Glardon, E.-H. (1893) 'De Valdezia a Lourenço Marques – Journal de voyage', *Bulletin de la Société Neuchateloise de Geographie* 7.

Schoeller, W. (1992) 'Mosambik in der strukturellen Anpassung', in P. Meyns (ed.), *Demokratie und Strukturreformen im portugiesischsprachigen Afrika*, Freiburg: Arnold Bergstraesser Institut.

Seidel, H. (1898) 'Die Ba-Ronga an der Delagoabai', *Globus*, vol. 74, no. 12: 187–93.

Shilubane, R.P.M. (1958) *Muhlaba – Hosis ya va ka Nkuna Nkanyi wa le Ndzilakaneni*: North-Eastern Transvaal: The Nkuna Tribe.

Silva e Cunha, J.M. (1952) *O sistema português de política indígena – Princípios gerais*, Lisbon: Agência Geral do Ultramar.

Smith, A.K. (1970) *The Struggle for Control of Southern Mozambique, 1720–1835*, Berkeley: University of California Press.

Spittler, G. (1996) 'Ethnologische Arbeitsforschung in Afrika', in K. Beck and G. Spittler (eds), *Arbeit in Afrika*, Hamburg: Lit Verlag.

Thomas, K. (1980) *Religion and the Decline of Magic: Studies in Popular Beliefs in Sixteenth and Seventeenth Century England*, London: Weidenfeld.

Toennies, F. (1957) *Community and Association*, Michigan: Michigan State University Press.

Vail, L. and L. White (1980) *Capitalism and Colonialism in Mozambique*, London: Heinemann.

Van Butselaar, J. (1984) *Africains, Missionnaires et Colonialistes – Les origines de l'Église Presbytérienne du Mozambique (Mission Suisse)*, Leiden: E.J. Brill.

Vilhena, M. da Conceição (1996) *Gungunhana no seu reino*, Lisbon: Edições Colibri.

Weber, M. (1980) *Wirtschaft und Gesellschaft*, Tubingen: J.C.B. Mohr.

Webster, D. (1978) 'Migrant Labour, Social Formations and the Proletarianisation of the Chopi of Southern Mozambique', *African Perspectives* 1: 157–74.

White, L. (1993) 'Vampire Priests of Central Africa: African Debates about Labor and Religion in Colonial Northern Zambia', *Comparative Studies in Society and History* 35: 746–72.

White, L. (1995) 'Tsetse Visions: Narratives of Blood and Bugs in Colonial Northern Rhodesia, 1931–9', *Journal of African History* 36: 219–45.

Wiese, C. (1907) 'A Labour Question em nossa casa', *Boletim da Sociedade de Geografia de Lisboa* 6: 241–7.

Wittrock, B. (2000) 'Modernity: One, None, or Many? European Origins and Modernity as a Global Condition', *Daedalus*, vol. 129, no. 1: 31–60.

Wuyts, M.E. (1989) *Money and Planning for Socialist Transition: The Mozambique Experience*, Aldershot: Gower.

4

Mozambican Convert Miners: Missionaries or a Herd without a Shepherd? The Anglican Mission of Santo Agostinho, Maciene,[1] 1885–1905

Alda Romão Saúte

Two of the ten men [Mozambican migrant miners] searched had two Bibles each, indicating the result of missionary propaganda in the Transvaal. Now, the blacks carrying these will attempt to spread in their districts the doctrines, which they [the missionaries] had instilled in their spirit.... In addition, one of the Bible-carrying mine workers had a pen and pencils, one slate, seven bottles of ink and one packet of envelopes.[2]

Contemplating the Bibles, slate, bottles of ink, pen and pencils in the miners' boxes, the governor general of Mozambique, Freire de Andrade, knew from previous experience as governor of Inhambane that the Bibles were going to be read and expounded upon in the home villages of those workers. Using the slate, the Mozambican miners would teach others to read and write, motivating them by showing how the 'signs' on the Bible pages could 'speak'.[3] Andrade saw the Bibles as proof that Mozambican miners had been influenced by Protestant missionaries, and hence were 'de-nationalizing' Mozambicans and in active opposition to Portuguese colonialism.

Andrade's statement on the impact of Mozambican miners from the Transvaal on local communities allows us to reflect historically on the African–mission encounter[4] in southern Mozambique. Andrade's statement also suggests that Mozambican convert miners not only posed a serious threat to the stability of the Portuguese and Roman Catholic colonization agenda but also challenged the assumption that the establishment of Christian missions and the spread of Christianity and literacy in southern Mozambique were products of the white missionaries' efforts.

This chapter on Mozambican convert miners explores the experiences of returning African miners from South Africa. The growth, expansion and development of Christianity in southern Mozambique, particularly in the Maciene district, has depended on, and been distinctively moulded by, Mozambican miner initiatives. Without training or commission by the missionaries, Mozambican miners were manifestly proclaiming Christianity and building Christian communities imbued with meaning within the context of their own values and experiences. The central premiss of the chapter is that the Word of God and the gospel in Maciene came not from the sea aboard the big ships representing civilization, nor from the Anglican European mission stations through catechists, nor from the returning refugees of Ngungunhane[5] campaigns; rather, it was spread by returning Mozambican miners on their own initiative.[6] It was also the effort of the returning miners that facilitated the presence of Protestantism/Anglicanism in Maciene, notwithstanding the Portuguese and Roman Catholic alliance to weaken the presence of Protestantism in Mozambique.

Before turning to this issue it is necessary to explore the political and economic conditions of Mozambique in the early stage of Portuguese colonialism in order to provide a context for understanding evangelical work in southern Mozambique, particularly in Maciene district.

On the Eve of Colonial Rule

Portugal's status as the colonial power of Mozambique was confirmed for the Europeans at the Berlin Conference (1884/5), but more as a result of the competition for position between Germany and Britain than because of its independent strength.[7] The Berlin treaty simultaneously obliged Portugal to 'effectively occupy' its colonies. Thus, at the political level, Portugal organized the colonial administration not only to annihilate its most refractory 'vassals', such as the leader of the Gaza kingdom, but also to establish the colonial state apparatus (army, police, court of justice and jails) which would guarantee Mozambican labour by force. Three levels of Portuguese administration operated subordinate to the governor-general of Mozambique. At the highest level were the district governors, usually military officers. Each district was divided into European and non-European areas. European areas were administered as *concelhos* (councils) with limited self-government, while Mozambicans lived mainly in the rural areas, which were administered as *circumscrições* (circumscriptions) and *posto de localidades* (local offices). A Portuguese official called *chefe* or *administrador do posto* governed each of these *circumscrições* and *posto de localidades* with the help of the *régulos* (usually members of local royal families). Mozambicans were coerced to pay taxes, and to perform *chibalo* (forced labour).[8]

At the economic level, Portugal, lacking the required financial resources to bring about development, responded by drawing Mozambique into the global network and playing the *rentier* role by leasing out its colony and its resources to various interests, in particular to British capital.[9] This process took different forms in different parts of Mozambique. In the centre and north, under the system of chartered companies, the Portuguese leased out great tracts of the country as concessions to private foreign capital, which had rights not only of economic exploitation but also of administration and political control. The Companhia do Niassa had jurisdiction over an area of 190,000 square km, and the Companhia de Moçambique controlled a concession of 155,000 square km. While northern and central Mozambique were leased to foreign capital, southern Mozambique, the regions more than 22 degrees south of the Save river, were turned into a service economy for South Africa.[10]

Portugal organized the supply of Mozambican workers to the mines of South Africa and, by extension of this service role, labour was bartered for transport services: the Mozambican railways and labour facilities were guaranteed a proportion of South Africa's import–export traffic.[11] A transport infrastructure was built to serve as an outlet for South Africa's raw material exports, and it also facilitated the easy flow of men to and from the mines. That flow of men was necessarily a constant and highly regulated one. By the late 1890s, *chibalo*, labour conscription, and emigration had become intimately linked in a continuously reinforcing spiral. The more labour the gold mines drew from Mozambique, the more Portugal, a weak colonial power, was compelled to rely on cheap, compulsory labour. But forced labour also served to push increasing numbers of males to South Africa, where as 'volunteers' they could earn wages far higher than at home. Mozambique consistently provided the highest proportion of migrants for the gold mines, although many other countries also furnished labour.[12]

Table 4.1   Male Mozambican immigrants to the Witwatersrand mines, 1902–06

Year	Maputo	Gaza	Inhambane	Total
1902	5,220	19,297	13,168	37,685
1903	3,150	19,531	18,586	41,267
1904	3,432	11,795	11,817	27,044
1905	5,766	17,564	13,894	37,224
1906	4,676*	14,166	17,056	35,898
Total	22,244	82,353	74,521	179,118

* Including six migrants from West Africa.

The development of mining in South Africa totally transformed the Mozambican class structure. A class of worker-peasants was formed in the south of Mozambique. In addition to those recruited through the official channels, there was much clandestine emigration, with Mozambicans working in various other sectors of the South African economy. Katzenellenbogen reports that, 'as early as October, 1889 a survey of forty-four mines in the Transvaal revealed that, out of a total of 8013 African mineworkers, 4657, or 58 percent, were Mozambicans'.[13] The report by the governor of Mozambique, Freire de Andrade, points out the steady flow of Mozambican migrant miners to the Transvaal during the period 1902–06, as shown in Table 4.1.[14]

From the data, Andrade comments that the native population of southern Mozambique, particularly of Gaza and Inhambane, were robbed of over 150,000 males, who lived almost permanently in the Transvaal. Their labour, in other words, was used to build up South Africa's economy and not that of their own country, even though the export of labour provided the Portuguese government with a dependable source of income. Portugal received payments in gold in exchange for each emigrant legally contracted by the WNLA (Witwatersrand Native Labour Association). The persistent absence of a large percentage of the fittest section of the Mozambican workforce contributed to the underdevelopment and peripheralization of the country. In fact, the high rate and steady labour migration to the South African mines exercised a crucial influence not only on reproduction but also on labour pressure and the reorganization of gender roles in southern Mozambican households. To ease the labour bottleneck, women and older children (girls) performed tasks that their own male relatives and later Portuguese colonial officials often presumed they were biologically incapable of doing. In this labour-exporting zone, women helped by their older children hewed and cleared heavy stumps. Moreover, women, besides farming, cooking, fetching water and fire, bearing and raising children, began to be responsible for all the duties in the household in the absence of the husband or man. Thus, one can infer that the principal productive forces of southern Mozambique were shaped not only according to Portugal's need to accumulate capital but also according to the needs of capitalist accumulation in South Africa.

Notwithstanding Andrade's concerns, male Mozambican immigration continued to be the distinguishing feature of this region and a major source of colonial revenue. This export of cheap labour continued even after 1926, when Salazar's regime came to power in Portugal and inaugurated a policy of 'economic nationalism' that was intended to create conditions to serve the accumulation needs of the Portuguese bourgeoisie.[15] It was in this political and economic context that Mozambican miners met the missionaries, converted to the Christian faith, built Christian communities and, later on, spread Christianity in southern Mozambique.

Building Christian Communities in South Africa's Mines[16]

The discovery of diamonds at Kimberley in 1870 and of gold on the Witwatersrand in 1886 brought, in succession, a period of prosperity to the economy of southern Africa, the migration of tens of thousands of Africans to South Africa, and the propagation and emergence of Christianity both in the compounds and in southern Africa as a whole. The propagation of Christianity in the diamond and gold mines began as early as 1880 and 1890, respectively. Congregationalists, Methodists, Anglicans, Presbyterians, Lutherans, Baptists, Calvinists, the South African Compound Mission (SACM) and Catholics saw the African workers housed in the compounds as a potential source of new converts.[17] It was, in fact, on the South African compounds that Mozambican workers were initially exposed to the Christian message and later built Christian communities.

The compounds where African miners were living were more centres of workers' organization and institutions of social control. The compounds generally consisted of four attached buildings forming a square, with a large open area in the centre. These buildings were divided into rooms, each containing from ten to twenty Africans. The doors of the rooms all opened onto the square, and there were gates guarded by African policemen which the African workers had to pass through in order to get out of the compound. African workers were supplied with maize meal from the steam pots of the compound and meat rations which miners cooked in the compound courtyard. Anything else, like beer or other types of food, had to be purchased out of their wages in the compound or at neighbouring eating houses. Life in the compounds was mainly organized around work, with only Sundays or special days like Easter and Christmas off.[18] To illustrate the alienating and dehumanizing conditions of the compounds, Agnew, a Free Methodist missionary stated:

> the work of visiting the rooms in these compounds would not perhaps suit the high-toned preachers. Some Wesleyan preachers have said that they do not like native work… Some of the rooms to be visited are very dark, very dirty, [very noisy], and the inmates thereof are not anxious to hear the gospel. To go into these rooms and sit on an oil can or an empty dynamite box and endeavour to explain the mystery of godliness is something in which there is little earthly glory, and which wins but little earthly applause.[19]

It is not surprising that some African miners living in these conditions, and far from their families, communities and environment, would turn to beershops and brothels in the nearest urban locations. Other groups of miners would involve themselves in faction fights, riotous quarrels or dances. Others would attend schools, churches and brass bands to escape boredom, homesickness and the generally dehumanizing living conditions.[20]

These descriptions of the living conditions of African miners in South Africa help us to understand when, why and how Mozambicans encountered Christianity and joined or built Christian communities. For example, Philip Nyampule, a Mozambican miner, described his encounter with the Christian faith as follows:

I came from Gazaland an absolute heathen, to work in the mines. I had
never heard about Jesus Christ. I was working in the Wemmer compound.
One Saturday night three of my roommates and I went out on a drunken
spree. On Sunday morning our thirst drove us out for more. As we were
entering the gate of the compound, I noticed a circle of natives gathered
around a European, so I remarked to my chums, 'Hallo [Hello]! What
is up there?' 'Don't go near them,' replied my companions, 'they are the
people of the *Abafundizi* [priest] and the schools!' I was just sufficiently
under the influence of the intoxicant to make me obstinate and combat-
ive, so I said: 'Who are you, to dictate to me what I must do? and went
straight over the group.... Then the white man [missionary Baker] said:
'they [the Mozambican miners] seem to understand nothing at all; their
heads are as hard as stones, you can get no sense into them.' I [Philip]
was furious and marched off to our room.... The following Sunday I
went to the open-air meeting. His [Abafundizi] address was principally
about the evils of indulgence in intoxicating liquor. He had convinced
me that we are fools, and I decided to give up the drink.[21]

Later on Nyampule was baptised and chose the name Philip. His
experience was not unique. Gastão Pene Manave, although not one
of the first to go to the mines, told a similar story:

On Sundays, during our worship in the church, drunken miners often
entered and disrupted the services. The members of the church council,
evangelists or catechists (including me) would persuade them to keep silent
or to leave. Later on, we would visit them to explain that beer makes
people stagger, and swear, and fight and steal, and often lands people in jail,
while their wives and children go about naked and starving at home. If
they would like to change, we could do something for them, that is, help
them to believe in God as we believed. I really remembered Michaque
Tsangane, a Xhosa miner, who after my talk said: 'My heart was pressed
with what you said in the church. I had drunk, but I wanted you to pray
for me.' Later on, he converted to the Church of England.[22]

In another account, Agnew, a missionary worker in the compounds,
commented sadly in his diary: 'Sometimes in the out-of-door meetings [on Sundays] we would be disturbed by drunken characters and
others.... So we always invited them into our school and indoor
meetings.'[23] These disturbances were generally stopped by either the
African compound police or other miners. Similarly, Baker explained
that one Saturday night he walked around the Wholhuter compound,
and going from room to room could not find a single miner to
whom he could address the issues of God because of the ongoing
beer drinking. 'I stood outside and wept',[24] he stated.

As the accounts by Nyampule, Manave, Agnew and Baker reveal, an appreciable number of Mozambican miners encountered missionaries and Christianity during their leisure-time activities, particularly on Sundays. They accepted the new faith because the missionary message touched on their failures and weaknesses, namely intoxicating liquor. Their accounts also demonstrate that propagation of the gospel on Sundays in the compounds competed with other leisure-time activities.[25]

Like many other southern Mozambicans, Estevão Uamusse crossed the border into South Africa to seek work and training. According to his son, Noé Estevão Uamusse, when his father arrived in the compound he was accommodated in a heathen dormitory. Their life consisted of noise, drunkenness and the absence of respect. One day his father complained about the awful life in his room in a talk with his underground co-worker. After a while the co-worker took his father to visit his dormitory.

> My dad, astonished with the order, neatness and warm welcome from the miners' dormitory asked the co-worker: 'How did you manage to keep your room clean and quiet?' The co-worker replied: 'Here we are Christians.' My dad: 'What is it to be a Christian? I would like to be a Christian and live in this pleasant place.'

Soon his father was invited to live in a Christian dormitory and learn the Christian faith.[26]

Pedro Zimila, an old man, remembered that when he, too, went to the mines, during the trip he was advised to inform the manager of the mine that he was a Christian of the Church of England. 'I did not ask why I should say this because I was afraid.' Once in front of the manager he repeated the message. The manager said: 'There is your room Shangaan boy.' 'I went there and I found my future mates knelt and mumbled something. I stood shaking, sweating at the door because I thought it was a mining regulation.' One mate walked to the door and welcomed him. This was the way Zimila became acquainted with Christianity.[27]

Some elderly miners recalled that their fathers and uncles had described their experiences of a somewhat later period. Brass bands, magic lantern shows, open-air religious services and, mostly, the enthusiastic literacy classes were the activities where their fathers, uncles and they encountered Christianity. The missionaries, evangelists and catechists, they remember, taught them salvation, about prayer, the blood of Jesus, how it washed the earth, mercy and forgiveness; to sing the hymns, and to pray. Teachers focused their lessons on reading and writing skills, using blackboards or wall charts, slates and pencils, and the Bible for reading. Thus the missionaries, evangelists and catechists introduced the word of God and converted Mozambican miners to the Christian faith. A very interesting case is that of João Manuel Nhavotso. He remembered that

> One day a Mozambican miner appeared in my room and said, 'I have a class for Ba-chopis in my school, and I am looking for scholars.' I replied, 'I will come.' In spite of my advanced age I wished to go school. I started to spell out the syllables, ba, be, bi, bo, bu. When I could read and write a word on the chart I would fairly laugh with joy. I would say, 'I love books', 'I love it here', pointing to my eyes, ears and chest. When I received my salary I bought a spelling book, Bible and hymnbook. After three months I was able to spell out words in the Zulu language.[28]

A similar memory was held by Zacarias Paindane, a miner, who explained that even though he attended the Sunday prayer meetings, he felt his Christianity unfulfilled. He wished to be able to read the Bible and therefore he asked a dormitory mate to teach him to read and write. He paid one shilling per month.[29]

These Mozambican accounts are confirmed by missionaries of the SACM. For example, Albert Walklett said that in the 1890s Rev. Morris and he often had magic lantern lectures[30] at the De Beer's, Central and British United compounds. They established schools in four compounds where the miners were instructed in the mysteries of the three Rs. This work was on the whole interesting and encouraging; the miners made rapid progress and all seemed eager to learn.[31] Galley, who was from the same mission, but worked three years later, recorded a similar impression of the assertiveness of migrant miners in Kimberley:

> The morning-schools in the compounds still continue to give me encouragement. I have now thirty scholars at the Central and twenty at the De Beer's compounds; fine, stalwart men they are, and all eager to learn.... However, De Beer's, containing over 2,800 souls was always to us and other missionaries a place of many difficulties for native conversion.[32]

The foregoing testimonies illustrate the diverse ways Mozambican miners encountered the gospel and joined or built Christian communities in the Kimberley and Witwatersrand compounds. For instance, some Mozambican miners were drawn to Christianity because they had concluded that the Word of God had saved them from an evil life. Others perceived Christianity as a path to enter into a community marked by a new respectability evidenced by cleanliness, order and respect. Still others understood Christianity as an avenue to learn how to read and write – that is, a new way of perceiving the world. There is no indication that these individuals rejected Mozambican beliefs.

Another point well worth noting is that Mozambican miners were not a *tabula rasa* in this encounter, but creatively selected, adapted and manipulated Christianity for their own benefit in the brutal compound regime. Zacarias Paindane's and SACM missionaries' accounts suggest that Mozambican miners were capable of turning the tables and manipulating literacy classes to suit their own ends. While the missionaries perceived the literacy classes as vehicles for dis-seminating the gospel and the ethic of industrial work, Mozambican miners understood these classes as a source of economic advantages and social prestige. Thus, some literate miners received some shillings from workmates for teaching them how to read and write or for writing a letter. At the Randfontein compounds, two Mozambican miners from Bilene and Catembe taught classes for workmates; at Clydesdale Collieries, another Mozambican from Manjacaze also taught night classes for his workmates. Harries and Maloka asserted that small literacy groups proliferated in the compounds and most of them worked under the guidance of church elders.[33] Other literate miners stood a chance of getting white-collar jobs or clerical and other better-paid jobs at the mine.[34] Gastão Pene Manave bluntly explained that he spent fifteen years working as a list checker for the underground miners because he was literate.[35] The encounter with Christianity offered Mozambican miners an education that permitted them to manoeuvre in the material world or climb out of it, and to avoid the most dangerous work underground.

Once Africans had accepted conversion, the Mozambican migrant encounter with Christianity and the creation of Christian com-munities in the compounds became the consequence not only of missionary activity but also of the zeal of the recent converts, who worked tirelessly to spread the faith among their workmates. One such convert was Noé Estevão Uamusse, a Mozambican miner, who explained that,

One day, I was underground working when my Xhosa co-worker, Temussana, insulted another colleague. I was astonished with the rude behaviour but kept silent. After two days I told him that I wanted to have a conversation with him but out of the working place. In fact, I went to his dormitory and I spent an enjoyable time listening to him and asking him about the verbal fight he had had with the other colleague. After that, I explained to him that to avoid trouble a man needed to be patient, to listen and to forgive. Before finishing my talk he said: 'Ah! I have really never seen you mad at or insulting anybody.' And I promptly replied: 'Because I am a Christian. I behave this way because I follow Jesus' teaching about mercy and forgiveness. In fact, I came here to invite you to come to where I learned these values.' He bluntly asked me: 'Did you learn these values in the church?' I replied: 'Yes.' Then he asked me: 'But do you want to prevent me from beer drinking on Sundays?' I answered: 'No. First we will go to the church and later on you can go to the beershop.' Sunday we went there and the Xhosa preacher addressed Jesus' mercy and forgiveness and the evils of drunkenness using daily experiences in the compounds and the Xhosa homeland. My Xhosa co-worker was so deeply touched that he told me that he wanted to quit drinking and come to church every Sunday. The following Sunday he came to collect me in the dormitory. Later on, he asked me to teach him the catechism.[36]

David Vumuca Langa, an Anglican convert, recalled that during thirty years of nursing in the compound hospital he convinced many patients to give up their charms (amulets and protective charms) and believe in God's teachings. For example, Alberto, a patient who came with a big wound in the leg, believed that the accident that had caused the wound, was a result of a *muloi*'s attack (witchcraft), and hence the charms around his wrist were protecting him. 'Using Evangelical and health knowledge I told him that he could never be saved by charms. We [human beings], of course, I assured him could do nothing; that only the Holy Spirit could change our hearts and subdue our natures.' Underground mining, Langa stressed, was dangerous work. The patient listened very respectfully to what he said in regard to Jesus and salvation, and handed the charms to him.[37]

These reminiscences reveal that, as time passed, the recent Mozambican converts made the work of proselytization their own business. Any time and any place were used by recent Mozambican converts to approach their workmates in the compound. What appeared at first to be a scattered and small group of 'intruders' or 'fanatics' were actually manifestations of new communities manoeuvring themselves into being, of small groups forging new links, manipulating, being manipulated and ultimately reconstituting themselves. Part of the success of the recent converts, I argue, was a result of converts' ability to combine evangelical teachings and everyday life experiences as a means to gain new converts. The reminiscences also shed light on the ways in which eventual Christian work was undertaken by Mozambican miner converts in southern Mozambique.

A number of African converts who had been promoted as evangelists and catechists also catalysed the process of conversion and the establishment of Christian communities in the compounds. African evangelists and catechists gathered fellow Christians in their rooms for frequent prayers and religious services. Saturday and Sunday afternoons they visited 'heathen' dormitories, prayed for the sick and held catechism classes. A quarter-century later the process was similar. For example, David Vumuca Langa, an Anglican evangelist in the mines in the 1930s, related that on Sunday mornings, accompanied by some of the African Anglican Christians, he would visit the heathen rooms and hold a short prayer service and sing hymns. Then they would go to the church for mass. According to him, during the procession sometimes a 'lost sheep' would be rescued and other people would follow the group to the church. Usually after the mass 'we asked the strangers to introduce themselves to the church community. Some stated that they were there because they liked the Anglican preaching; others said because they wanted to be Anglicans rather than Catholics.'[38] Besides the Sunday morning procession from dormitory to dormitory, Langa explained, oftentimes 'he [Langa] moved from one compound to another preaching in dormitories, counselling miners about their personal problems and preparing work-mates for baptism'.[39] Most of his teachings were filled with daily experiences from the compound.

Another interesting account of conversion and the building of Christian communities was told by Bonifácio Macie, a Mozambican miner, living in Manave's catechist room. Bonifácio Macie, reminiscing on his mining life forty years ago, related:

> I am so proud of catechist Gastão Pene Manave, who lives here in Maciene. In Jone, he was the catechist in our room. In spite of labouring all day in the mine, every evening Manave [as other catechists and evangelists] not only held an evensong but also taught catechism to the heathens. On Saturday, he visited new converts, the sick or the heathens in various compounds. On Sunday, he held matins and after that a procession from

room to room. He sang and preached to the heathens. Then he would lead his group to the church. During the mass he acted as *turukela* [interpreter] of the Shangaan or Xhosa languages. Many people loved and respected his preaching. I knew some Mozambicans who became Christians because of his teachings.[40]

Like Bonifácio Macie, Baker narrated a story about Titus Ndaba, a Chopi convert and evangelist from Gazaland. According to Baker, during a Sunday morning service Titus Ndaba attempted to interpret the Scripture: '[T]here is a way that seemeth right unto man, but the end thereof are the ways of death.' He preached:

> My brothers, there is a serpent on every path, and the man who trifles with it is a fool. If you play with sin it will bite you. A habit may seem very small and harmless, but indulged in, like the use of strong drink, or immorality, it ends in death. The only safe path is to follow Jesus Christ's, and then the end will be eternal life.[41]

Ndaba's sermon, as well as those of other Mozambican evangelists or catechists, was not merely picturesque. Behind the simple, figurative talk was the sincerity of one who knew the people to whom he was talking, their failures and weaknesses as well as their kindly and generous qualities of heart. Knowing and loving the people whom they were addressing and their besetting sins, they denounced the wrongs of everyday life and warned their listeners about the danger of disregarding the manifold calls which God had vouchsafed to them. Simon Nkomo, a Shangaan convert, preaching to his workmates, gave the example of a young man from Gazaland who during three years in a mine, collected pieces of corncobs, bones, rags, bits of coal, and other odds and ends and deposited them in two beautiful trunks. After he ended his term he went home. Once there and before the excited family and welcoming neighbours, he opened the trunks disclosing the odds and ends. When his father saw them he shouted: 'Get rid of this, you idiot!' Simon interpreted:

> [M]y dear friends, you have another Father, Who is in heaven. He sent you into the world to work for him. If you spend your life in accumulating earthly treasures, when you get up there into the presence of God, and your boxes are opened, God will say to you, 'you idiot! … And He will bundle you and your rubbish into the outer darkness. You better begin to find out what kind of things pass current in heaven, and lay up treasure where the moth and the rust cannot corrupt, and where thieves do not break through and steal.[42]

In sum, the testimonies of Mozambican and other African[43] evangelists and catechists and Baker's account highlight the varied means they employed to gain a growing number of converts. It was through their commitment that Africans with ethnic and language differences could worship and belong to the same Christian community. Maloka states that at Knights Deep mine in Germiston, for example, the Sothos and Shangaans held a joint Christmas service. Ethnic and language differences were not barriers to such efforts, since many Africans spoke more than one language and could translate for those who could not understand the services.[44] Thus, ethnic and language barriers were not obstacles in the process of building Christian communities in the compounds. Another point explicit in these accounts is that it was Mozambican and other African catechists and evangelists who made Christianity shine and live in the compounds. Their zeal and commitment to the work of God did not fade when they returned to their villages. It found expression in setting up their own congregations at home.

Although not explicit in the Mozambican miners' accounts, there was already in the African religions the requisite belief structure to which missionaries could appeal, and upon which they could enlarge and build the Christian faith. African/Mozambicans believed that the ancestor spirits, known in southern Mozambique as *Swikwembu*,[45] are the masters of everything: earth, fields, trees, rain, men, women, children, even wizards. They had full control over all these entities or persons. The *Swikwembu* would bless or curse and bring misfortune on their descendants. They were the most powerful spiritual agency acting on man's life; hence the necessity of propitiating them with prayers and offerings.

To compare the characteristics of African religions with Christian religion is to find significant similarities, which can be grouped as in Table 4.2. These similarities, I would argue, help us understand how the conception of *Swikwembu* as both transcendence and possessing divine moral attributes made it easy for some Mozambicans to accept Christianity into their lives. God was one more spirit to help and protect them. In this context, two general ideas grew out of the ferment of evangelization in the mines and had a considerable impact on Mozambican miner converts. First, it is clear that Mozambican miner converts perceived that, in principle, they suffered no ritual or cultural stigma from participating in Christian religious life. Second, they conceived a narrative continuity in religion more pervasive,

Table 4.2 Similarities between Christian and African religions

Characteristic	African religion	Christian religion	Meaning
Spiritualistic religion	Yes: *Swikwembu*	Yes: God	Spiritual entities worshipped
Omnipresence	Yes: *Swikwembu*	Yes: God	Present everywhere but not physically
Omniscience	Yes: *Swikwembu*	Yes: God	Acknowledge what their people do although spatially and physically distant
Omnipotence	Yes: *Swikwembu*	Yes: God	Absolute control over living and non-living entities
Sacerdotal religion	Yes: eldest brother	Yes: priest	
Religious acts	Yes: *Swikwembu*	Yes: God	Prayers and offerings
Animistic religion	Yes	No	Various gods

all-embracing and comprehensive than the Western view of religion as a separate department of life. They related Christianity to the whole system of life. For instance, some Mozambican converts saw Christianity as a path to learning to read and write. Literacy allowed them to understand the mine managers in the mine workplace and the Portuguese colonial administrators. Some Mozambican converts learned and practised professions such as evangelist, catechist and teacher in the compound. Others understood conversion as a way to entitle them to run their Christian communities themselves and to gain secular advantage. Other Mozambican converts used Christianity in those areas of life over which their community felt little of control, such as beer drinking, praying for the sick, and comforting the relatives of the dead. In sum, they considered Christianity as a path to spiritual, educational, economic and/or social advantages.

The process of conversion and building of Christian communities in the compounds was not a linear but rather a complex one characterized by resistance, struggles and acceptance. Having demonstrated the success in Mozambique of converting and creating Christian communities, we can now consider some unsuccessful attempts at conversion. Accounts show that there were Mozambican and other

African miners who refused conversion. Perhaps they reacted this way because Christian activities took place in the miners' leisure time or because they did not understand what the African catechists and evangelists and missionaries were doing since the Africans were there only to dig diamonds and gold. The most common forms of open resistance or sabotage of a church service or meeting were the playing of drums and xylophones and shouting. Noé Estevão Uamusse, Mozambican evangelist, recalled that on different occasions when visiting the rooms of heathens he heard words of contempt and mockery. One miner asked: 'Who are you? What do you want here? How much are you going to pay me? We are here for mining.' Other miners would laugh and shout hurrah [good idea, very good]! Suca! Huma [get out]![46] Similarly, Latimer Fuller, an Anglican missionary who gathered his group at a corner in the compound courtyard, explained:

> When we start preaching, there is a band and a thump from the corner and you know that the pianos have begun: six men with a sort of drumstick in each hand start to belabour the pianos, and we perceive an evident unsteadiness in the congregation.... [Meantime] a terrific yell comes from a distant doorway ... in a moment he is joined by a twenty dancing natives stamping, shouting and yelling till perspiration runs off them in streams, and the congregation moves off to the dance while we proceed to another and quieter mine.[47]

Even physical attacks and acts of vandalism on converts were not uncommon. Philip Nyampule, Baker's Chopi convert, who had given up beer drinking, found his books ripped apart, his writing slate broken, and his way to a Sunday service barred by dormitory mates and former beer-drinking friends.[48] A similar experience was related by Gastão Pene Manave, who explained that one day when trying to advise a colleague who had had a drunken fight he was told rudely: 'Let me alone guy. I never care about your preaching', and the colleague covered himself with a blanket.[49]

Yet, despite resistance and setbacks, Mozambican miners built Christian communities in the South African mine compounds at the turn of the nineteenth century. Brass band performances, magic lantern shows, open-air religious services, conversation among work-mates and literacy classes were the various ways in which Mozambican and other African miners were converted to Christianity and new communities created in which ethnic and language differences were overcome. Moreover, it is worthwhile to note that even though the European missionaries had played an important role in the conversion of the first Africans to Christianity, African converts were the key players in the process of conversion and building of Christian communities in the mine compounds. Africans contracted as evangelist, catechist, pastor or simply convert used any opportunity to preach and convert more co-workers to the Christian faith.

Returning with the Bible to the Countryside

[Diamane] with a Bible and a hymn book in his haversack, and a mackintosh over his shoulders, off he went.[50]

While in the Kimberley and Witwatersrand compounds, thousands of Mozambican miners acquired some knowledge and practice of Christianity, and when they went back to their villages they began to preach the Christian message. It may be that they only grasped the most elementary rudiments of the Christian faith; nevertheless, one-third of returning miners started to propagate their new-found faith. Within two to three years some miner converts had already created tiny congregations of believers, members of their households or simply neighbours. This section will demonstrate that miners also spread Christian ideas through the reading charts, literature and writing material that they read or offered on arriving home. Still others returned to their villages with the intention of starting a day school. Yet, by and large, the Mozambican miners' activities were not planned or prepared by the European congregations operating in the compound mines. It simply happened because of the zeal and commitment of Mozambican miner converts, at a time when the training of African agents was still far from high on the normal missionary agenda.

The experience of Titos Baúle, a miner converted to Christianity, provides a fine example of the process of Christianization in mining compounds and in southern Mozambique. According to his son, Titos Baúle was probably born in 1861. He was captured during Ngungunyana's raids in the Chopiland and taken to Chaimite to work as a slave. From there Titos Baúle fled to South Africa. In South Africa he converted to the Christian faith while working on the mines. Upon his return, and before settling at Baúle–Chidenguele, he went to Bilene to marry Lina Maxaeie, the sister of his friend and workmate in mining and religion. Afterwards he went back to Baúle alone for a short time and then returned to Bilene to fetch his wife. He started to sing and pray alone in his hut. After that he invited his relatives and neighbours to pray. Jonatana Titos Baúle recalled:

> When my dad arrived at Baúle, the people were heathens. My dad did not face obstacles in converting the Baúle community because he asked permission from the chief of the land, called Mavilane, and had family connections with the majority of this community's members. When the number of women and men grew, he built a small hut in his yard. He prayed and sang in Zulu but interpreted into Chopi. He never returned to South Africa.[51]

Estevão Mulate Baúle, an Anglican convert, corroborated Jonatana Titos Baúle's account: 'When Titos Baúle arrived, he held a meeting with his brothers and relatives where he explained that he had found Christ in South Africa, and had returned home to act as missionary among his heathen community.'[52] His denomination was the Church of England. He started to preach at Kokola La Mahoo where the Baúle community lived near the swamp to hide from the Ngungunyana's attacks.[53] Indeed, in 1951 Francis Boatwright, an Anglican missionary, acknowledged publicly that Titos had taught his people even before Bishop Smyth was consecrated the first bishop of the diocese in 1893. Titos was therefore one of the grandfathers of the Diocese of Lebombo. Blind for the last ten years of his life, he never ceased teaching the gospel; he knew all the prayer book and most of the Bible by heart.[54]

Titos Baúle's experience was strikingly similar to other Mozambican miners, varying only in time, space and the quality of personal relationships with Mozambican chiefs.

Djobe Mucavele and Jeremias Mucavele, too, carried the Gospel to Maciene. Paulo Estevão Macie recalled:

> The Anglican religion in Maciene was brought by the Mozambican miners who went to the Rand by foot. When they left Maciene they were heathens. In the compounds beside eating and sleeping, repair work or mending, they were learning to read and write from the Bible. When they arrived home, they talked about their adventures. Among other things they discussed the *Bava Mfundissi* [the priest], and what he taught about Jesus and the resurrection. After that, they prayed and invited the wives,

children and the neighbours to learn what they had learned in the Rand. In time, these men went back to the Rand and asked the missionaries to follow them, to go to their country and baptise their converts. Djobe Mafumo [Mucavele] and Jeremias Mucavele were the Mozambican miners who started to teach and spread the Gospel in Maciene well before the English Anglican missionaries. They were also the ones who invited the missionaries to go to Maciene.[55]

Similarly, Felisberto Chinhamane Chilengue described Djobe Mucavele preaching and successfully converting and gaining followers. He eventually moved from open-air meetings to a hut that he built and set up a *chiluvelo*, an altar for worship. During the service, Djobe Mucavele stood and preached in front of the *chiluvelo* with lighted candles.[56] Jeremias Mucavele,[57] Chicogo Djobe's brother-in-law and workmate from the mines, read and interpreted the Bible during the mass. In these early days, Felisberto Chilengue concurred that 'God's prophets did not wear a special cloth, instead they used regular clothes brought from South Africa.'[58] Later on, Djobe Mucavele travelled to Jone, where he reported to the missionaries on the flock that had joined him.[59]

Although many Maciene informants asserted that Djobe Mucavele and Jeremias Mucavele, among others, were the key players in the propagation of Christianity in Maciene, some offered a slightly different version. For example, Matilde Chicogo, supporting Paulo Macie's and Felisberto Chilengue's accounts, stated that although Djobe Mucavele and his male collaborators did not teach women and children to lead the prayers, in their absence women and children prayed and sang. And hence women and children also played a significant role in propagating or maintaining the Christian faith.[60] Celita Uamusse, stressing the same point, explained that from the very beginning of Djobe Mucavele's preaching women constituted the majority of attendants. 'We, children were not allowed to attend catechism classes because sometimes we played during the work.'[61] Both women asserted that Djobe Mucavele had never baptised anybody.[62]

Titos Baúle's and Djobe Mucavele's[63] experiences demonstrate the ways in which Mozambican miners built Christian communities in Maciene district. Second, their experiences of conversion in the compounds in some ways were replicated in the countryside of Mozambique. For instance, the process of conversion and subsequent formation of Christian communities at the mines started in open-air meetings, in evangelist visits to the dormitory or in talks with a co-worker. In the Maciene district, in small face-to-face settings, miner converts talked about Jesus to close relatives, and demonstrated how to pray. In addition, the church hierarchy they had known in the South African compounds was implemented in the Maciene district: positions of leadership in the church were confined to men. Nevertheless, in the context of Maciene, women had begun unofficially to play these roles.

Finally, these miners' experiences also suggest that while Mozambican converts were preaching the gospel, at the same time they were introducing new values to their communities. These included:

1. *The meaning of special space and time* To pray to God there is a need for a chapel (with *chiluvelo*, candles, crucifix, cassocks) and a specific time to worship. Mozambican miner converts built a small hut where they set up an altar for worship.[64] Consequently, people had to plan their daily activities knowing that they should make time for their prayers. For example, Sunday was no longer a field-working day.

2. *The new notion of hierarchy in the church* There was a community of believers, preachers, evangelists, priests and bishops with specific tasks to perform.

3. *The new principles of dressing* The dress of the miner converts leading or attending the religious services led Mozambican new converts to accept the convention of wearing European clothes rather than Mozambican muchecas and tangas when in church services. Thus women would exchange the Mozambican culture of tangas, a single strip of cloth round the waist, for Western dresses, which covered the shoulders and the upper part of the body. This visible distinction would apparently mark off the Christians from the rest of the community for many years, providing missionaries with a rough but convenient method of identifying their adherents. Missionary Stowell, visiting Maciene district, noted that on a Sunday there would be seen, in some of these 'straw' churches, as many as fifty or sixty people, dressed in 'clean' and 'beautiful' clothes, while outside would be sitting a few 'heathen' women, dressed in a single strip of cloth round the waist, their hair and bodies smeared with bright red earth.[65] Mozambican miner converts were important agents of change in their home regions both culturally and religiously.

Unlike in Chidenguele and Maciene, where the chiefs generally permitted miner converts to spread the Word of God, in Nhamavila miner converts oftentimes experienced their rude and brutal power. Under the threat of conscription to *chibalo*,[66] Zaqueu Machai and Isaías Nhatave spread and built Christian communities. According to Noé Estevão Uamusse, Zaqueu Machai left home for the Witwatersrand. It was during his sojourn in the Rand that he encountered Christianity, and was baptised and confirmed. Back home, Zaqueu Machai asked permission to preach to the chief. The chief sent his messengers to watch Zaqueu's performance. Zaqueu gathered his family and stood up, holding the crucifix, praying and preaching. The messengers were impressed, and asked him the meaning of the figure on the crucifix. Zaqueu Machai explained that it was Jesus Christ crucified, and added: 'for God so loved the world that He gave His only begotten Son, that whoever believes in Him should not perish but have everlasting life'.[67] The chief authorized Zaqueu Machai to preach all over the land. Nevertheless, on various occasions, the messengers would secretly appear to check on Zaqueu Machai's activities, according to Noé Estevão Uamusse.[68]

Isaías Nhatave's experience was different from that of Zaqueu Machai in one important aspect. Nhatave and his Christian community had ended up in *chibalo*. Ribeiro Nhatave, nephew of Nhatave, explained:

> [My] uncle Isaías suffered a lot to spread Christianity because of Portuguese persecution. When my uncle and other converts were praying, frequently the chief of the land would appear and arrest the people and take them into *chibalo*. My uncle ended up working at *chibalo*. Despite these Portuguese persecutions, my uncle continued to preach the gospel. Later on, he went to Maciene to invite the missionaries to baptise his converts.[69]

Zaqueu Machai's and Isaías Nhatave's experiences demonstrate the vulnerability of the miners' evangelization and the response of miner converts, depending upon local circumstances. These events might explain the long period spent forming a Christian congregation.

Contrary to the situation in Nhamavila, in Zandamela in spite of some chiefs' claims of authority, miner converts had room to preach, to create Christian communities, as well as to establish contacts and friendship with other miner congregations. Often a miner convert would visit or invite another miner convert to preach in his congregation and/or talk about his work and community. Among themselves they might exchange religious material, ideas or information. For example, Naftal and Marta Buque and Artur Massochane Chibuque recalled that Josefa Mutiwa Buque, who brought Christianity to Buquene, had links with Djobe Mucavele, Titos Baúle, Unkuanovane, Daniel and Júlio Dumangane. In looking back, Marta Buque thought that these networks were not only the seeds of the formation of the Anglican community but also provided evangelical and secular news and support to the Mozambican miner converts scattered all over the country.[70] Her husband, Naftal Buque, one of the oldest Mozambican Anglican priests, asserted that it was through these networks that Josefa Mutiwa Buque contacted the Anglican missionaries at Maciene.[71] Similarly, Jonatana Titos Baúle recalled that several times Josuel Maxaeie, his uncle from Bilene Macie, went and preached at Baúle.[72] David Vumuca Langa also remembered that Isaías Cossa and Mateus Cossa were oftentimes guest evangelists from Nhocoene-Chongoene to Bahanine.[73]

These reminiscences suggest that the brotherhood, which grew out of the dormitory or church in South Africa, was extended to a much broader community of Christians. Shangaans from Bilene and Chopis from Zandamela felt as close as siblings, a phenomenon that might have seemed almost impossible given the divisions left during the Ngungunyana regime. Christianity was breaking down ethnic and language barriers and creating a community of Christians. In fact, the evangelical teachings had enabled Mozambican converts to perceive that the derogatory names or distinctions of people according to ethnic group was the work of men. Every human being had the same constitution. In these new Christian communities Mozambican converts were able to travel and exchange ideas with other converts – that is, to broaden their world-view. Moreover, these communities were also used as a network for the selection of a good marriage partner, family alliances and help in case of need. It was the practice of parents far from the schools to house their children with a fellow Christian family while they were educated. Finally, the reminiscences imply that the converts' links facilitated the Anglican and other missionaries' efforts to establish their congregations and legitimize leadership in the region.

Missionary Donald F. Stowell echoed the Mozambican accounts. He asserted that every petty chiefdom had Christian villages, and many of these had a specially built church of mud and wattle, with an altar, crucifix, candlesticks, pictures and vestry in which to hang cassocks and store supplies for the catechists, preachers and helpers. There, a dozen people, particularly the miner converts, prayed to Jesus every morning and afternoon but especially on Sundays. These little centres of Christian life that Stowell recognized had sprung up all over Maciene district, despite the absence of white missionaries.[74] Missionary Philip Mkize, remembering the early days of Anglican mission work in Maciene, stated that by the time Maciene became the biggest centre in the diocese, the Shangaan miners, who alternated between Maciene and the Rand, were mostly responsible for the rapid growth of the work in Maciene. Many of them, Mkize explained, converted on the Rand, and when they returned to their homes 'they not only stuck to the religion taught to them by the missionaries at the mines, but passed it on to their people, when whole families were converted.'[75] Matias James (Jaime) Chicogo, former student, teacher, catechist and priest of Maciene, eulogizing the life of Bishop William Edmund Smyth, who passed away on 5 April 1950, wrote:

> [B]ishop Smyth came to us while I was young. I can hardly call to my mind and I heard and saw him doing at Maciene.... Bishop Smyth's last visit to Maciene was in 1912. He arrived at Maciene and found almost the largest congregation he had had during his visits to Maciene. He said, 'I met some of you at the diamond mines, Kimberley. I followed you to your country.'[76]

In other words, the first Anglican work in Maciene district was a result not of the evangelization of the European missions, but rather of the Mozambican miner converts.[77]

Parallel to the miner converts' proselytization, miners with a knowledge of literacy and a desire to teach reading and writing also promoted Christianity in southern Mozambique, particularly in the Maciene district. On their departure from South Africa they took with them supplies of catechisms and Bibles, spelling books and slates, bottles of ink, pens and pencils, so as to be able to start teaching as soon as they arrived home. Titos Baúle, who had been converted and instructed in the mysteries of the three Rs in the mines, back home taught *ba, be, bi, bo, bu* to women and men. According to Jonatana Titos Baúle, his father was conscious that a strong Christian community needs people knowledgeable in catechism and the Bible, and hence he undertook the teaching of these, besides preaching the Word of God. Lucas and Joel Nhangave were some of Titos's pupils and later on helpers in evangelization.[78]

A similar point of view was expressed by a group of informants from Maciene. Matilde Chicogo remembered that from the time she was very young she saw some Maciene women attending Djobe's catechism classes. Djobe had a guidebook with questions and answers. He instructed the women that if he asked, 'Who created you?'; they would answer: 'God created me'; and to 'What did God create you for?', they would respond: 'God created me to know, to believe and to love Him on the earth and in the heaven.' And so on. Women learnt by rote.[79] Felisberto Chinhamane Chilengue concurred that Djobe asked questions of, and taught the answers to, men and women. He also taught the Lord's Prayer and Holy Mary's Prayer by rote. Finally, Paulo Estevão Macie added, Djobe started to teach catechism to his family and relatives and then to neighbours and people from the Maciene community. Back in Jone he told the missionaries that members of his village, including his own family, knew the catechism. Djobe used Xilengue as the language in which to teach them.[80]

Others, like Ambrósio Langa, had worked for several years in Kimberley where he had learned to read and write Zulu, and where he had converted. When he returned to Bahanine in early 1900, he attempted, successfully, to bring literacy to his community. Simultaneously with preaching, Ambrósio Langa gathered some boys and taught them how to write and read in Zulu. David Vumuca Langa remembered hearing from his brother from Joni:

Father and mother
I am writing this letter to let you know how I am doing. I live in a Christian dormitory, there are so many of us, I meet people from all over Africa. People I live with come from all corners of southern Africa – including countries like Lesotho, Malawi, Botswana and South Africa. Every evening we meet for a prayer meetings…

This is all I have for today. Send my regards to everyone at home. May God protect and bless you all.[81]

David Langa said that it was typical of those who wanted to show that they had mastered the Zulu language. However, Ambrósio Langa, not satisfied with his level of education and eager to spread literacy in the community, enrolled his son Stefani in the Swiss mission boarding school at Ricatla – Marracuene. There Stefani studied secular and ecclesiastical subjects. Back in Bahanine, Stefani combined evangelical and literacy work teaching boys as well as adults. By using the book *Lições de Coisas* (*Lessons of Things*), boys were taught Portuguese while adults were instructed in Shangaan through *Buko La Vaxaheie* (*The Speaker's Book*). At that time, David Vumuca Langa explained, the Anglican church did not have a boarding school, and therefore, the only option was to enrol at the Swiss mission school.[82]

Notwithstanding the scarcity of detailed records, the evidence suggests that the people of Maciene district were first introduced to literacy or Western education through the efforts of Mozambican miner converts. In their evangelization, Mozambican miner converts started a rudimentary school, teaching catechism and the Bible, as well as reading and writing African languages. In fact, the education was *ipso facto* biblical. The early students were ordinary men, women and children. Some adults were nearly sixty. The classes were held under trees or in the small chapels.

Mozambican miner converts, using their experiences of literacy on the Rand, thought that catechism, Scripture and the Bible were textbooks for schooling. To be literate meant to know the catechism by rote and, later on, to read the Bible. Indeed, this approach was validated by the Anglican missionaries when they arrived and began to examine the Maciene/Nhamavila/Zandamela/Baúle candidates for baptism. In the eyes of these people education was the learning of religious subjects. As a result, in Maciene and other parts of southern Mozambique, religious teachings preceded the formal Western conception of education.

In sum, oral accounts of the spreading of Christianity in the Maciene district reveal that Christian congregations existed there from the very early days of the Diocese of Lebombo, around 1894, mostly along the two main routes from the Limpopo to Inhambane. They were founded by those who returned from work in Kimberley and the Witwatersrand. Mozambican testimonies and missionary records indicate that Mozambican miner converts asked the missionaries in Kimberley and the Witwatersrand to follow them home and to baptise their converts, because they did not have the authority to perform such ceremonies themselves. However, it is still difficult to assess the size of the Mozambican congregations in those days due to scanty statistical data. To some extent, these accounts allow the reader to infer that what Mozambican miner converts preached might be a combination of what they learned and saw in the compound proselytising process, as well as what they interpreted through their own cultural filters. Nevertheless, these Mozambicans with a leadership capacity, which was then honed through evangelistic work on the mines, became important agents of change in their home regions, both culturally and religiously. The establishment of Christian congregations by Mozambican miner converts was not a smooth process, but rather a complex one characterized by struggle, negotiation and adaptation. These Mozambican congregations were seeded by the arrival of Mozambican miner converts and consolidated both by women and by the labour of Mozambican evangelists who devoted themselves to Christian teaching.

Portuguese State Efforts to Blunt Evangelization

As already indicated, returning Mozambican miners from Kimberley and the Witwatersrand were posing a serious threat to the stability of the Portuguese and Roman Catholic colonization agenda. Governor-General Freire de Andrade, contemplating the Bibles in the miners' boxes, asserted not only that it was out of character for Catholic missionaries to sell Bibles to these miners, but also that those Bibles were going to be used in the propagation of gospel and literacy, and hence expand the world-view of the people of the countryside. Moreover, Portuguese administrators and governors of southern Mozambique saw the labour migration to South Africa as a potential political danger to the whole region, and therefore, tried to thwart the Mozambican miners 'de-nationalizing' activities.[83] Thus, in July 1902, in an official letter to the governor-general of Mozambique, the governor of Gaza advised that the Chongoene and Muchopes lands had been granted to the Franciscan mission.[84] This was a move to counter the presence of Mozambican congregations commonly called Protestants. The Portuguese viewed the Protestant work as de-nationalizing, and hence undermining of official attempts at colonization. The governor of Gaza wanted to close the 'Protestant road' for the sake of Portugal's own imperialistic interests. In fact, by December 1903, in a exploratory visit, Franciscan priest Camilo Gaveta found many Protestant schools (reed chapels) in the interior of Gaza led by catechists (maybe evangelists) teaching in the Zulu language. He also met the Bishop of the Diocese of Lebombo, William Eduard Smyth, visiting the so-called schools. Thus, in January 1907 the Franciscan mission settled at the *cabo* (headland) Nhadamel, 1 kilometre from Chongoene and 15 kilometres from Xai-Xai.[85]

From 1901 to 1905, in a friendly and cooperative correspondence between the governor of the Military District of Gaza and the head priest of the Roman Catholic mission of S. Paulo de Gaza, Messano, the officials discussed and planned how to frustrate the proliferation of the Protestant missions. While the governor asked the mission to establish a station and schools in the Muchopes region, the head priest of the mission solicited the governor to order the *régulos*[86] to forcibly recruit Mozambican children to study in the Roman Catholic schools. In 1903 the mission opened five day schools for Mozambican children, so-called *indígenas*.[87] In 1908/9 the Franciscan mission opened schools at *régulo* Makupulana (Muchopes circumscription) and *régulo* Xiahlo (Xai-Xai circumscription), the places where Mozambican miner converts such as Titos Baúle, Isaías Nhatave, Zaqueu Machai, Ambrósio Langa, Djobe Mucavele and their helpers spread the gospel.

The Portuguese tried to thwart these Mozambican miner convert initiatives further by arresting the converts and sending them to forced labour. Isaias Nhatave's experience, described elsewhere, provides a classic illustration of Portuguese brutality and anti-Mozambican policy. Events of this nature were also reported in Anglican records. A letter addressed to the Bishop of Lebombo in 1905, complaining about the Portuguese brutalities, including the fact that the local commandant had been sent to arrest an Anglican subdeacon in church during a Sunday service that he was conducting.[88] A similar event was described in a bishop's report, which stated that one of his pupils was arrested at the church while he was conducting a service.[89]

While it is difficult to know from the limited sources available to what degree the Portuguese attempts to frustrate the Mozambican initiatives succeeded, it is at least clear that the Mozambicans continued singing loudly, praying and preaching openly in daylight every Sunday, under a tree or in a small chapel. The data strongly support my contention that it was Mozambican miner converts of the Maciene district who were responsible for the main work of proselytising.

Conclusion

This chapter has focused thus far on the diverse strategies that Mozambicans used to straddle the European mission and the colonial world, to cope and struggle to construct a Christian religious experience rooted in their culture and identity. I have identified and analysed the process of the Mozambican encounter with Christianity and the building of Christian communities both in South African compounds and in southern Mozambique, especially in the Maciene district. As has been shown, Mozambicans were clearly the key actors in the process of appropriating Christianity and literacy, interpreting it for other Mozambicans as well as building new communities for their own ends and interests.

In South Africa, Mozambican miners were introduced to Christianity and the building of Christian communities in brass band performances, magic-lantern shows, open-air religious meetings, conversation among co-workers and literacy classes. Although there were compound motivations behind the Mozambican desire to be Christian, it was the Mozambican/African perception of the world based on spirituality that provided the conditions in which the Christian message was heard, accepted and transmitted to other Mozambicans. Mozambican miner converts related Christianity to the whole system of life: for them, Christianity was a path to attain spiritual, educational, economic or social advantages.

In southern Mozambique, particularly the Maciene district, it is clear that Mozambican miner converts, not Europeans, introduced the gospel and literacy. The gospel and literacy did not arrive by sea in big ships with 'civilization': they were spread by Mozambican miner converts. Mozambican miner converts were not a 'lost herd' or simply 'converts'. They were integral actors in the founding of the Anglican mission of Santo Agostinho – Maciene. Goodall recognized this in the early 1950s: '[A]s a matter of history, the faith was first carried to Lebombo by migrant miners.'[90] Notwithstanding Portuguese attempts to diminish Maciene miners' evangelical and literacy efforts, their initiatives grew throughout the Maciene district, and helped to establish the Protestant presence there.

Notes

1. The Anglican mission of Santo Agostinho – Maciene is a geographical area that includes Chongoene, Maciene, Zandamela, Nhamavila, Cucuine, Cumbene, Nhacutse, Manjacaze, Chidenguele, Nhatsembene and Xai-Xai. Sometimes it is called the Central District of the Diocese of Lebombo. It is a cathedral of the Anglican mission in southern Mozambique. In this article 'Maciene district' refers to this geographical area. 'Maciene' refers to the headquarters.

2. Freire d'Andrade, *Relatório sobre Moçambique*, Lourenço Marques, 1907, p. 232.

3. Ibid., pp. 229–32.

4. Throughout this chapter I use the phrase 'African–mission encounter' as shorthand for the multi-level, multifaceted, complex engagements, avoidances, accommodations and interpretations that developed at the interfaces of Christian teaching and initiatives and African peoples, cultures and societies. The term embodies great complexity, and is not intended to essentialize any specific modality. On the contrary, the chapter is broadly concerned with teasing out these very complexities.

5. Ngungunhane was the king of the Gaza empire in the late nineteenth century.

6. For instance W.H. Malton and the testimonies of the first Anglican missionaries to arrive in Mozambique asserted that the latter introduced the Anglicanism in the region and in Maciene: 'it will be remembered that at this time (1895) many of the Chopi were at Delagoa, and that John Matthews, himself a Chopi, was beginning work among them; their return to their own country created the nucleus there of a Christian community, but Chopiland had to wait.' W.H.C. Malton, *The Story of the Lebombo Diocese*, London, 1912, p. 112. Other literature supporting Anglican missionaries as pioneers is: Latimer Fuller, *Light on Lebombo*, Westminster, 1920; Eduardo Moreira, *Portuguese East Africa: A Study of Its Religious Needs*, New York, 1936; John Paul, *Mozambique: Memoirs of a Revolution*, Harmondsworth, 1975.

7. Since the Methuen Treaty of 1703, the Portuguese economy had been beholden to British manufacturers. Under this agreement, British textiles could freely enter the Portuguese market, thus effectively hampering the growth of Portugal's own domestic industry, and in return Portuguese wine had preferential entry to Britain. Portugal paid for this uneven trade balance with Brazilian gold, and this helped to consolidate London as the financial centre of Europe. Departamento de História, *História de Moçambique*, vol. 2, Maputo, 1983; F. Félix Lopes, *Missões Franciscanas em Moçambique*, Braga, 1972; José Manuel Garcia, *História de Portugal: Uma Visão Global*, Lisbon, 1986; Walter C. Opeelo, *Portugal: From Monarchy to Pluralist Democracy*, Boulder CO, 1991.

8. Allen Isaacman and Barbara Isaacman, *Mozambique: From Colonialism*

to Revolution, 1900–1982, Boulder CO, 1983, pp. 29–31; Departamento de História, *História de Moçambique*, vol. 2, pp. 89–92, 242; Alf Hegelsson, *Church, State and People in Mozambique*, Uppsala, 1994, pp. 94–5, 127. For more details, see Jeanne Marie Penvenne, *African Workers and Colonial Racism: Mozambican Strategies and Struggles in Lourenço Marques, 1877–1962*, London, 1995.

9. There is much literature discussing this issue but the most important include: Ruth First, *Black Gold: The Mozambican Miner, Proletariat and Peasants*, Hassocks, 1983; Isaacman and Isaacman, *Mozambique*; Gervase Clarence-Smith, *The Third Portuguese Empire 1825–1975: A Study in Economic Imperialism*, Oxford, 1985; Departamento de História, *História de Moçambique*, vols 2 and 3; Malyn Newitt, *A History of Mozambique*, London, 1995.

10. Departamento de História, *História de Moçambique*, vol. 2, pp. 109–17, 131–52, 166, 173–84.

11. Even before the discovery of the Witwatersrand goldfields many Mozambicans travelled to Natal and the Cape, largely in pursuit of relatively higher wages. In fact, men began selling their labour for a wage before the final conquest and establishment of the colonial state. Three factors can be identified to explain why this should have occurred: the early impact of merchant capital; the Ngoni invasion; and the development of plantation agriculture and mining in South Africa. In 1857 authorization was given for voluntary migration from Lourenço Marques to Natal by sea (Decree no. 152, 2 August 1857). In 1875 the authorization was extended to permit Mozambicans to work in the Cape Province (Decree no. 246, 18 July 1875). The first statute governing migration regulations for the employment of Mozambicans in the South African Republic (Transvaal) was enacted in 1897 (Decree no. 100, 18 November 1897) issued by the colonial governor of Mozambique, Mouzinho de Albuquerque. For a detailed discussion on the issue see First, *Black Gold*; Departamento de História, *História de Moçambique*, vol. 2; Patrick Harries, *Work, Culture and Identity: Migrant Labourers in Mozambique and South Africa, c. 1860–1910*, Johannesburg, 1994.

12. First, *Black Gold*; Penvenne, *African Workers and Colonial Racism*.

13. S.E. Katzenellenbogen, *South Africa and Southern Mozambique: Labour, Railways and Trade in the Making of Relationship*, Oxford, 1982, p. 38.

14. Andrade, *Relatório sobre Moçambique*, p. 59. First argues that in the period 1896–98, 60 per cent of mineworkers employed by WENELA (Chamber of Mines) were Mozambicans. By 1906, the figure had risen to 65 per cent. First, *Black Gold*, p. 16.

15. The need for and control of the Mozambican labour force brought competition, conflicts and tensions among South African mining capital, the colonial Portuguese administration, Portuguese colonial settlers and Portuguese metropolitan capitalists. Important literature to consult: Katzenellebogen, *South Africa and Southern Mozambique*; First, *Black*

Gold; Clarence-Smith, *The Third Portuguese Empire*; Departamento de História, *História de Moçambique*, vols 2 and 3; Harries, *Work, Culture and Identity*.

16. Although I was able to draw on the ideas and experiences of old miners because of the similarities of the process, their accounts were limited to the period in living memory and I was obliged to use, for my evidence, third- and fourth-generation miners' experiences and documentary sources.

17. For instance, in Kimberley by 1883 the Congregationalists were installed at the Kimberley mine and Du Toit's Pan; by 1885 the Methodists had nearly 200 members in the mines. The Anglicans, Dutch Reformed, Roman Catholics and Lutherans soon followed. It is worthwhile to note that in 1878 nearly 8,000 Mozambicans, so-called Shangaans, made up about 30 per cent of the workers in the diamond diggings. In the gold mines of the Witwatersrand (a region that stretches from Springs through Johannesburg to Randfontein) although missionary efforts had begun as early as the 1890s, they increased after 1896, when Albert Baker established the interdenominational South African Compound Mission (SACM). There Baker established halls for worship, schools and cottages for evangelists. By 1899, out of 100,000 African miners, 20,000 were Mozambicans, the so-called East coast boys. Harries, *Work, Culture and Identity*, p. 49; Albert W. Baker, *Grace Triumphant: The Life Story of a Carpenter, Lawyer and Missionary in South Africa from 1856 to 1939*, London, 1939, pp. 101–2; C.F. Pascoe, *Two Hundreds Years of the S.P.G.: An Historical Account of the Society for the Propagation in Foreign Parts, 1710–1900*, London, 1901, p. 358.

18. W.T.G. Hogue, *G. Harry Agnew: A Pioneer Missionary*, Chicago, 1905, pp. 214–17; Harries, *Work, Culture and Identity*, pp. 195–8; T. Maloka, 'The Struggle for Sunday: All-male Christianity in the Gold Mine Compounds', in Richard Elphick and Rodney Davenport (eds), *Christianity in South Africa: A Political, Social and Cultural History*, Oxford, 1997, pp. 242, 248.

19. Hogue, *G. Harry Agnew*, pp. 215–16.

20. Harries, *Work, Culture and Identity*, pp. 195–7, 212–15; Maloka, 'The Struggle for Sunday', pp. 244–8, and the following accounts of Mozambican elder miners of Maciene district.

21. Baker, *Grace Triumphant*, pp. 308–9.

22. Interview with Gaspar Pene Manave, Navene, 19 July 1999.

23. Hogue, *G. Harry Angew*, p. 233.

24. Baker, *Grace Triumphant*, p. 107. Indeed, a stronger drink, very intoxicating, was usually supplied on Sundays by the owners of the mines. Latimer Fuller, *The Romance of a South African Mission*, Leeds, 1907, p. 16; John Wesley Haley, *Life In Mozambique and South Africa*, Chicago, 1926, p. 124. This evidence contradicts Charles Van Onselen's essay 'Randlords and Rotgut 1886–1903: The Role of Alcohol in the Development of

European Imperialism and Southern African Capitalism, with Special Reference to Black Mineworkers in the Transvaal Republic'. The mine owners may have used alcohol to draw and hold Africans to the mines, but they soon tried to control the kind of alcohol available, keeping it as weak as possible because otherwise they had drunken workers or workers too drunk to work. The first was a serious safety hazard and the second produced a labour shortage.

25. Maloka also stressed that the gospel competed with the miners' leisure-time activities. Maloka, 'The Struggle for Sunday'.
26. Interview with Noé Estevão Uamusse, Nhamavila, 17 July 1999.
27. Interview with Pedro Zimila, Cumbene, 3 March 1999.
28. Interview with João Manuel Nhavotso, Baúle, 4 August 1999.
29. Interview with Zacarias Paindane, Buquene, 19 March 1999.
30. The magic-lantern lectures consisted of evangelization and display of slides on the 'life of Christ', 'Joseph', the 'Prodigal Son' and crucifixion scenes. A. Walklett, 'Kimberley', South African Pioneer, vol. 4, no. 3, May 1890: 63.
31. A. Walklett, 'Black Diamonds–Kimberley Compounds', South Africa Pioneer, vol. 4, no. 3, May 1890: 42.
32. T.J. Galley, 'Kimberley Compounds', South Africa Pioneer, vol. 6, no. 4, April 1893, p. 6.
33. Maloka, 'The Struggle for Sunday', p. 251; Harries, Work, Culture and Identity, pp. 216–17.
34. Maloka, 'The Struggle for Sunday', p. 251; Harries, Work, Culture and Identity, pp. 216–17.
35. Interview with Gastão Pene Manave, Navene, 7 March 1999.
36. Interview with Noé Estevão Uamusse, Nhamvila, 17 July 1999.
37. Interview with David Vumuca Langa, Ntetene, 23 March 1999.
38. Interview with David Vumuca Langa, Ntetene, 21 August 1999.
39. Ibid.
40. Interview with Bonifácio Macie, Maciene, 5 March 1999.
41. Baker, Grace Triumphant, pp. 302–4.
42. Ibid., pp. 305–7.
43. The experiences of other African miner evangelists and catechists are described in depth by Hogue, G. Harry Agnew; Fuller, The Romance of a South African Mission; A. Granjean, La Mission Romande, Lausanne, 1917; Baker, Grace Triumphant; Helgesson, Church, State and People; Harries, Work, Culture and Identity; Maloka, 'The Struggle for Sunday'.
44. Maloka, 'The Struggle for Sunday', p. 243.
45. Swikwembu: the spirits of departed members of the family.
46. Interview with Noé Estevão Uamusse, Nhamavila, 17 July 1999.
47. Fuller, The Romance of a South African Mission, p. 18.
48. Baker, Grace Triumphant, p. 106.
49. Interview with Gastão Pene Manave, 7 March and 19 July 1999.
50. Baker, Grace Triumphant, p. 124.

51. Interview with Jonatana Titos Baúle, Baúle, 4 August 1999.
52. Interview with Estevão Mulate Baúle, 4 August 1999.
53. Ibid.
54. In the first quarter of 1951, missionary Francis Boatwright recorded with regret the death of catechist Titos Baúle, who was about 90 years old. F. Boatwright, 'A Maciene Digest', *Lebombo Leaves*, vol. 50, no. 141, 1951: 12. Lebombo diocese was created on 5 November 1893 with the consecration of the first bishop, William Edmund Smyth. It was the ninth diocese of the Church of the South African Province.
55. Interview with Paulo Estevão Macie, 30 July 1997; 28 January 1999. Events of this nature were commonplace throughout southern Mozambique. For instance, in 1889, while Baker and Agnew were travelling to Inhambane they found Diamane, one of Baker's converts in the Rand at Koseni-Gazaland. According to Agnew, Diamane had quite a number of young people who could sing hymns in Zulu. He had taught a number of them the Lord's Prayer [Testament]. 'The harvest is great, but the labourers are few.... We feel that there is a rich harvest of souls awaiting us', Agnew stated. Hogue, *G. Harry Agnew*, pp. 254–6.
56. Interview with Felisberto Chinhamane Chilengue, Maciene, 1 February 1999.
57. Some interviewees told me that Djobe and Jeremias were brothers but others argued that they were just relatives.
58. Interview with Felisberto Chinhamane Chilengue, Maciene, 1 February 1999.
59. Ibid. However, the Anglican mission records are contradictory regarding Christianity at Maciene. For example, Bishop Smyth, in reporting about Lebombo's work, said that he had confirmed a man who had joined the Anglican church although he lived eight or ten miles from their station in the Chongoene district. This man had built a chapel close to his own house, which the Bishop inaugurated and dedicated to All Saints. The place was Maciene. His priest, Philip Mkize, acknowledged that it was Jobe Mkabela [Djobe Mucavele] who helped the Anglican missionary Peak to choose a suitable site outside the Roman priests' area (Chongoene), and therefore Maciene was chosen. Report from William Edmund Smyth about Lebombo Work, 1905, Diocese dos Libombos, Lb29b: Fundo do Distrito de Maciene; P. Mkize, 'Some Recollections of the Early Days', *Lebombo Leaves*, vol. 37, no. 94, 1939: 13.
60. Interview with Matilde Chicogo, Maciene, 30 January 1999.
61. Interview with Celita Uamusse, Maciene, 2 February 1999.
62. Ibid.; interview with Matilde Chicogo, Maciene, 30 January 1999.
63. Djobe Mucavele was a more prominent figure in Maciene people's memories than Jeremias.
64. Mozambicans I interviewed described how and where Djobe Mucavele, Titos Baule and others worshipped.

65. Rev. Donald Stowell, 'In Lebombo with the Chopi', *Lebombo Leaves*, vol. 27, no. 56, 1929: 9.

66. *Chibalo*, or *xibaro, shibalo, chibaro*: conscripted contract and/or forced labour.

67. Interview with Noé Estevão Uamusse, Nhamavila, 17 July 1999.

68. Ibid.

69. Interview with Ribeiro Nhatave, 22 March 1999.

70. Interview with Marta Buque, Buquene, 18 March and 3 August 1999.

71. Interview with Naftal Buque, Buquene, 18 March and 3 August 1999; interview with Artur Massochane Chibuque, Buquene, 5 August 1999.

72. Interview with Jonatana Titos Baúle, Baúle, 4 August 1999.

73. Interview with David Vumuca Langa, Ntentene, 23 March 1999.

74. D.F. Stowell, 'In Lebombo with the Chopi', *Lebombo Leaves*, vol. 27, no. 56, 1929: 9.

75. P. Mkize, 'Some Recollections of the Early Days', *Lebombo Leaves*, vol. 37, no. 49, 1939: 13–14.

76. Matthias James Chicogo, 'My Dear Friends', *Lebombo Leaves*, vol. 49, no. 139, 1950: 14.

77. Even Gonçalves, a Portuguese missiologist, analysing the history of Protestantism in the Portuguese colonies, located the origins of Protestantism in Mozambique with the unorganized, unofficial, but vigorous evangelical work of Mozambican miner converts. José J. Gonçalves, *Protestantismo em África: Contribuição para o Estudo do Protestantismo na África Portuguesa*, Lisbon, 1960, pp. 115, 128.

78. Interview with Jonatana Titos Baúle, Baúle, 4 August 1999.

79. Interview with Matilde Chicogo, Maciene, 30 January 1999.

80. Interview with Paulo Estevão Macie, Maciene, 28 January and 4 February 1999.

81. Interview with David Vumuca Langa, Ntetene, 23 March 1999.

82. Ibid. The Swiss mission boarding school located in Ricatla was founded by missionary Henri Junod in 1907. Its aim was to offer a full training of evangelists and teachers not only in religious matters but also in basic techniques of giving lessons in literacy. Teresa Cruz e Silva, 'Protestant Churches and the Formation of Political Consciousness in Southern Mozambique', London, 1995, p. 59.

83. Andrade, *Relatórios sobre Moçambique*, pp. 229–32; Harries, *Work, Culture and Identity*, pp. 167–91; Jeanne Penvenne, *African Workers and Colonial Racism: Mozambican Strategies and Struggles in Lourenço Marques, 1876–1962*, London, 1995, pp. 24–7.

84. Officio de 24/7/1902 do Governador de Gaza ao Governador Geral de Moçambique. *Arquivo Histórico de Moçambique (AHM)*, Fundo: Administração Geral. Caixa 102, p. 467.

85. Lopes, *Missões Franciscanas*, pp. 148, 150.

86. *Régulo*: petty Portuguese officials, usually Mozambican members of local royal families.

87. Letters dated 19 April 1901; 26 July 1903; 12 June 1905 and 15 August 1905. AHM, Fundo: Governo do Distrito de Gaza – Diversos: Instrução e Cultos. Caixa 359. Indígena: 'native' of Mozambique, the majority of Mozambicans.

88. Letter from unknown to the Bishop, 21 October 1905. Diocese dos Libombos, Lb29b: Fundo do distrito de Maciene.

89. Report from William Eduard Smyth, the Bishop about Lebombo work, 1905. Diocese dos Libombos, Lb29b: Fundo do Distrito de Maciene.

90. C.E. Goodall, 'Ships Pass in the Night', *Lebombo Leaves*, vol. 49, no. 140, 1950: 14.

PART II

...to Globalization

5

Globalization and the Political Economy of the African Migration to the North

Francis Njubi Nesbitt

This chapter examines the political economy of the African brain drain to the North from a historical perspective. It builds on an earlier work, 'African Intellectuals in the Belly of the Beast: Migration, Identity and the Politics of Exile', which argues that migrant African intellectuals in the North face different realities, which engender specific politics and possibilities for engagement with Africa and the African diaspora. They are forced to come to terms with the indelible mark of Africanness on their bodies, creating an identity crisis, the resolution of which is a political act that produces three types of intellectuals: the comprador intelligentsia, the postcolonial critic and the progressive exile (Nesbitt 2002).

This chapter examines the formation of this intellectual African diaspora through three periods of globalization: slavery, colonialism and neocolonialism. It traces the varied intellectual responses of transplanted Africans, from the first 'slave narrative', published in 1789 by Olaudah Equiano, 'The African', to the emergence of negritude and pan-Africanism as political philosophies that engendered the anti-colonial and anti-apartheid movements, to current theorizations around notions of truth and reparation.

Rethinking the 'Brain Drain' Theory

It has become fashionable to decry the 'brain drain' and to demonize African intellectuals for seeking greener pastures in the North instead of staying at home to serve the communities that educated them at great expense. Some blame the North for poaching African health-care workers in the midst of an AIDS pandemic. Others claim African countries are to blame for underpaying and devaluing their professionals. Most blame the migrants themselves for leaving. Instead of seeking scapegoats, however, African stakeholders need to create institutional frameworks for the diaspora to contribute to development processes. First they need to understand what motivates African brains to migrate and, more importantly, why they maintain ties with their country of birth.

The disastrous effect of the brain drain is undeniable. Recent studies show that the migration of Africans has accelerated. The World Bank estimates that 70,000 highly qualified Africans now leave their home countries every year. (During the 1990s the number of professional emigrants was estimated at 20,000–30,000 a year.) Meanwhile the continent spends US$4 billion a year on importing 100,000 expatriates from industrialized countries to perform tasks that could have employed thousands of Africans at a fraction of the cost. Thus it is not surprising that UN reports indicate that 30,000 Africans with Ph.D.s are working outside the continent and that 60 per cent of Ghana-trained doctors left the country in the 1980s, or that a University of Cape Town study showed that skilled workers who migrated to other countries have cost South Africa an estimated US$7.8 billion in lost human capital. The role of expatriates in Africa's underdevelopment highlights the role of the Northern governments and multilateral institutions, which routinely reserve a minimum of 20 per cent of bilateral and multilateral assistance for expatriate 'consultants'. This preference for expatriate control of development projects sponsored by international agencies is demoralizing for African professionals and increases the likelihood of emigration.

While the negative impact of these skilled labour migrations is often emphasized, it is crucial to examine how the 'brain drain' can be turned into a 'brain gain', or 'brain mobility', and what the migrations tell us about Africa's insertion into contemporary processes of globalization. Instead of blaming the emigrants, African governments and the North for poaching skilled labour, stakeholders need to focus on how to harness the intellectual, material and financial capital of the African diaspora that is embedded in the North. This process resembles what Ali Mazrui calls the 'counter-penetration' of Africans in the North. Counter-penetration occurs when African intellectuals embed themselves 'in the belly of the beast' and strike back at the empire from within. Although this theory may sound utopian, the African diaspora has successfully influenced bilateral and multilateral policies in the North and can be mobilized to serve as an African lobby in Europe and the United States. Governments, civic organizations and institutions of higher education should consider creating policy frameworks that make it easier for the diaspora to contribute to Africa's development.

Before urging intellectual migrants to 'stay home' or 'come home', African stakeholders need to understand the complex relationships the migrants develop with their old and new homes. Drained brains become active members of their new communities in the North while maintaining strong ties with their communities of origin. They develop relationships with family, schools and universities, professional and ethnic organizations. These ties cut across geographical and national boundaries, giving rise to translocal societies without a fixed territorial definition. These relationships depend on the ability to maintain society despite mobility. Thus it is possible for the brains to take Africa with them and create it anew in the diaspora. This diaspora perspective makes it possible to move beyond the hand-wringing, recriminations and bribery that have characterized the 'brain drain' discourse to date.

Translocal Communities

Maintaining ties with the homeland is a political act tied to the migrant's identity, the reasons for migration and the ease of assimilation. The white migrants from South Africa and Zimbabwe may not be interested in returning to southern Africa. They reject Africa and exchange their national identities for a racial (white) identity. These avenues of assimilation are closed to the black migrant, who is locked into a lower caste reserved for black Africans. The designation 'African' itself has evolved from a strictly geographical definition to a racialized definition that equates 'African' and 'people of African descent' with 'black' Africans. A white or coloured born in South Africa, or an Arab in Morocco, is identified as 'white' in the United States. They are not considered 'African'. In contrast, a black person from the United States, South America or the Caribbean would be considered 'African American', even though their ancestors were brought to the new world five hundred years ago. More recently, of course, we have had the introduction of new immigrants from the continent, whom Ali Mazrui designates 'American Africans'. This represents an expansion of the designation 'African' beyond its strictly geographical connotation to include affective associations with the estimated 200 million people of African descent in the diaspora.

The recent immigrants from the continent are themselves new to 'African' identity. On the continent, most people live under ethnic categories like Kikuyu, Ibo, Hausa and Acholi. Some educated, middle-class and/or urban dwellers may see themselves as members of a nation like South Africa, Kenya or Tanzania. In some countries, like South Africa, which has recently emerged from the crucible of apartheid, national consciousness is still strong. For most, however, 'national' consciousness emerges only occasionally during Independence Day celebrations, international soccer matches or at election time. 'African' consciousness, however, is a rarity. It is in exile that the Nigerian–Ibo, South African–Zulu, Kenyan–Kikuyu person suddenly and unequivocally becomes an 'African'.

What does it mean to be an African in Europe and America? The migrant quickly learns that the image of Africans is not attractive. It is written in the faces of obnoxious waitresses, the teacher who slams the door of opportunity, the policeman who treats you like a criminal. It is reflected in the floods of negative media images that poison people's minds with racist stereotypes. Just when the migrant thought he was free of the travails of the African condition, he is forced to confront the indelible mark of Africanness on his body. He is forced to wear, explain and even defend a badge of inferiority. This predicament tears at his identity. It creates a duality that is the root of the existential crisis faced by the migrant African intellectual. The postcolonial flight from the African continent ironically reinforces the worst stereotypes of Africanness. A half-century on, Frantz Fanon's description of the black migrant's experience in his classic *Black Skin, White Masks* still holds true:

> You are in a bar in Rouen or Strasbourg, and you have the misfortune to be spotted by an old drunk. He sits down at your table right away. 'You, African? Dakar, Rufisque, whorehouses, dames, coffee, mangoes, bananas.' You stand up and leave, and your farewell is a torrent of abuse. (Fanon 1952)

This chapter examines the formation of this new African diaspora through three phases of globalization. The objective is to produce an intellectual history of this specific group of highly skilled African migrants, their experiences, their connection to African Americans, their reflections on the condition of Africanity in exile and contributions to both host societies and Africa. I pay particular attention to the geopolitical forces that shaped the African intelligentsia, including slavery, colonialism and Cold War, and their response to these. The chapter is based on an examination of empirical research, theoretical analyses and personal reflections that address various dimensions of the 'brain drain'. I examine its causes, courses and consequences for Africa and the United States and investigate both its pitfalls and possibilities. The aim is to explore how these migrant scholars build expatriate knowledge networks and establish linkages between this new diaspora and institutions on the continent. I examine how the new African diaspora, building on the work of the older diaspora, can promote the globalization of Africa and the Africanization of globalization in productive ways.

The contemporary diasporas are following the migration patterns and practices of the older diasporas, strengthening and transforming the connections constructed over many generations. It is critical, therefore, to bring to the discussion a proper sense of history. Moreover, in so far as current African migrations are part of the uneven global flows of capital, commodities, cultures, information, ideas and individuals, it is important to understand them in the context of contemporary processes of globalization. The specific forces and conditions within each African country that have together produced the brain drain must be analysed and understood. In the North, likewise, the experiences of the African diaspora are quite varied, thereby engendering differing politics and possibilities for engagement with Africa.

Organic Intellectuals

The earliest cohort of African intellectuals (that is, black writers/intellectuals born in Africa) in the diaspora were writers such as Olaudah Equiano, Ottobah Cuguano and Phyllis Wheatley. They were organic intellectuals in the Gramscian sense, who participated in an anti-slavery discourse that stripped Western modernity of its liberal pretensions. They were 'organic' because they emerged from the enslaved population and were recognized as leaders in the abolitionist movement; they were 'intellectuals' inasmuch as they produced a remarkable collection of written works that would form the foundation for an international, transcontinental anti-slavery discourse. This discourse, which utilized the latest technology at its disposal, foreshadowed the civil rights movement and the human rights discourse of the twentieth century. In addition to its vision, the anti-slavery discourse also reflected a transnational and trans-continental network of African intellectuals participating in the first anti-globalization movement of modernity. The emergence of this intellectual movement among an enslaved population was all the more remarkable because people of African descent were prohibited by law from reading and writing. Nevertheless, the abolitionists mastered the art of writing and the technology of the printing press, producing an impressive collection of autobiographies, pamphlets and newspapers to inform the world about the inhumanity of slavery from the African perspective. Henry Louis Gates Jr. estimates that over one hundred ex-slaves wrote autobiographical narratives before the American Civil War and over six thousand told their stories through interviews, essays and books. According to Gates, 'The black slave narrators sought to indict both those who enslaved them and the metaphysical system drawn upon to justify their enslavement. They did so using the most enduring weapon at their disposal, the printing press' (1987: ix).

This anti-slavery discourse was Pan-African and internationalist from the outset. Two Africans, Ottobah Cugoano from the Gold Coast (modern-day Ghana) and Olaudah Equiano, an Ibo from an area of West Africa now known as Nigeria, pioneered the movement (Thompson, 2000). Cuguano's *Thoughts and Sentiments on the Evils of That Wicked Traffic Slavery in Human Species*, published in London in 1787, used a synthesis of his African background, Christianity and eighteenth-century humanism to expound on the equality of all humans. Cuguano's initiative was followed two years later by Olaudah Equiano's 1789 autobiography, *Narrative of the Life of Olaudah Equiano, the African*, which denounced the brutality of slavery and the hypocrisy of European and American 'civilization'. Both texts had a powerful influence on the emergence of the abolitionist movement in Britain. Equiano's impassioned protest went through several printings and was widely read by the British ruling class. It also made its way to the Americas where it had a major impact on black abolitionists, who modelled their protests on Equiano's pioneering effort. His autobiographical style, his title *Narrative of the Life of...*, and his assertion, 'Written by Himself', became the standard recognizable features of the genre. Thus, the genre of 'slave narratives' emerged as a Pan-African discourse, a literary dialogue among writers of African descent on three continents.

These Pan-African anti-slavery activists also founded a slew of anti-slavery newspapers including David Russwurm's *Freedom's Journal* (1827), Douglass's *North Star* and *Douglass's Paper*, which further disseminated the anti-slavery doctrine. This precedent set by black abolitionists would be used to great effect by many visionary anti-racist leaders throughout the twentieth century. Both the African-American W.E.B. Du Bois and South African Sol Plaatje, for instance, wrote autobiographical narratives rooted in the tradition of the slave narratives. Du Bois's *Souls of Black Folk* (1903) clearly influenced Plaatje's *Native Life in South Africa* (1916) (see Chrisman 2000). These texts are eloquent denunciations of racism and human rights violations on both sides of the Atlantic. Even more pertinent, Plaatje's monograph was initially serialized in Du Bois's *Crisis* magazine, reflecting the strategic and ideological collaboration between Africans and African Americans that had characterized the abolitionist movement.

Du Bois was probably the most accomplished appropriator of media technology to expose the violence of racism, colonialism and apartheid. Du Bois left his teaching position at Atlanta University in 1910 to become the editor of *Crisis*, which he turned into a formidable instrument in the struggle for human rights in the diaspora and on the continent. He made the magazine into the definitive record of black people around the world and, equally important, of the savagery of white racism in Africa, Europe and the Americas. Du Bois also used his tenure at the National Association for the Advancement of Coloured People (NAACP) to organize three Pan-African conferences, which were critical moments in the evolution of a black response to the new manifestations of white racism including segregation, colonialism and apartheid. These Pan-African conferences were an extension of the black abolitionist movement of the eighteenth and nineteenth centuries. Both used the printing press to disseminate their moral suasionist and humanitarian arguments against human rights violations.

Other Pan-African leaders were also accomplished anti-racism propagandists. Marcus Garvey, a printer by trade, founded a newspaper called *The Negro World* to promote his anti-racist movement. Garvey's newspaper surpassed even Du Bois's *Crisis* in terms of sales and geographical distribution between 1915 and 1920. *The Negro World* was distributed throughout Europe, the Caribbean and the African continent, where colonial administrators tried to ban it without much success. In France, Pan-Africanists from West Africa and the Caribbean also promoted their human rights and anti-colonial struggle, *négritude*, through their influential magazine *Présence Africaine*. On the continent, Pan-Africanists also mastered the art of media counter-penetration. Kwame Nkrumah, Jomo Kenyatta, Nnamdi Azikiwe, Julius Nyerere, Sekou Toure – all launched newspapers, journals and magazines in their campaigns against the racial violence perpetrated against Africans and people of African descent by Euro-American racism. Thus the history of Pan-African movements is replete with the successful appropriation of communications technology to expose human rights violations that accompanied slavery, colonialism and apartheid.

The Cold War and African Intellectuals

The African intellectual presence grew considerably during the Cold War as the United States tried to counter the spread of socialist ideas, recruiting African students to study at historically black colleges and other US universities. During the Second World War, Africa had become critical to US foreign policy as the source of strategic minerals like uranium, industrial diamonds and cobalt. Some of these minerals, found in abundance in southern Africa, were critical to the production of nuclear weapons. Consequently, intelligence agencies, the military and philanthropic foundations began to finance studies of African societies by cold warriors designed to ensure that the United States would maintain control of these strategic resources. They also established 'African Studies' programmes at major universities and provided scholarships for selected African students to study in the United States. The aim was to develop a new generation of pro-capitalist African leaders by reaching out to African students in the United States.

As a result of these policies, many of the leaders of African decolonization spent years – sometimes decades – in the North. Some, like Leopold Sedar Senghor, Sekou Toure, Kwame Nkrumah, Sylvanos Olympio, Nmandi Azikiwe, Kamuzu Banda, Amilcar Cabral, Eduardo Mondlane and Julius Nyerere were scholar-activists who studied for advanced degrees in Europe and the United States before eventually returning home to lead their countries to independence. Many of these leaders developed their political skills and personae in the West, where they formed student associations and joined Pan-Africanist groups dedicated to overthrowing colonial powers in Africa. Many also flirted with leftist political thinking – socialism, Marxism and communism. It is this generation that gave us positive theories like African personality, Consciencism and African Social-ism. Yet, once they returned home from exile and seized the reins of power, a disturbingly large number abandoned their progressive politics for the worst forms of neocolonial clientelism and despotism. Of this group of independence-era leaders, only Cabral, Mondlane, Nyerere, Nkrumah, Toure and Olympio maintained their progres-sive perspectives. Few others resisted the lure of power and client relations with the same colonial powers they had once denounced in the streets of London, New York and Paris. More recently we have seen the emergence of a new African intelligentsia in the West. This postcolonial generation faces a new reality and new options of negotiated identity. Both groups were confronted with the spectre of racism and the resulting double consciousness, but the postcolonial generation has the benefit of more favourable immigration policies and greater educational and professional opportunities created by the civil rights movement and African independence movements (Arthur 2000: 7–10). This new dispensation has allowed the African migrants to seek employment at major universities and settle in the United States. Thus, despite the continuing problem of racism, these migrants can and do make new lives for themselves in exile.

This new reality has allowed the African migrant scholar to participate in both American education and politics in areas that were closed to the independence-era exiles. This generation of scholars has produced a new genre of reflective works that explore the experience of exile from a variety of vantage points. Yet the condition of Africanness both marginalizes and expands the migrant's horizons at the same time. He is no longer Acholi or Ugandan but African – a member of that mythical race created by the white imagination as a foil and a justification for the holocaust of slavery and colonial exploitation. He is not only responsible for Somalia, Congo and Sierra Leone, but also tied inexplicably to inner-city gang culture, street hustlers and drug addicts. In the likely encounter with the police profiler, skin colour will trump national origin every time. Colour also trumps education, erudition and accomplishment. None of these means anything in a late-night encounter with the police. In the New World, a man is no longer an Acholi or even a Ugandan; he is an African, or, more accurately, a black man, thus automatically a suspect and a target for any white racist policeman, waitress, teacher or taxi driver.

It would be a mistake, however, to give the impression that 'the fact of blackness' creates a collective race consciousness, a natural unity among the African migrants and the native black populations of Europe and America. Such race consciousness is the perception, often limited to the politicized Pan-Africanist community. Most African-descended peoples continue to see each other, and themselves, 'through the eyes of others', as Du Bois put it. Unable to penetrate the veil of racism, many migrants consider African Americans lazy, violent and obsessed with race, while many African Americans see migrants as inferior, ignorant and uncivilized (Askia 1997; Waters 1992). According to John Arthur 'The cultural barriers and social and economic differences separating the Africans and African Americans are sometimes the cause of a simmering hostility and misunderstanding between them. Sharing the common physical characteristic of skin color has not ensured cultural and economic unity between African immigrants and American-born blacks' (Arthur 2000: 78).

These tensions are compounded at historically black universities and Black Studies programmes at mainstream universities, where most African scholars are forced to find employment because of the lack of opportunities at historically white universities and departments. Although there are countless cases of African scholars working in harmony with African Americans in historically black universities, the increasing numbers of African migrant scholars have intensified competition for the few positions set aside for black scholars in the academy. Recent struggles at Virginia State University, a historically black institution, epitomize the problem. Virginia State has been hit by a slew of lawsuits from African and African-American professors, with both groups alleging discrimination (Wilson 2001). The lawsuits have so far cost the state US$4 million, with several suits still pending. The suits pit Africans and African Americans against each other in struggles over leadership and control of departments and research dollars. Initially, three African-born professors sued the university, claiming they were denied salary increases and promotion by African-American department heads. Two Nigerians and an

Egyptian won their cases. One of the Nigerians settled out of court and left the university; the other two professors received settlements totalling US$1.6 million.

Following a major administrative reorganization in 1999, which replaced several African-American department heads, however, the lawsuits this time came from African-American professors. The reorganization sparked vicious infighting, reflected in an email that circulated on campus and leaked to the national press. The email, authored by an African-American faculty member, accused the administration of appointing 'unqualified' foreign-born professors as department heads for fear of further lawsuits. The email complained that the number of African-American department heads had decreased from 15 to 4. The administration argued, however, that the numbers were 12 before and 5 after. African-American faculty member F.S. Farley told the *Chronicle of Higher Education* that the foreign-born department heads were 'not experienced or well trained', even though the *Chronicle* reported that most of them had doctorates. Farley also claimed that black students seeking their roots at historically black colleges faced the 'extra burden' of dealing with foreigners.

Thus migrant African intellectuals, who probably left neighbouring African countries because they were unable to overcome their images as outsiders, find that they face the same problem in the United States. In this case, however, the tension is between diasporic blacks and Africans who are forced to compete over the few jobs set aside for black scholars (African, African-American and West Indian) in the American academy. The problem, therefore, is the segregation of most black scholars in historically black universities and African Studies and African-American Studies departments. The fact that 49 per cent of African immigrants have college degrees while only 14 per cent of African Americans graduate from college adds a class dimension to the problem. The Bureau of Census reports, for instance, that the median household income of African immigrants is US$30,907 compared to US$19,533 for black Americans (Bureau of Census 1997).

These tensions are increasingly being reflected among students as the growing presence of people of African descent from other parts of the world begins to redefine the 'fact of blackness'. Although universities across the United States continue to lump all people of African descent together as 'black', students from Africa, the Caribbean and the United States make finer distinctions. Harvard University, for instance, reports that 10 per cent of its student population is 'black' but does not distinguish among the numerous subdivisions within the category. Yet these subdivisions loom large among the students and are reflected in their organizations: the Harvard African Students Association draws Africans; the Caribbean Club draws West Indians; and the Black Students Association is predominantly African American. As increasing numbers of African and Carib- bean-born students are admitted to universities around the country, African Americans are beginning to feel like a 'minority within a minority'. They resent the fact that many immigrants from Africa and the Caribbean do not immediately define themselves as 'black' or understand the history and politics of race in the United States. Many of these immigrant students will take their experiences with them to graduate school and some to teaching positions, guaranteeing a continuation of the process.

Thus migrant African scholars must negotiate new identities that can no longer depend on the security of nationality and ethnicity but are not exactly Afro-European or African-American either. This dilemma of being not exactly African, but not Afro-European or African-American either, is the peculiar challenge of migrant African scholars. Elsewhere I have described the resolution of this identity crisis as a political act that manifests itself in the lives and work of academics, producing three 'types' of migrant intellectuals: the comprador intelligentsia, postcolonial critics and progressive exiles (Nesbitt 2002). In this chapter I will focus on the political activity of African intellectuals in exile including their roles in the anti-colonial, anti-apartheid and reparations movements.

The Allegory of the Cave

In 'The Allegory of the Cave' Kenyan scholar-in-exile Ngugi wa Thiong'o discusses the role of exiles in African liberation. The allegory tells of members of a cave-dwelling community who have had the opportunity to see the outside world and return to the cave, where they try to explain what they have learned to the cave-dwellers (Ngugi 1998). Some return as agents of the outsiders, using their knowledge of the cave to facilitate the extraction of natural and human resources. Others return with the knowledge gained from their travels on the outside but refuse to speak in the language of the cave and instead insist that the cave-dwellers learn the language of the outsiders if they want to benefit from the new knowledge and technology. Only a few return to the cave dedicated to relearning the cave dwellers' language so that they can teach the insiders the new techniques effectively.

Ngugi's allegory of the cave captures the migrant scholars' political dilemma in stark terms, making it clear that they have the choice of either serving the neocolonial system as witting or unwitting agents or using the knowledge they have gained from their sojourn in the West to liberate their fellows. The progressive exiles resolve the crisis of double consciousness by learning from the experience of exile while maintaining their identity as Africans. As Amilcar Cabral put it, it is only through a spiritual and physical 'return to the source' that Africans in the diaspora can build an 'identity with dignity in the context of national liberation' (Cabral 1973). This dignified identity is what Du Bois was referring to when he wrote that he wanted to merge his 'double self into a better and truer self' (Du Bois 1903). Du Bois manages to build this dignified identity through Pan-Africanism and the commitment to the liberation of all people of African descent, whether in the diaspora or on the continent.

This Pan-African identity allows the migrant scholar to join the struggle for liberation while in the diaspora. Ngugi wa Thiong'o himself epitomizes the successful resolution of double consciousness through the development of a Pan-African identity. Because of his outspoken support for human rights and opposition to neocolonial domination in Kenya, Ngugi was detained without trial by the Kenya government in December 1977. Eight months after his release from prison in December 1978, the University of Nairobi informed him that his post had been terminated by 'an Act of State' the day he had been detained. Despite an extended battle to regain his position as an associate professor of literature at the university, and in spite of the support of the university staff union and supporters around the world, Ngugi was unable to resume his duties at the university. In 1982 he was forced into exile, first in London and then in the United States where he taught at several universities before accepting a position as Erich Maria Remarque Endowed Chair in Languages at New York University. Today, Ngugi is at the forefront of the debate about the role of indigenous languages in the struggle for decolonization. His artistic and theoretical writings have inspired anticolonial struggles around the world. But it is in the Pan-African community that Ngugi has found a home. Since joining New York University, he has become a leading member of the progressive bloc of the African Studies movement in the United States, which provides a counterpoint to the accommodationist perspective espoused by the Appiah school of Black Studies located at Harvard University. Thus we see the politics of exile determining the perspective and location of African scholars across the ideological spectrum. Kwame Anthony Appiah, a descendant of the Ashante ruling class who was schooled at Oxford University, chooses to associate himself with the conservative, accommodationist strand of Black Studies, while Ngugi wa Thiong'o, a descendant of Kenyan peasants, associates himself with the progressive strand of Black Studies. More interesting than any vulgar economic determinism is the transcendence of class, political and educational background here. The question is how and why these individuals from dramatically different political and educational backgrounds ended up in Black Studies. Both Ngugi and Appiah were accomplished and respected scholars in traditional disciplines before taking the plunge into the murky and unstable waters of African Studies. The fact that they chose to work in the same garden despite their ideological differences demonstrates the power of Africanness in determining the politics of exile, even among the most able of the talented tenth.

The Anti-apartheid Movement

It is this power of Africanness; this 'fact of blackness', as Fanon put it, that compelled African exiles and members of the African diaspora to join black people on the continent in the successful struggle to liberate South Africa from the jaws of apartheid. The global anti-apartheid movement emerged in the progressive Pan-African communities of the United States and Britain. It was sustained by strong ties that had been forged among black activists around the world during the anti-colonial movements of the 1930s and 1940s. The first anti-apartheid organization in exile, for instance, was the leftist Council on African Affairs, led by Paul Robeson, W.E.B. Du Bois and Alphaeus Hunton. At the height of the movement in 1978, Leslie O. Harriman, the Nigerian chairman of the United Nations Special Committee Against Apartheid, reminded activists of the roots of the movement in Pan-Africanist circles:

We have today anti-apartheid movements in many countries playing a crucial role in the campaign against racial discrimination in South Africa. These are all fairly new, and the first of these movements, we must recall, was founded by Paul Robeson and the black people of the United States. (Harriman 1978: 78–79)

During the 1970s Africans and African Americans reestablished ties that had been severed by the anti-communist hysteria of the 1950s. These ties were cemented by the increased mobility of people of African descent and in particular the presence of African exiles in the United States. The theories and activities of exiles and revolutionaries like Julius Nyerere, Amilcar Cabral, Agostino Neto, Nelson Mandela and Eduardo Mondlane heavily influenced African-American activists (Walters 1995: 59–65). In 1962 Amilcar Cabral addressed the United Nations and then met with African Americans, with whom he discussed his ideas on revolutionary nationalism. Julius Nyerere's African Socialism was also a major influence, leading to support for the armed struggle in South Africa, Angola and Mozambique; the study of Kiswahili by African Americans, and the formation of Maulana Karenga's Kwanzaa movement (Walters 1995). These practical and theoretical ties were parlayed into a highly successful global movement for international sanctions in the 1980s led by new Pan-Africanist organizations like TransAfrica and the Free South Africa Movement (Robinson 1998). In the 1970s, radical groups espousing ideologies ranging from black nationalism to Maoism to Marxism–Leninism played an important role in pushing the movement to support armed struggle. This was demonstrated in the 30,000-strong crowd that attended the Africa Liberation Day (ALD) march on Washington DC in 1972 and the large crowds that returned for ALD activities throughout the 1970s. These groups reflected a revival of Pan-Africanist sentiment, which created the conditions for the emergence of an anti-apartheid culture in the United States. Like the civil rights movement of the 1960s, the anti-apartheid movement introduced a new culture, with its own language, values and heroes, to the United States. A specific discourse on sanctions, divestment, divestiture, disinvestment and krugerrands was clearly associated with the movement. Images of Nelson Mandela, Robben Island, Soweto and Sharpeville became tools for galvanizing outrage against the racist regime. The Student Nonviolent Coordinating Committee (SNCC) and the Black Panthers evolved into anti-imperialist and

Third Worldist organizations. SNCC formed an international affairs desk under James Forman in 1966 and organized sit-ins at the South African Embassy in Washington DC. Forman attended the International Conference on Apartheid, Racial Discrimination and Colonialism in Southern Africa in 1967, where he presented SNCC's position paper on apartheid. By its demise in 1970, SNCC had taken on a strong Pan-Africanist orientation although it was split between the 'back to Africa' emigrationists and those who saw their future in the United States. This latter group became very important in moving the anti-apartheid movement from a pacifist orientation to unequivocal support for the armed struggle.

It was also this upsurge in popular anti-apartheid sentiment in the African-American community that led the Congressional Black Caucus (CBC) to take up the issue of apartheid. Ron Dellums drafted the first sanctions bill introduced in the US Congress in response to a petition from the Polaroid Revolutionary Workers Union (PRWM). It is this bill that became the basis for US sanctions against South Africa thirteen years later when Congress passed the Comprehensive Anti-Apartheid Act over President Reagan's veto. The PRWM's access to Congress demonstrates how the black freedom movement in the United States created the conditions for the success of the anti-apartheid movement. It is the passage of the Voting Rights Act in 1965 and the election of African-American legislators that led to the key turning point in the US anti-apartheid movement. Before the election of African Americans to Congress, anti-apartheid activists were outsiders with no access to the decision-making process. It is the establishment of the Congressional Black Caucus in 1969 that made the institution of a black lobby (TransAfrica) possible in 1977. The CBC included South Africa in its legislative agenda from the outset. The Black Caucus was also the source of the Comprehensive Anti-apartheid Act of 1986, which transformed US policy towards South Africa.

This collaboration between congressional leaders and human rights activists was reflected in the Free South Africa Movement, which organized the arrests of thousands of demonstrators outside the South African Embassy in Washington DC in the early 1980s. Numerous African-American congressmen were arrested along with ordinary citizens and celebrities in the sit-ins outside the South African Embassy. This loose coalition of politicians, activists, scholars, students, ministers and journalists was established to implement one of the most remarkable examples of grassroots human rights groups influencing the foreign policy of a major superpower (Nesbitt 2003). The movement forced the pro-apartheid Reagan administration to change its foreign policy and debunked the myth that foreign policy is the preserve of national elites.

Prior to the emergence of the CBC, anti-apartheid organizations were limited to disseminating information to the media and the public, without having any access to Congress, where decisions were being made. With the election of African-American legislators following the Voting Rights Act of 1965, however, the anti-apartheid movement acquired important allies in Congress and moved onto a different level. The CBC itself also recognized the need for a partnership between black legislators and activists in an effort to change domestic and foreign policies. This need stemmed from the fact that CBC initiatives like sanctions against South Africa were not likely to be sponsored by corporations or the traditional lobby groups that control interest-group politics in Washington. Thus the CBC was involved in the formation of advocacy organizations like TransAfrica and the Free South Africa Movement as an alternative source of influence and power. This collaboration between legislators and activists was the key to the transformation of US foreign policy towards South Africa. This global anti-apartheid movement demonstrated that perspective was more important than space or time, and that progressive African exiles could use their location 'in the belly of the beast' to transform the international system for the benefit of all. These global solidarity movements demonstrate that a united front of people of African descent, as imagined by pioneering Pan-Africanists like Du Bois and Nkrumah, is still possible, even critical, in the New World Order of global markets and corporate domination.

Reparations and Transformation

Like the anti-apartheid movement of the 1980s, which forced the West to acknowledge that apartheid was a 'crime against humanity', the African reparations campaign is gaining momentum and transforming human rights discourse in the global public sphere. Led by African and African-American intellectuals, the black reparations campaign raises critical moral and ethical questions about human responsibility and restitution that the North has refused to acknowledge despite the efforts of nineteenth-century abolitionists and twentieth-century anti-colonial, anti-apartheid and civil rights activists.

Northern recalcitrance was demonstrated once again at the World Conference Against Racism, Racial Discrimination, Xenophobia, and Related Intolerance (WCAR), held in Durban, South Africa, from 31 August to 7 September 2001. Delegates from Africa and the Diaspora came together to demand that the West acknowledge that slavery and colonialism were crimes against humanity with serious contemporary effects that required reparatory compensation. Despite resistance from the United States, the conference adopted a declaration acknowledging that slavery and the slave trade were 'crimes against humanity' and 'should always have been so'. The resolution also acknowledged the wrongs of slavery and colonialism and recommended that the international community take measures to alleviate the impact of these crimes. The declaration fell far short of the African demand for an explicit apology and reparations for the enslavement of millions of Africans and the bloody coloniza-tion of the continent, the cancellation of illegitimate debt, and the return of Africa's material and cultural treasures. Nevertheless, the acknowledgement that slavery and colonialism are crimes against humanity provides the international reparations movement with a foundation on which to build the case.

Since the WCAR, the black reparations movement has gained considerable momentum. Activists have adopted legal, political and mass-movement strategies. A follow-up conference, the African and African Descendants' World Conference Against Racism, held in Bridgetown, Barbados, in October 2002, demonstrated the strength of the mass-movement strategy. The conference, which attracted over five hundred participants, discussed a plethora of issues including taking legal action, AIDS and affirmative-action strategies. A Pan-African Movement was formed to deal with issues ranging from racial profiling to poverty, to reparations for slavery, colonialism and apartheid (Wilkinson 2002). It was agreed to initiate lawsuits, first against Britain, Germany, France and Belgium, and then against Portugal, Spain and the Netherlands.

The movement showed both its strengths and weaknesses at the Bridgetown conference. On the plus side was its mobilization of hundreds of participants from all parts of the world to discuss the issue of reparations. This and the formation of a Pan-African organization to facilitate communication and collaboration among activists across world demonstrate the growing maturity of the movement. On the minus side, however, was the tendency of activists to indulge in tangential gestures that had little practical value. This was evident, for example, in the majority floor vote – demanded by the vocal and organized Afro-British and African-American delegations – calling for the expulsion of non-Africans from the conference. The motion was carried at an unacceptable cost: the loss of delegates from Cuba, South Africa and Colombia, who could not accept the decision despite their African heritage. Given the minuscule presence of non-Africans at the conference, the vote was self-indulgent at best.

The legal strategy has been the most successful to date in obtaining reparations for people of African descent. The lawsuits have spread from the United States to Haiti, Kenya and Jamaica. In 1999, lawyer Alexander Pires won US$1 billion for 24,000 black families who charged discrimination by the Department of Agriculture. According to Pires, the US Department of Agriculture provided no loans to African-American farmers until 1997. 'Ninety-five percent of all farm loans went to white farmers. And until the 1960s, the USDA had a special section called Negro Loans, which ensured that black applicants were rejected. It's amazing' (Harper's 2000). In March 2002, a reparations lawsuit was filed against Aetna, CSI and Providence Bank, along with 100 other companies, charging that they had profited from slavery (Cox 2002). Also planning class-action lawsuits is a group of high-powered lawyers led by civil rights attorney Johnnie Cochran and Harvard University law professor Charles Ogletree. The precedent for these lawsuits is the US$6 billion settlement won by the World Jewish Congress on behalf of Holocaust slave labourers.

In Kenya, survivors of the War of Independence and the concentration camps established by the British have sued the British government for war crimes. According to the *Daily Nation*,

Among incidents likely to be top of the agenda are the Hola massacre, where seventy detainees were beaten to death; castrations at Nyangwethu Screening Camp; and the Lari massacre, in which civilians, mostly women and children, were allegedly killed by colonial and loyalist forces. Colonial officials estimated that 10,527 LFA fighters were killed and 2,633 captured by the British forces between 1952 and 1956, when the insurgency against colonialism peaked. Some 1,826 'loyal African' soldiers were killed and 918 wounded. At least 2,000 innocent black people were also killed. After failing to track down the freedom fighters, the colonial government turned on the African population, arresting thousands and detaining around 77,000 in what was called 'Operation Anvil'. When the state of emergency was lifted, about 38,449 Kenyans were still in detention, convicted of being either 'Mau Mau' or sympathisers. (*Daily Nation* 2002)

In Jamaica, lawyers served a writ on Queen Elizabeth II when she visited Kingston in February 2002 (Wilkinson 2002). France is also being targeted because it forced Haiti to pay 150 million francs as compensation for French property lost during the slave uprising that led to the first black republic in the West. Although these reparations lawsuits are critical components of the movement, they need to be placed in perspective. Single-issue class-action lawsuits only benefit the parties affected by the particular, named crime against humanity. While it is critical that the Kenyan victims of detention, torture, castration and confiscation receive compensation, their case would be immeasurably strengthened by a formal association with similar suits in Jamaica, the United States and Namibia. This collaboration would allow the aggrieved to share experiences and collaborate on the broader challenge of restoring Africa to its rightful place as an equal in global affairs.

A third strategy is the political campaign for reparations that seeks to convince governments to acknowledge their role in human rights violations and provide compensation for property and lives lost. The role of government has been prominent during periods of reconstruction after major wars, genocide, and other mass human rights violations. Union Army General William Tecumseh Sherman's Field Order #15, for instance, required military officers to provide black families with 40-acre plots on former slave plantations as compensation for unpaid labour. On 11 March 1867 Thaddeus Stevens of Pennsylvania introduced H.R. 29, which called for the redistribution of former slave plantations among the freed slaves. President Andrew Johnson reversed Sherman's field order and vetoed H.R. 29. One hundred and nineteen years later, Representative John Conyers of Michigan introduced H.R. 891 in the 104th Congress, calling for a commission to be established to study the question of reparations. Despite the conservative tenor of its request, in contrast with Stevens's call for redistribution of property, Conyers's mild proposal received little support, and as a result has yet to make it out of committee.

On 4 May 1994, the state of Florida passed the Rosewood Compensation Act, acknowledging the state's responsibility for failing to prevent a massacre of the black town's residents in a white rampage in 1923 (Brooks 1999). The pogrom lasted for days, leading to charges that the State of Florida could have intervened and saved lives and property. The Rosewood Compensation Act provided compensation of up to US$150,000 for victims and their families (a total of US$7 million), and established scholarships for minority students with preference given to Rosewood residents (Brooks 1999).

Reconstruction after colonial rule in Africa sometimes involved land redistribution schemes that resembled General Sherman's field order. In Kenya, British settlers were forced to vacate Kikuyuland after a ten-year guerrilla war, but not before they had been 'compensated' for land taken by force from African peasants. The British also secured a promise from Kenya's first African president, Jomo Kenyatta, that he would not pursue compensation claims for war crimes. A similar agreement between Zimbabwe's Robert Mugabe and the British in 1980 failed to materialize, leading to the current crisis as war veterans attempt to take back their lands from settlers.

In Brazil and Colombia, people of African descent continue to seek title to lands they have occupied for hundreds of years. In 2000, Brazil's Congress voted that residents of Quilombos in northeastern Brazil should receive title deeds to lands they had occupied in some cases since the fifteenth century, when Africans created independent communities of fugitive slaves. Afro-Colombians also received title to lands occupied by former slaves, but have been displaced by right-wing paramilitary gangs linked to the Colombian military. The Afro-Colombians had the misfortune to occupy land near oilfields and mineral deposits. Massacres and forced displacement are pulling the population out by the roots. According to Mary Jo McConahay, the Chocó province on the Pacific, home to 400,000 people, has been hard hit by the Colombian war. The area is the source of mineral deposits critical to the aerospace and nuclear industries; of oil, gold and silver; and of most of the timber felled in Colombia. In 1998, Afro-Colombian Governor Luis Murillo declared Chocó off-limits to all armed groups, including the army. Within months, courts had stripped him of office, and he was kidnapped and held by a death squad in Bogotá. He escaped, and is now living in exile in Washington DC (McConahay 2002).

The biggest challenge for the growing movement is to develop a global structure that will bring together different parts of the movement for dialogue and development of a global vision and strategy for reparations. There is no doubt, for instance, that the mass kidnapping and deportation of millions from the African continent is at the core of the reparations claims of all parties, be they from the Caribbean, South America, the United States or even the African continent itself. This global trade in Africans and the products of their labour also underpins the second pillar of the reparations campaign, which is the claim that the West received unjust riches from the centuries of unpaid labour of Africans and their descendants in the diaspora. Africans and people of African descent in the diaspora were and continue to be targeted as a racial group, not as individuals. Slavery, Jim Crow laws, apartheid and colonialism created a racial caste system that continues to determine the life-chances of people of African descent, based primarily on their colour. Thus a Pan-African effort is imperative if the campaign is to encompass the global implications of slavery and its legacies of segregation, colonialism and global apartheid.

These efforts at the national and international levels are commendable, but they require a more developed critique of capitalism, and thus a strategy to tie the campaigns to the global anti-capitalist movements. These movements would be natural allies of the reparations movement, if the issue were framed as part of a multifaceted attack on race and class oppression, instead of centring itself on calls for an apology and a cheque. Reparations must be seen not as an end, but as a means to achieve a more equitable distribution of wealth and power, the creation of a democratic culture, and the dismantling of structures of global apartheid. As Robin Kelley puts it:

> The reparations campaign, despite its potential contribution to eliminating racism and remaking the world, can never be an end in itself. Money and resources are always important, but a new vision and new values cannot be bought. And without at least a rudimentary criticism of the capitalist culture that consumes us, even reparations can have disastrous consequences. (Kelley 2002: p. 133)

References

Allen, R.L. (1998) 'Past Due: The African American Quest for Reparations', *Black Scholar*, vol. 28, no. 2: 2–17.

Apartheid Debt and Reparations Campaign Media Statement (2002) 'Major Apartheid Reparations Suit Filed in US Court', 12 November; see full text of filed complaint at /www.cmht.com/casewatch/civil/apartheid.html.

Arthur, J. A. (2000) *Invisible Sojourners: African Immigrant Diaspora in the United States,* Westport CT: Praeger.

Askia, N. (1997) 'Africans, African-Americans Say Color Doesn't Ensure Unity. Cultural Barriers Can Even Breed Hostility', *Atlanta Journal Constitution*, 24 August, p. B7.

Asmal, A., and S. Roberts (eds) (1996) *Reconciliation through Truth: A Reckoning of Apartheid's Criminal Governance*, Cape Town: David Phillip.

Boraine, A., and Levy, J. (eds) (1995) *The Healing of a Nation?*, Cape Town: Justice in Transition Project.

Brooks, R.L. (ed.) (1999) *When Sorry Isn't Enough*, New York: New York University Press.

Cabral, A. (1973) *Return to the Source*, New York: Monthly Review Press.

Clarke, B. (2002) 'We Must Touch On the Real Issues', *Barbados Advocate*, www.barbadosadvocate.com/NewViewNewsleft.cfm?Record=10273.

Cox, J. (2002) 'Corporations Challenged by Reparations Activists'. *USA Today*, 21 February.

Chrisman, L. (2000) 'Rethinking Black Atlantism', *The Black Scholar*, vol. 30, nos 3–4: 12–17.

Daily Nation (2002) 'Mau Mau Veterans to Sue Britain for War Crimes', 28 October.

Du Bois, W.E.B. (1940) *Dusk of Dawn: An Essay towards an Autobiography of a Race Concept*, New York: Harcourt, Brace.

Du Bois, W.E.B. (1994) *The Souls of Black Folk,* New Jersey: Gramercy Books.

Fanon, F. (1967) *Black Skin, White Masks*, trans. C.L. Markmann, New York: Grove.

Gates, H., Jr. (ed.) (1987) *The Classic Slave Narratives*, New York: Mentor.

Harper's Magazine (2000) 'Making the Case for Slave Reparations', November.

Harriman, L. (1978) Introduction to J.H. Clarke (ed.), *Dimension of the Struggle against Apartheid, A Tribute to Paul Robeson. Proceedings of A Special Meeting of the Committee Against Apartheid on the 80th Anniversary of the Birth of Paul Robeson*, New York: African Heritage Association.

Horowitz, D., et al. (2001) 'David Horowitz's Ten Reasons Why Reparations for Slavery is a Bad Idea for Blacks – and Racist Too', *The Black Scholar*, vol. 31, no. 2: 48–55.

Human Rights Watch. (1993) *Accountability and Human Rights: The Report of the United Nations Commission on the Truth for El Salvador*, August.

Ignatieff, M. (1996) 'Articles of Faith', *Index on Censorship*.

Kelley, R. (2002) *Freedom Dreams: The Black Radical Imagination*, New York: Free Press.

Labaton, S. (2001) 'New F.C.C. Chief Would Curb Agency Reach', *New York Times*, 7 February.

Munford, C. (1996) *Race and Reparations: A Black Perspective for the 21st Century*, Trenton NJ: Africa World Press.

Maga, T.P. (1998) 'Ronald Reagan and Redress for Japanese American Intern-ment, 1983–88', *Presidential Studies Quarterly*, vol. 28, no. 3: 606–19.

Mazrui, A.A. (1994) 'Global Africa: From Abolitionists to Reparationists', *African Studies Review*, vol. 37, no. 3: 1–18.

McConahay, M. (2002) 'For Afro-Colombians, the War is Not About Drugs', *NCM Online*, 12 June.

Maki, M.T., et al. (1999) *Achieving the Impossible Dream: How Japanese-Americans Obtained Redress*, Chicago: University of Illinois Press.

Nesbitt, F.N. (2002) 'African Intellectuals in the Belly of the Beast: Migration Identity and the Politics of Exile', *Mots Pluriels* 20, February.

Ngugi wa Thiong'o (1998). 'The Allegory of the Cave: Language, Democ-racy And A New World Order!', *Black Renaissance/Renaissance Noire*, vol. 1, no. 3: 25–46.

Nkrumah, K. (1966) *Neo-colonialism: The Last Stage of Imperialism*, New York: International Publishers.

Reich, R.B. (1991) *The Work of Nations: Preparing Ourselves for 21st Century Capitalism*, New York: A.A. Knopf.

Robinson, R. (2000) *The Debt: What America Owes to Blacks*, New York: Penguin Putnam.

Rodney, W. (1974) *How Europe Underdeveloped Africa*, Washington DC: Howard University Press.

Thompson, V.B. (2000) *Africans of the Diaspora: The Evolution of African Con-sciousness and Leadership in the Americas*, Trenton NJ: Africa World Press.

UNHCR (2002) 'Declaration of the World Conference against Racism, Racial Discrimination, Xenophobia and Related Intolerance', Durban, South Africa, 31 August–8 September 2001, www.unhchr.ch/huridocda/huridoca.nsf/(Symbol)/A.Conf.189.12.En?Opendocument.

U.S. Bureau of Census (1997). 'Educational Attainment of the Foreign-born Population 25 Years and Over by Region of Birth and Gender: 1997', Table 13–1D, www.census.org.

Walters, R. (1995). *Pan Africanism in the African Diaspora: A Study of Modern Afrocentric Movements*, Washington DC: Howard University Press.

Waters, M.C. (1994) 'Ethnic and Racial Identities of Second Generation Black Immigrants in New York City', *International Migration Review*, vol. 28, no. 2: 795–820.

Westley, R. (1998) 'Many Billions Gone: Is It Time to Consider the Case for Black Reparations?', *Boston College Law Review*, vol. 40, no. 429, December.

Williams, E.E. (1961) *Capitalism and Slavery*, New York: Russell & Russell.

Wilkinson, B. (2002) 'Blacks Consider Suing France for Wrongdoings in Haiti', *IPS*, 27 September.

Wilson, J. (2001) 'A Battle over Race, Nationality, and Control at a Black University', *Chronicle of Higher Education*, 27 July.

6

From Civil War to Floods: Implications for Internal Migration in Gaza Province of Mozambique

Inês Macamo Raimundo

This chapter examines the internal migration in Gaza province, Mozambique, between 1992 and 2000. This period is significant for two major reasons. First, the civil war in Mozambique, which began in 1976, ended in 1992 with the signing of the General Peace Agreement. Second, the year 2000 is important in that floods added impetus to internal movements of people in the area studied. The overall aim of the chapter is to examine the implications of these internal movements in one of Mozambique's provinces: Gaza, once known as the granary of Mozambique.

Due to a series of events, Gaza province today has experienced changes that have given impetus to rural-urban migration – from rural areas to the province's capital city of Xai-Xai. The unprecedented movement of people to the overburdened city of Xai-Xai has implications in terms of urban development and management. Based on fieldwork research, combinations of qualitative and quantitative methodologies were used in this study. It is difficult to quantify in population terms the rural-urban migration and its specific contribution to the growth of the city of Xai-Xai for two reasons. The main reason is the lack of official published data on the subject. Second, the city is still receiving internally displaced persons as a result of the 2000 floods, and the municipality still does not have an accurate figure of how many people are involved.

According to data from the 1980 and 1997 censuses (Gabinete Central do Recenseamento 1992; INE 1999), there has been an unprecedented growth of population in the city of Xai-Xai. In fact, with reference to data from the other cities of Mozambique, the rate for the period 1980–97 was one of the highest in the country. The significance of this is that 'the rapidly increasing growth of population in Xai-Xai is resulting in important movements of people trying to survive' (Arão Sibinde, city planner, Xai-Xai, 23 April 2001). In spite of this growth in population, Xai-Xai continues to receive more and more people from other parts of Gaza province and also from the neighbouring province of Inhambane. Some 75 per cent of those consulted in the study were born outside the city, particularly in the neighbouring districts such as Chibuto, Manjacaze, Alto Changane and Guijá.

Like many cities in Mozambique, Xai-Xai has been confronted by growing pressure to provide adequate housing, water supply, electricity, schooling and hospitals. As a consequence of the civil war and the impact of the structural adjustment programme operational since 1987 (Lattes 1990; ACNUR/PNUD 1997a; Araújo 1997, 1999) and of the 2000 floods (Christie and Hanlon 2001), Xai-Xai has experienced even greater inflows of migrants from the districts of Gaza. Due to the lack of employment, many have had to resort to street vending, which has created severe problems in terms of overcrowding, waste management, obstruction of traffic, inadequate public health, inadequate building stock, poor housing provision and an array of social, economic and political problems that plague many other Third World cities (Gilbert and Gugler 1992; Knauder 2000).

Although research findings paint a picture of migrants who are poorly educated and unskilled, with a high dependence on agriculture for subsistence and some dependence on small-scale economic activities, this chapter uses case studies to examine the experience and livelihoods of migrants in the city of Xai-Xai who make a living despite all odds.

Urban Livelihoods in Gaza Province

The data collected for analysing the urban livelihoods of migrants in the city of Xai-Xai demonstrate the way that the migrants adopt coping strategies for survival and how rural–urban migration has impacted on their lives. It is worth noting, however, that although Xai-Xai's urban population has increased over the past twenty-five years, showing how the city has served as a receiving area for migrants, caution should be exercised in treating growth simply in relation to migration, because the number also reflects the expansion of the territorial administrative division, which gave the city more space and, therefore, more people.

In its assessment of urban livelihoods in Xai-Xai, with a view to understanding how the migrants have been integrated, this chapter demonstrates that it is not the rate of employment, or housing, or other facilities such as transport that assist migrants in settling down, but rather the likelihood of their adopting a viable, sustainable livelihood strategy.

The city of Xai-Xai: an overview

What makes people move out of Gaza province to the city of Xai-Xai is that it is the capital of the province, situated in the coastal zone with regular rain. It therefore has higher income levels, higher levels of education and better opportunities – hence the attraction for migrants.

Xai-Xai is situated in southern Mozambique, 210 kilometres from Maputo, the capital. The city covers an area of 130 square km representing 0.15 percent of the area of the province (Pililão 1989) and 9.3 per cent of its total population (INE 1999). Xai-Xai consists of a 'downtown' area and an 'upper town'. It was the downtown area that in 2000 was flooded by the Limpopo river, which affected 30,000 families (Arão Sibinde, Xai-Xai, 23 April 2001; Christie and Hanlon 2001). In terms of administration, Xai-Xai is a municipality divided into a 'cement city' of ten districts; a semi-urbanized area made up of the villages of Patrice Lumumba, Marien G'Ngouabi, the administrative posts of Inhamissa and Xai-Xai Praia; and non-urbanized areas, which include the outlying villages of Macamwine and Xilunguine (Arão Sibinde, Xai-Xai, 23 April 2001).

In terms of environment, Xai-Xai has a tropical humid climate, and sandy soil poorly suited to agriculture because of its coastal dunes. In terms of education, the city possesses one high school, which teaches up to twelfth grade; two secondary schools; and one technical school. There is a single provincial hospital, which has ten doctors, and two medical centres, supported by one doctor (Arão Sibinde, Xai-Xai, 23 April 2001). The health sector in Gaza province is supported by projects run by the Confederation of Save the Children Fund (US), such as the construction of hospitals and residences for health workers (Samuel Maibasse, the program manager of the Save the Children Fund in Gaza province, Xai-Xai, 8 June 2001). The water supply in the city is variable. In the 'cement city' there is tap water, but in the 'reed city' water is sourced from both holes and wells.

In terms of principal economic activities, many of Xai-Xai's inhabitants are involved in processing fisheries, urban agriculture and small businesses. In the words of the city's planner: 'Because Xai-Xai is a coastal zone, this advantage allows us to develop tourism activity. Xai-Xai is mainly an agriculture region where more than 50 per cent of its population is involved in agricultural activities, cattle rearing and fishing' (Arão Sibinde, Xai-Xai, 23 April 2001).

Culture as a push and pull factor in migration

In the rural areas, and in small cities such as Xai-Xai, migration is strongly influenced by cultural practices which force people constantly to move back and forth. The life histories of Mbaecane Z. Fungane, abandoned by his wives and children, and Jaquelina J. Macuácua, widow, support this conclusion.

Mbaecane was born in Fungane in 1915 (Alto Changane-Chibuto district). He attended school up to fourth grade. He is a former carpenter who now survives on agriculture. He married two wives, but his wives and children have now abandoned him because they are convinced that their father was involved in witchcraft. The community supports this view. The basis of the accusation is the local common-sense belief that people over 80 can only stay alive with the help of witchcraft. Before Mbaecane settled in Xai-Xai in 1988, his migration history, in reaction to the RENAMO (National Resistance of Mozambique) armed attacks during 1980s, was that of constant movement in flight from the Matsangas (as RENAMO guerrillas were called in Gaza province during the civil war). Before moving to Xai-Xai, Mbaecane tried to settle successively in Saúte, Chiare and Banganhane localities in the district of Chibuto. Lack of security led him to move to Xai-Xai. He meanwhile lost his land, cattle, goats, lamb, house and clothing. According to him, none of his relatives stayed in Chibuto, where they had lived most of their lives. When he arrived in Xai-Xai the leader of the village of Marien N'Gouabi took him in and gave him some land for building and cultivating. Nevertheless, after the signing of the General Peace Agreement in

1992, Mbaecane decided to return to his homeland. However, his sons refused to allow him to do so, arguing that it was not safe and that he had lost everything there during the civil war. Mbaecane does not know where his wives are. He knows only that his four sons are migrant labourers in South Africa (Xai-Xai, 15 May 2001).

Mbaecane Fungane's case illustrates how culture can be a push-factor in migration in a situation where he is retired and his relatives abandon him and forced him to return to a non-viable homeland because of the belief in witchcraft.

For most people who have settled in Xai-Xai there is little desire to return to the homeland. Some women do wish to return, but for cultural reasons they are unable to do so. Married women must stay where their husbands live (focus group discussion: Maria J. Mate, Jaquelina Macuácua, Atália Chungwane, Elina Maluleque, Xai-Xai, June 2001). The following life history confirms how cultural factors act in these situations.

Jaquelina was born in 1954. She lives in a household of eleven. The head of the household is her husband, a mineworker in South Africa. He has been away for ten years. Jaquelina's family settled in Xai-Xai in 1987. They were forced to move from Alto Changane, where she was born, mainly in response to RENAMO's armed attacks but also due to the 1980 drought. Although her husband has been away for a long time, Jaquelina still awaits his instructions concerning day-to-day running of the family's affairs. This has made Jaquelina's life somewhat difficult: she has been unable to earn a livelihood for her family back in her homeland. Because of cultural beliefs that prevent her from making any decision without her husband's consent, she cannot go anywhere. In Xai-Xai she is involved in the cultivation of family plots. However, in the floods of 2000 she lost her entire crop, Her land is still flooded. Although her husband does not visit, he sends money to meet the family's needs (Xai-Xai, 1 May 2001).

Survival strategies of rural-to-urban migrants in Xai-Xai

Migrants in the city have been involved in a number of activities that allow them to survive in an urban economy, such as working as street vendors, selling soup, hawking, and working with a *xitique* (a women's association that runs a rotating credit system, which also commonly serves as a mechanism for its members to participate in market activities), and obtaining land for urban agriculture. The following case studies demonstrate how migrants fashion their own means of achieving social inclusion in the city.

Urban agriculture

Fernando Magude Macamo (Xai-Xai, 1 May 2001) was born in 1937. He is a former mine labourer who was involved in agriculture to support his family of nineteen. His first-born son, who has worked in the mines of South Africa since 1990, committed a crime, and is now serving a seven-year sentence in a South African prison. This means that the family cannot expect any financial help from him. Fernando migrated from his homeland in 1983 in response to RENAMO's armed attacks to Chibuto, to Chókwè and, finally, to Xai-Xai in 1990. He is from the village of Mudjequene, Panda district (Inhambane province). When he migrated, nobody was left behind in the village as a result of the civil war. Before the war, Fernando had owned cattle, goats, chicken, donkeys and a large farm. He notes that during this time it was common to produce an agricultural surplus, which his family would sell. When he arrived in Xai-Xai he continued in agricultural activity, in addition to performing odd jobs and providing reed and straw for villagers. He currently owns a house with toilet facilities and a well. Fernando also owns a piece of land where all the family engage in agricultural activities. However, Fernando lives under the fear of losing this land. He worries that 'white' people will confiscate his land, claiming that it belongs to them, even though it was nationalized following independence. He says that he would not have this kind of problem if he were still living in his homeland. Yet, according to the city planner (Arão Sibinde, Xai-Xai, 23 April 2001) the only white farmer living in this village is Mr Carvalho, who during the 2000 floods gave his land over to displaced people and donated eighty oxen. Despite his fears, Fernando is not interested in returning to his homeland because he is too old. Fernando's experience shows that villagers can face land tenure worries when they migrate to the city.

Selling soup

Maria José Mate (Xai-Xai, 30 April 2001) is 23 years old, a typical example of a migrant who by step migration arrived in Xai-Xai and has survived in the city in spite of many setbacks. A common practice for many unskilled women is to sell soup by the bowl to construction workers at building sites. Maria was involved in this activity until February 2000, when the floods washed away her house and everything she owned. She had lived in downtown Xai-Xai since she arrived in 1990. Maria was born in Alto Changane (Chibuto district) in 1976. Because she wanted to carry on her studies, Maria moved in 1987 to Ngulelene, a village located about 30 kilometres from Xai-Xai. At this time, she was living with her married cousin. She attended primary school in the village of Chicumbane, 10 kilometres from Xai-Xai. In 1990 she moved to Xai-Xai in order to carry on her studies at the high school. When she arrived she rented a house (hut) in downtown Xai-Xai at the edge of the Limpopo river. Maria's parents supported her for two years. In 1992 she became pregnant and was suspended from her studies. In order to survive, Maria resorted to urban agriculture and sold soup from 1993 to February 2000. Her cousin, who lives in Maputo and also survives by selling soup to workers, introduced her to the soup idea. Maria assured me it is not a profitable activity, but it allows her to feed herself and her two children. Maria recalls how the 2000 floods affected her life, washing away everything she had. She is now dependent on assistance.

Membership of a xitique

Melita Solomone (Xai-Xai, 30 May 2001) survives by being a member of the rotating credit association commonly known as a *xitique*. Melita is a 31-year-old single mother. She used to be a member of a *xitique* when she was living in downtown Xai-Xai. Melita was born in Chibuto district. RENAMO's armed attacks forced her to move to Xai-Xai. For seven years she was employed as a housemaid. In 1998 a friend convinced Melita to join the credit association. Five women were involved at that time. When the group disbanded due to the floods membership stood at ten. The money that accumulated per month was a million MT on average. Melita was able to furnish her own house and buy dishes and pots. Some of the money Melita invested in small businesses relating to buying and selling items such as *capulanas*, sandals and underwear. As she notes, selling women's clothing is more profitable and secure because women like to be well dressed. In the 2000 floods Melita lost her house and furniture; worse, though, was that they brought about the dissolution of the credit association – her main source of income.

The three case studies above demonstrate that migrants possess a degree of resilience that is sometimes not taken into account, even in the grandest migration policies. They also show that the desire to build a life out of the ashes of Mozambique's civil war has driven migrants to find ways of surviving in the city rather than return to the countryside. The problems of living in the city are insignificant compared to the chaos and destruction that Mozambique's civil war caused in their lives. Such are the unquantifiable and intangible factors that will continue to see African cities as the destination for growing numbers of migrants.

Links between migrants and rural relatives

Although many migrants claim no longer to have relatives in the rural areas since everybody fled from the war or hazardous conditions, in fact the concept of family in the Changana culture is very broad, and tends to have no geographical boundaries (see Junod 1974). Significantly, migrants deem the practice of sending remittances to family extremely important: it is seen as an act that will result in a blessing. The literature on migration has overlooked the non-economic purposes of migrant remittances. My findings are that the practice in the province of migrants sending remittances back to the homeland has grown over time. One participant, Zacarias Chissaque (Xai-Xai, 2 May 2001), stated that he has sent products home to his relatives since he settled in Xai-Xai, as it is the only way not to forget ancestors. At the end of the year he would send goods to Maniquenique such as *capulanas* (a kind of sarong), as well as petrol; he celebrates such traditional ceremonies just to keep in mind his absent relatives.

Another case is that of Lourenço Machava (Xai-Xai, 1 June 2001). Lourenço was born in 1957 in Chibuto, and moved to the downtown area of Xai-Xai in 1977 in order to study, although he was unable to do so. Lourenço is an agricultural machine operator. He has not earned a salary since 1999, however, as his company ran into financial problems. His household consists of seven people, who are his responsibility. He recently became a widower. Contrary to expectations he did not follow the culturally allowed practice of remarrying. Lourenço lost everything in the floods. The NGO WorldVision and neighbours who gave his family furniture, food and two tents to accommodate his young children assisted him. The problem he currently faces is that he has no land, which means that he cannot undertake any urban agriculture, and no bank is willing to grant him credit to start a business. Despite these harsh living conditions, Lourenço still assists the family he left behind in Chibuto. He hopes that his life will soon improve.

How the 2000 floods affected people in the city

Once Mozambique had signed the General Peace Agreement in 1992, the country started to rebuild its economy in the wake of the devastating war. Attempts at re-establishing social and economic stability included repatriating Mozambican refugees who were living and working outside the country, and introducing development projects by opening up to foreign investment (Knauder 2000; Christie and Hanlon 2001). In Gaza province, huge investments were made in both the cashew nut and tourist industries, especially between 1992 and 2000. However, disaster struck in early 2000 when the southern and central parts of Mozambique were hit by the tropical storm Connie and the passage of cyclones Eline and Gloria, which produced heavy rainfall, causing in turn the flooding of rivers (Christie and Hanlon 2001). These floods displaced thousands of Mozambicans, particularly in the cities of Chókwè and Xai-Xai. People were forced to move out to search for safe havens. The following case studies reveal how the floods forced people to move and show how the displaced coped with this disaster.

Baptista Simango (Xai-Xai, 26 May 2001) was born in the city of Maputo in 1965. He was a victim of the 2000 floods because he was living in the downtown area of Xai-Xai, the area most severely affected. Now Baptista is still living in a hut (since October 2000) built by Auxílio Mundial, a local NGO. He is still waiting for a permanent house from the government. Before the floods, Baptista owned two brick houses and a large farm, but everything was washed away. His household consists of six people, including his niece, who is an orphan. The children were badly affected by the floods because their schools were washed away. They now study in tents without blackboards, textbooks or exercise books. Baptista is a mine labourer in South Africa, although he was in Mozambique when the floods struck. Then his work permit expired and he experienced difficulties with the company for whom he was working. Red tape has prevented him renewing his work permit, so he is unable to return to his job in South Africa. This, of course, has serious implications for the financial viability of his family. He now has no employment. However, he has skills in electrical repair and has used them to assist many people living in the 'cement city'. Baptista cannot own land at present because the government is still resettling those displaced by the floods. He believes that this time it will be difficult to satisfy everybody. The floods of the 1970s, which he remembers, affected relatively few people; it was then easy to obtain land on which to build or engage in agriculture.

The floods forced many people to move from the downtown area to uptown Xai-Xai. The main problem created was land scarcity: somehow it had to accommodate 30,000 displaced people. Some have occupied the 'reserved' areas in the city such as dunes and the green spaces, thereby creating environmental problems – waste management, water supply, electricity, unemployment, informal market trading – and other consequences of intensive unscheduled land occupation. The unavailability of land has been a major constraint to the establishment of viable urban livelihoods, in spite of the victims' best efforts. The mounting urban poverty crisis remains a pressing problem for the government of Gaza province.

Espreciosa Ivone (Xai-Xai, 29 May 2001), a single mother, is 31 years old. She was born in Manjacaze district. Espreciosa is the head of her household. She attended school up to seventh grade. Her household comprises five people. In fact, for Espreciosa as a single mother it is hard surviving as a street vendor. Espreciosa is the main breadwinner. She has been selling her goods by crossing districts, and bartering other goods. Espreciosa used to live in downtown Xai-Xai, but because of the floods she moved to the 2000 village under the auspices of the World Vision, the Save the Children Federation, Cruz Vermelha de Moçambique and the government. From these organizations and the government, she received building materials, food, blankets and land for building. Comparing the reasons for migration she declared that she never would have moved out because of the war. However, because of the floods she has had to rebuild her life in a new environment, with a new house and new neighbours.

What are the major findings of this research? First, migrants in the city of Xai-Xai are still not confident that war is, finally, over. This has made them reluctant to return to their homelands. Second, the scale of the 2000 floods and their devastating impact have created a reluctance among migrants to settle in downtown Xai-Xai for fear of further flooding. Thus the Xai-Xai municipality is confronted with the problem of settling this huge mass of people in a situation where the city has only 130 square km of land at its disposal, high unemployment, and too little land available for agriculture. Yet, paradoxically, Xai-Xai is a tourist attraction because of its beaches. The question the Xai-Xai municipality must face up to is, how can the municipality settle victims of the flooding given that there is no spare land? Returning to the rural areas is not an option, unless the government provides them with land to start again, before another flood strikes. The alternative seems to be urban poverty.

Conclusion

Studies have considered the effects of rural-to-urban migration on the lives of migrants in the city of Xai-Xai. One such effect is unemployment, which they seek to compensate for by engaging in informal activities. Another is lack of accommodation, which stretches the resources of the municipal authorities to the limit as they seek to resettle flood victims. Throughout, migrants have maintained relations with their homelands. Informal activities as well as keeping relations with the homeland can be seen as survival strategies.

The situation in Xai-Xai worsened in the wake of the 2000 floods. This happened against the background of land scarcity, for both building and farming, and a shortage of formal employment. Migration to the city of Xai-Xai was also fuelled by the continuing relevance of culture as well as the harsh living conditions in the rural areas. Older people account for a considerable number of the refugees, as their longevity is often seen a sign of witchcraft. The desire to move to the city also rests upon the belief that Xai-Xai, in its capacity as a provincial capital, offers more opportunities for a better life. Popular wisdom has it that it is better to live in the city under harsh conditions than to live in the countryside without schools, electricity and hospitals.

From a gender perspective, women are increasingly joining the ranks of internal migrants. There are differences, however. According to custom, those who are widows are still constrained by the cultural practice that insists a male relative must take over the responsibilities of a dead husband – and this includes deciding whether or not a woman may move away from her home.

Migration to Xai-Xai is, as we have seen, inextricably linked to Mozambique's political upheavals of the past two decades, particularly in response to RENAMO's armed attacks. The floods of 2000, like those of earlier decades, attracted worldwide attention. However, there remains an urgent need for human assistance in the city of Xai-Xai, where the flooding has exacerbated the precarious living conditions of the majority of people, making them even more vulnerable in terms of housing, water supply, sanitation and land tenure.

References

ACNUR/PNUD (1997) 'Perfis de Desenvolvimento Distrital – o distrito de Xai-Xai', Maputo: Alto Comissariado das Nações Unidas para os Refugiados Programa das Nações Unidas para o Desenvolvimento.

Araújo, M.G.M. (1999) 'Cidade de Maputo, Espaços Contrastantes: Do Urbano ao Rural', Finisterra, vol. 34, no. 67–8: 175–90.

Araújo, M.G.M. (1997) Geografia dos Povoamentos, Assentamentos Humanos Rurais e urbanos, UEM/Maputo: Livraria Universitária.

Araújo, M.G.M. (1996) Urban Settlements: National Report to Habitat II, Maputo, Maputo: Comissão Nacional para os Assentamentos Humanos, Ministério das Obras Públicas e Habitação.

Araújo, M.G.M. (1992) Distribuição Geográfica da População e Processo de Urbanização, Maputo: UPP/DNE.

Araújo, M.G.M. (1988) 'O Sistema das Aldeias Comunais em Moçambique: Transformações na Organização do Espaço Residencial e Produtivo', Ph.D. thesis, Lisbon: Universidade de Lisboa.

Bertle, M. (1992) 'The Witwatersrand', in J. Smith and I. Wallerstein (eds), Creating and Transforming Households: The Constraints of the World-Economy, Cambridge: Cambridge University Press.

Brown, B.B. (1980) 'The Impact of Male Labour Migration on Women in Botswana', South African Labour Bulletin, vol. 6, no. 4.

Chant, S. (1991) Women and Survival in Mexican Cities: Perspectives on Gender Labour Markets and Low-income Households, Manchester: Manchester University Press.

Chant, S. (1992) 'Migration at the Margins: Gender, Poverty and Population Movement on the Costa Rica Periphery', in S. Chant (ed.), Gender and Migration in Developing Countries, London: Belhaven Press.

Chant, S., and S.A. Radcliffe (1992) 'Migration and Development: The Importance of Gender', in S. Chant (ed.), Gender and Migration in Developing Countries, London: Belhaven Press.

Christie, F., and J. Hanlon (2001) Mozambique and Great Flood of 2000, Indiana: Indiana University Press.

Gabinete Central do Recenseamento. (1992) *I recenseamento geral da População*, Maputo.

Gilbert, A. and J. Gugler (1992) *Cities, Poverty and Urbanization in the Third World*, Oxford: Oxford University Press.

Hanlon, J. (1986) *Beggar your Neighbours: Apartheid Power in Southern Africa'*, London and Bloomington: Catholic Institute for International Relations in collaboration with James Currey and Indiana University Press.

INE (1996) *Anuário Estatístico, Província de Gaza*, Maputo: Instituto Nacional de Estatística.

INE (1999) *II Recenseamento Geral da População e Habitação, 1997: Resultados Definitivos*, Maputo: Instituto Nacional de Estatística.

Junod, H.A. (1974) *Usos e Costumes dos Bantos: A Vida duma Tribo do Sul de África*, vol. 1, *Vida Social*, 2nd edn, Lourenço Marques, Imprensa Nacional de Moçambique.

Knauder, S. (2000) *Globalisation, Urban Progress, Urban Problems, Rural Disadvantages: Evidence from Mozambique*, Aldershot: Ashgate.

Lattes, A.E. (1990) 'Distribuição Espacial, Urbanização e Migrações, Dinâmica e Processos Económicos, Sociais e Culturais', Série População e Desenvolvimento 2, Maputo: UPP/DNE.

Miles, M.C. (1997) 'Migration and Development in Post-colonial Swaziland: A Study of Women's Mobility and Livelihood Strategies', Ph.D. dissertation, Johannesburg: University of the Witwatersrand.

Pililão, F. (1989) *Moçambique – Evolução da Toponímia e da Divisão Territorial 1974–1987*, Maputo: DINAGECA.

7

Land Reform in Kenya:
The Place of Land Tribunals in Kombewa

Samwel Ong'wen Okuro

The literature on land dispute resolution in Kenya is very limited. What there is points either to the growth in such disputes or to the inability of the land dispute resolution mechanisms to solve land disputes at the local level. For example, Kanyinga (1997) examines the sociopolitical consequences of land tenure reforms, particularly during the Moi era. He observes that after the Moi regime had drained the public resources in previously rich agricultural corporations, it used land as an important resource for establishing and maintaining patronage relations with leaders and groups considered strategically significant in terms of political support. As a result, political elites accumulated more land at the expense of the poor. This has not only generated a situation of landlessness in Kenya; it has also increased the number of disputes on restricted land, resulting at times in crisis, as exemplified by conflicts along the Rift valley and in the coastal region of the country. Similarly, Shipton (1988), Wanjala (1990) and Kanyinga (1998) identify, although only in passing, the recent move in Kenya to decentralize land management and, particularly, issues concerning land disputes. They argue that the process, on the whole, has been riddled with corruption, unclear legal provision and a lack of knowledge about the working of the tribunals. These authors agree that the decentralization of land dispute resolution in Kenya had more to do with tightening government control over local land dealings than with improving efficiency.

The struggle over land is taking place across the African continent. Most countries have been witness to the same pressures of increasing competition and contestation over land, caused by rapid population growth, environmental degradation and low rates of economic development. As a result, many people have been left dependent on small-scale farming, livestock raising and foraging. These processes have combined to transform Africa from a continent of land abundance in the first half of the twentieth century to one of increasing land scarcity. This pressure has not only made a priority of land reform where it had not been initiated but has also questioned its legitimacy in those areas where it has taken place. For example, the land reform programme in Kenya initiated in the 1950s, encountered, and continues to encounter, myriad problems at the local level. Some problems are not new but have existed since the beginning, and have only been exacerbated by the deepening economic crisis found in much of Africa today.

In Africa, competition over land has occurred at all socio-economic levels and followed multiple fault lines, pitting national and local elites against ordinary citizens, neighbour against neighbour, kinsmen against each other and husbands against wives. Equally, local officials, village councils and traditional authorities have vied with one another to sell land to anyone willing to pay for it. Neighbours and kinsmen have encroached on others' fields or farmland, or, in some cases, have argued fiercely over inheritance and the claims of absentees. Boundaries have been fiercely contested by family members or the whole clan, leading at times to violent conflict. Similarly, in some cases customary rules long honoured in the breach have been revived and reinterpreted to exclude others, particularly descendants of 'strangers', from land they have occupied for many years. In the agriculturally rich areas and within the urban centres, land-grabbing has become everybody's business. This competition over land has not only driven up prices and sharpened real and perceived inequalities of income and wealth but has also intensified public debate over the legitimacy and accountability of institutions relied on during land arbitration. These events have not only served to question the view that indigenous or communal systems of land rights impede agricultural production and that private right in land boosts agricultural production; they have also forced a re-examination of the existing institutions for resolving land disputes. The issue has moved to centre stage because the question of land tenure and land reform and its impact on poor and vulnerable groups is now of such pressing importance. Although there is a rich literature on land tenure and land reform in Kenya, there is an inadequate historical record of how land disputes arising from land reforms have been addressed, and hence little is known of how to build strong and reliable arbitration mechanisms.

This chapter examines the role of divisional land tribunals in settling land disputes in rural Kenya, particularly in Kombewa. The aim is to point up the limitations inherent in the system of formal courts and divisional land tribunals. I argue that, as tenure security is a necessity on viable smallholder plots, constituting an important precondition for increasing agricultural productivity, supporting and sustaining rural livelihoods and enhancing overall food security, when that security is questioned or contested by others who lay claim to the same land, the time and effort spent in litigation play a part in determining the productivity of that land. Thus, even in areas where fully developed property rights have been established, particularly with regard to land, a straightforward legal process is the precondition for achieving agricultural productivity and food security. I argue further that land tenure in rural tenure,[1] as in other parts of Africa, is very fluid. People obtain access to land through a variety of means: social networks, customary institutions, family relations, service and renting arrangements and, occasionally, the law. It follows that the law should not have exclusive authority in arbitrating land cases. Land tribunals constituted by the Minister of Lands and Settlement should not have excessive powers to determine land disputes. I argue for, instead, the establishment of independent tribunals, comprising elders of 'integrity', who draw their legitimacy and authority from the entire community. These tribunals should be based on a common understanding of respect for human rights and local socio-economic and political realities.

Topography

Kombewa is an administrative division of Kisumu district, Nyanza province. It was originally called Central Seme Location. It borders Lake Victoria on the eastern side and Maseno division to the northeastern side, and was carved from the former Maseno division in 1987. It is inhabited by a section of the Luo community called Joseme and by a few immigrants (*jodak*) from neighbouring clans, such as Jo-Asembo, Jo-Gem, Jo-Kisumo, Abaluyia and, especially, the Banyore. Low ridges, seasonal rivers and scalps characterize the division's topography. There are also huge overhanging granite rocks in most places – for example, Kisian and the legendary Kit Mikayi. The granite rock is worked by the local population to produce ballast; the varying types of soil and riverbed sand deposits are used in construction and for making bricks.

Kombewa division has shorelines to the east. Consequently fishing takes up the greater part of the people's time. Other economic activities include subsistence farming and rearing cattle. Crops include maize, millet, cassava, groundnuts and cowpeas. The mean annual rainfall is 1,630 mm. The mean annual temperature ranges from a maximum of 25–30° Celsius to a minimum of 9–18° Celsius. Economically, Kombewa, like other parts of Nyanza province, is largely poor, with fishing as the only major economic activity.

Theoretical Framework

In 'The Land Question in Sub-Saharan Africa', Havnevik (1997) outlines the major theoretical positions on land tenure in Africa. This chapter draws on this work extensively. Havnevik argues that discussion has revolved around individualized tenure systems versus customary tenure systems, with the emphasis laid more recently on so-called community rights. The individualized land tenure system is supported by neoclassical economics literature on the grounds that a system of land title, or fully developed property rights, including the right to dispose freely of land without approval, is the only way to restore the growth potential of African regions subject to high levels of population and increasing commercialization of agriculture. By thus reducing the uncertainty surrounding land transactions, land can be more readily transferred to more dynamic farmers, and the excessive fragmentation encouraged by traditional land allocation and inheritance patterns will be avoided. More efficient cropping choices and more long-term investments in land will further evolve from enhanced tenure security. Credit supply will automatically increase through the potential for using land as collateral. This thinking was reflected, not surprisingly, in the World Bank's sectoral work and structural adjustment programmes. The World Bank has been supporting titling efforts on the assumption that this will ensure secure land rights, activate markets and increase agricultural production (Plateau 1996; Kanyinga 1998; World Bank 1998).

However, the more structural, institutional and empirically oriented economic theory has shown that very few countries in sub-Saharan Africa have followed the path described, except in the case of Kenya, which has been engaged in an extensive land registration programme since 1956. The presence of continuous opposition to the granting of land title is attributable to the fact that accumulated evidence has raised serious doubts about its effectiveness in enhancing agricultural growth and increasing the security of tenure (Hazell 1992; Bruce 1993; Bruce and Migot-Adhola 1994; Cornia 1994; Havnevik 1997). This perspective has reached a number of conclusions as follows. Land registration creates increased insecurity for vulnerable parts of the population. It does little to activate the land market, and where it does it is mainly for speculative ends. It does not reverse the process of land fragmentation; nor does it improve land allocation. It does not in significant ways improve smallholders' access to credit and there is no significant correlation between granting land title and increased agricultural yields. The position in Kenya is similar, as Kanyinga's report *Re-distribution from Above: The Politics of Land Rights and Squatting in Coastal Kenya* (2000) makes clear. This report argues that the practice of granting individual rights over public land has served to increase the number of landless people and has generated new types of dispute over ownership. At the same time, titling appears to have had little effect on credit as few people use their title to secure loans. Furthermore, it has not had a positive environmental effect anywhere in Kenya.

The policy implication emerging from this theoretical strand, argues Havnevik (1997: 6), is not that land registration is an inappropriate measure, but rather that it needs to be accompanied by other types of reform that can break down the various constraints acting on African agriculture, such as the lack of suitable technological packages, weakly developed infrastructure including roads, and poor input delivery services, output marketing systems and extension services. The changes brought about by structural adjustment policies, in particular substituting state structures with private-sector ones and the withdrawal of various forms of subsidy related to agricultural production, have not realized significant improvements. In some areas, smallholder market access and prices have improved, but outlying areas have experienced a worsening situation in the new liberalized context.

Land tenure reform in Kenya, particularly titling, is only one among a whole range of factors that have to be addressed in concert if agricultural production, food security and tenure security are to be improved. In Kenya, Kibwana (1993: 237) advises that we must pay appropriate attention to an number of factors: technological know-how, agricultural credit, managerial competence, appropriate training and agricultural labour, the establishment of viable agro-industries, and favourable pricing of primary agricultural commodities in international markets. To this list should be added the land dispute solution process, particularly at the local level. It is my contention that the effectiveness and legitimacy of this process affects not only agricultural production in Kenya but also smallholder tenurial security and credit acquisition. It follows that non-tenurial constraints (in this case divisional land tribunals) play an important role in holding back progress in agriculture, and that therefore reforms focusing exclusively on establishing formal property rights on land are doomed to fail.

Land Tenure Reform in Kombewa

Much confusion exists with regard to the precise nature of land tenure in pre-colonial Africa.[2] There are many reasons for this. Deliberate misrepresentation occurred, for instance, when some Western anthropologists refused to acknowledge the existence of communal land tenure in pre-colonial Africa. The fact of such tenure might conceivably have been used to justify socialism and communism (Kibwana 1993: 231). More generally, colonial efforts to govern Africans according to local customs were complicated by a contested understanding of African social realities. To acquire knowledge of 'native' customs, officials enlisted Africans as informants and commissioned anthropologists to help discriminate between 'authentic' customs and invented ones. Colonial officials also acquired information on 'native laws and customs' through their daily inter-action with chiefs and commoners, litigants and judges, witnesses and petitioners, labourers and vagrants, taxpayers and defaulters. To ascertain the rules of customary land tenure, or to sort out who did or did not belong to a land-holding family in the community or 'tribe', officials had to ask questions. And Africans gave conflicting answers, especially when the subject of inquiry was itself a point of contestation, such as claims to land or, chiefly, to office. If, as frequently happened, administrators sought to bypass the confusion and reinforce traditional authority by limiting their inquiries to a few chiefs and elders, they were likely to hear complaints not only from rival chiefs but also from 'young men', women or 'strangers' who had not been consulted. Officials dismissed individual complaints as based on jealousy or ignorance, but accumulated protests were harder to ignore. No sooner were authorities, boundaries and customs established than they had to be revised (Berry 1992; Gocking 1994; Ranger 1999). Traditions were 'invented', reworked, discarded or simply accumulated as colonial rulers and subjects debated their validity, or their relevance to the dilemmas and pressures of the moment. The chiefs, elders and others who were presumed to know customs often told conflicting stories.

It follows that the forty or so ethnic groups that inhabit Kenya could not be adequately represented when it came to the issue of land tenure. In the pre-colonial period there was great diversity in the forms of land tenure, reflecting the many, and changing, economic activities, settlement patterns, and social and political organizations. Nevertheless, it is undoubtedly the case (with the exception of the Wanga, the Nandi and Swahili states) that before colonialism, land in Kenya was owned communally and governed by customary law. Individuals did not own the land. A whole community owned the land, with each individual having the right to till it or use it in a manner acceptable to others. Land was not owned to the exclusion of everybody else. Individuals instead had rights to use communal land: for example, the right to graze one's domestic animals, the right to till and the right to collect firewood. Land was abundantly available and thus staking individual claims was superfluous. Furthermore, at this stage of development, experience taught that group activity and effort bore better results in productive work.

With the development of social and economic organization towards settled pastoralism and subsistence agriculture, as well as cohesiveness of social units within the ethnic group – lineage and clans – land belonging to an ethnic group was divided up into clan land and at the micro-level, family land. The head of the extended family exercised control over such family land. In exercising such powers, the head would, for example, subdivide the land into nuclear families (often polygamous). Such land was in turn divided into houses and/or given over to adult sons for cultivation. However, as time progressed, an individual was able to acquire personal land by his own efforts – by clearing virgin land in his area, by accepting a gift or by inheritance. Whereas the individual could not transfer or dispose of family land as self-acquired property, he had more or less a permanent interest in it, for his own benefit. However, to transfer self-acquired interests, he nevertheless had to seek the consent of the family. Thus individual autonomy in land matters was alien to pre-colonial tenure. This position is representative of land tenure in Kombewa before colonialism.

The establishment of colonialism halted the further spontaneous development of indigenous land tenure systems. An alien form of land tenure was introduced in the British East Africa Protectorate (as the interior of Kenya was initially named). From the time it was decided that the East Africa Protectorate would become a settlement colony, it became necessary to introduce a land tenure system similar to that existing in Britain so that the European settlers would be motivated to settle in the colony as well as to invest their financial resources without restraint. Thus, as early as 1897, individual tenure of land was introduced in Kenya by the Imperial British East Africa Company, albeit within delimited areas. But, as colonialism progressed, the official policy was individual tenure of land modelled on English law, although in practice the two systems of land tenure and agriculture coexisted. The indigenous system continued in the form of family tenure; indigenous agriculture was subsistence farming. The system for settlers was individual tenure; settler agriculture was oriented towards cash crops.

From 1945, the thinking about the development of African agriculture changed, particularly concerning practices within the native reserves, into which hitherto Africans had been bundled; the land was both marginal and, in terms of yield, grossly inadequate for the needs of the African population. Furthermore, Africans were viewed by colonial authorities primarily as providers of labour for European farms, and various ordinances were passed to this end – for example, the East African Hut Tax Ordinance 1903, Native Hut Tax and Poll Tax Ordinance 1910, Village Headmen Ordinance 1907, Native Authority Ordinance 1907, Native Registration Ordinance 1921, and so on. Official rethinking about African agriculture and its role in the colony was based on several factors. The colonial economy had been ravaged by the worldwide depression of the 1930s. The British government required colonies to be self-sufficient in agricultural production. In the early 1930s, demand for labour on European farms slackened; thus extra labour was available, which could be expended in African production. Also, it was deemed necessary for the African agricultural sector to augment the settler sector. These adjustments were followed by settlement schemes and improvement drives, which aimed at restoring and preserving land. When the remedies failed, colonial agronomic experts advanced the argument that the best way to correct the problem of land use among Africans living in the native reserves was to reform the tenure system (Kibwana 1993: 236).

The agronomists argued that African land tenure, which was predominantly communal in nature, undermined proper land use and rapid agricultural development because the system of access to land use rights encouraged fragmentation, thus cutting down returns to labour and time. It was also argued that African land tenure tended to encourage incessant disputes, thereby discouraging long-term capital investment and was not secure as the basis for generating agricultural credit. Lastly, the agronomists argued that the inheritance procedure of communal tenure encouraged the subdivision of holdings, a logic that rapidly produced units of sub-economic size. To cure these perceived ills, the agronomists recommended individualization of tenure among the indigenous people (Okoth-Ogendo 1976, 1986). This school of thought was further promoted by the East African Royal Commission of 1953–55, which recommended that individual tenure had the great advantage of granting individuals a sense of security in their possession of land and of enabling the community, by the purchase and sale of land, to move away from an unsatisfactory system of fragmented holdings to one based on units of economic size. It was envisaged that under individual tenure the psychological effect of owning land would catalyse the owner to work hard. It was argued, too, that consolidated individual holdings would facilitate proper farm planning on a mixed rotational basis.

In Kenya, land tenure reform began during the colonial period. The colonial government introduced individualization on the assumption that it would spur agricultural growth in the native areas and thereby undermine the ideological basis of the peasants' rebellion (the Mau Mau) that land hunger and political repression had aroused. A report in 1954 by the then deputy director of agriculture, R.J.M. Swynnerton, on *A Plan to Intensify the Development of African Agriculture in Kenya* inspired the reform (Kanyinga 1997). The Swynnerton Plan[3] (as the report was widely known) aimed at the displacement of the indigenous land tenure system with a system that entrenched private property rights, similar to what English Land Law provided in the native reserves. This began by identifying rights in land by way of recording rights over different fragments (demarcation and adjudication). Aggregation (consolidation) of such fragments into single units followed this phase. Registered titles concluded the procedure. This has remained the practice, except that consolidation does not apply to all areas (Wanjala 1990). However, it is important to observe that disputes over, for instance, the displacement of holders from one place to another despite their investment in the former location have prevented widespread consolidation (Kanyinga 1997).

The Swynnerton Plan posited that the security of tenure (a title deed) would enable a landowner to pledge his land as collateral for development capital, which would in turn enable farmers to pay more attention to their land instead of being drawn into a peasant rebellion. The Plan thus concluded that consolidation and farm planning would ultimately generate enough employment to absorb the dispossessed segment of the population. Further, the registration of land would convert African-owned land into a marketable commodity, and title to such land would then be freely transferable or chargeable as security for development credit. Registration would also increase the security of title, providing further incentive to investment.

It was as a result of these arguments that the Land Reform Programme reached Kombewa division. Kombewa began on 8 May 1956 as a pilot scheme for land consolidation in the whole of western Kenya. The DC of Central Nyanza, E.H. Risley, inaugurated the project. In his address he observed that

> the present system of land holding among the Luo was evolved when the tribe was much smaller in every way that it is now, and when they were constantly pressing forward to new lands. This system is now not suitable to a people now static. It prevents profitable farming, results in more poverty, than is necessary, and is steadily ruining the land. Seme location has been chosen as a pilot scheme since it contains examples of almost every type of soil formation found in the district as well it had a considerable element of progressive minded people. (DC/KSM/1/3/61, Land Consolidation, 1956, KNA; Okuro 2002a)

Women were central to agricultural production in Kombewa at this time. This was due to male labour migration to European plantations (see Okuro 2002a). In the same period, the district agricultural officer lamented that

> the Central Nyanza has been as in the past and is still a hunting ground of labour recruiters who entice away a very large proportion of young and

strong men, leaving nothing but old men, women and boys to cultivate the land. The Luo woman lives a life very apart from her husband. She is in matters connected with the running of the home and *shamba*, the executive partner. (DC/KSM/1/3/61, 1956, KNA; Okuro 2002)

Like any colonial project, land consolidation had certain drawbacks. The then assistant agricultural officer at Siriba Agricultural Centre acknowledged several problems arising from the process. He noted that some people were forced to destroy their houses, or sometimes a whole clan lost land, due to the demands of road construction. Some people were forced from fertile to less fertile land. Also there was the possibility of people being asked to leave a certain area in which they had long been tenant farmers and being forced to occupy tsetse-fly-infected areas. In some situations, they could even be moved to areas that lacked water. The other problem identified by the officer concerned absentee landlord and tenant farmers (DC/KSM/1/3/61, 1956, KNA; Okuro 2002). The land reform process in Kombewa also saw disputes over boundaries. These could only be sorted out by men, but since men were away labouring on the European plantations, it forced women to be at home not only to protect the crops but also to acquire and protect land rights. Adjudication and consolidation processes demanded that a person acquires land if only he/she had cultivated or was cultivating it. Married women and widows could only be given land to cultivate on behalf of the male children. It was observable from the beginning that the land reform programme in Kombewa was riddled with disputes requiring institutional arbitration.

Despite the many limitations and disputes, the post-independence Kenyan government simply retained the colonial land laws and pursued the same land reform programme without any major alteration (Okoth-Ogendo 2003). The 1966–70 National Development Plan had this to say about land reforms: 'it had been proved in the past that a significant number of farmers, registration, and where appropriate consolidation, of their holdings stimulate, increase efficiency and output far out of proportion to the cost of the process' (cited in Kibwana 1993: 236). The legislation vested the radical title – the ultimate ownership over land – in the state, thereby giving it unrestricted powers over control of land, public and private (Okoth-Ogendo 2003). This has had significant consequences, considering that, with the crystallization of the reform process, a set of land problems manifested themselves in earnest. The reform generated further disputes over land ownership and resulted in more skewed distribution of land ownership. It reproduced ethnic-based interests in land and made the land question more complex than ever. It further demanded the urgent establishment of sound and reliable mechanisms for solving land disputes in Kenya.

Land Tribunals in Kombewa

The formation of land tribunals in Kenya was initiated in consideration of the inapplicability of ordinary courts of law on issues surrounding land. It was also due to the rising number of unresolved land disputes in court registers. From independence, three systems of law governing land ownership existed in Kenya.[4] Initially there was customary law, which was unwritten and differed from ethnic group to ethnic group; it persists today. However, the establishment of colonialism ushered in two main Acts of Parliament and the importation of the English system of land ownership. First was the Indian Transfer of Property Act (ITPA) of 1882. This Act was used by colonialists to govern land ownership in the areas then called the 'White Highlands'. Much of the land in Kenya is still governed by the ITPA (Wanjala 1990). Second was the Registered Land Act (RLA) of 1963 found in the chapter 300 of the laws of Kenya. This Act governs land formerly held under customary law. It was enacted in 1963 as part of a result of a reform programme started by the colonial government and aimed at replacing the customary law system of communal ownership of land with the English system of individual ownership. It is therefore mostly applicable in those areas called 'reserves' and later 'trust lands'. This law is increasingly becoming the governing law even in areas that are not necessarily part of trust land. For this reason many people are converting their land ownership from ITPA to RLA.

It is important to observe, however, that before a piece of land is brought under the RLA, there must be registration, where one is issued with deeds and document or registration of title. This process of registration involves three important stages, each prone to disputes. The first is the adjudication. This is the process whereby the relevant officers from the Ministry of Lands and Settlement, with the help of the inhabitants of the area, go about ascertaining the right ownership of a given piece of land in an area. This process only takes place with regard to land that is unregistered and is still held under customary law. Second, there is what is referred to as land consolidation. This is the combining of small pieces of land to which rights of ownership have been identified into larger economic units. This process need not always follow land adjudication, since consolidation may not be necessary. Last is the process of registration, where appropriate entries are made in a land register and the land accordingly brought under RLA. Once land initially held under customary law comes under RLA, customary law no longer applies.

Most land disputes arise as a result of land adjudication. The processes of land adjudication initially occur after a government minister has given a declaration that trust land should be adjudicated. The minister then appoints an adjudication officer, who will appoint a demarcation officer, a survey officer and a recording officer. These appointments are made in consultation with the district commissioner of the area to be adjudicated. Those appointed should not be fewer than ten in number and must be persons resident in the area to be adjudicated. Any party having a claim to the land to be adjudicated must be present to show his boundaries to the demarcation officers. Any person who during the adjudication process feels that his rights have not been taken into consideration can complain to the adjudication committee, chaired by the adjudication officer, which will arrive at a decision based on customary law. A challenge to this decision can be lodged with the land executive officer, who will submit it to the arbitration board appointed by the provincial commissioner. Contestations based on the incompleteness or incorrectness of the adjudication register are referred to the minister of lands. The minister makes the final decision on an appeal; however, on the order of a high court, the minister's decision may be challenged.

One weakness of this procedure is that it gives the minister and the provincial administration excessive powers over land issues. Not only are these people government officers appointed by the president; they are not best placed to understand the realities of land cases in local areas. They must rely on the adjudication officers and other officials, who similarly are not neutral. Why should their decisions have legitimacy when those with claims on the land are not present. Customary laws have been twisted, reinterpreted and continuously contested, particularly when tenant landowners or illegitimate children have pressed claims to land. These absentee landowners, tenants and offspring do not seek arbitration through the provincial administration (which they claim is corrupt); they go straight to the courts. Thus, the land adjudication process has generated appeals and counter appeals, which have piled up in magistrates' courts.

Land disputes do not stop at the adjudication level. Disputes between registered owners of land and other people claiming an interest have also come to the fore. These disputes symbolize the clash between English law and customary law. Such disputes have arisen because individuals are registered as owners of land which is actually family land. The RLA provides that up to five people can be registered as owners of a piece of land. Families or houses can avoid future problems by dividing the land between themselves during the adjudication exercise to produce finality of individual titles.[5] These cases are common where people do not understand the legal implications of registration. In consequence, many people have found it difficult to accept the legal position. Long after registration, families, houses, brothers and relatives initiated endless cases in court over land ownership, distribution and boundaries. As a consequence of land registration, the land disputes arising were reported to the magistrates' courts. Nevertheless, these courts were unable to come up with a firm and final statement on the position of the law on land cases. On occasion the cases were customarily arbitrated, by evoking the concept of customary trust. An example of this is where the eldest son is registered as the owner of the land but is presumed to hold the land on trust for the younger sons in the family. In other cases, the magistrates have interpreted and enforced the law as it was.

In 1981 Parliament passed the Magistrates Jurisdiction Amendment Act, which established elders' courts, or panels of elders, and vested in them the power to hear and decide on certain land cases. These included beneficial ownership of land, the division and determination of boundaries of land, claims to occupy or work on land, and cases involving trespass. The panel comprised the district commissioner as chairman, or any other person appointed by him, and two to four elders agreed upon by the parties involved in the dispute. The judgement of the panel was then passed on to the resident magistrates' court entrusted with making the final decision. Appeals can be made, in which case a fresh tribunal is constituted. The law defines elders as persons in the country or communities to which the parties in the dispute belong who are recognized by the customs in the community or communities as being, by virtue of age, experience or otherwise, competent to resolve issues between parties. Where there are no such elders, the law defines an elder as meaning such a person as the district commissioner appoints (Wanjala 1990).

It is clear (and in this I agree with Wanjala) that the law contemplates an elder in the old style, who is presumed to be incorruptible, impartial and respected by the society. Such an elder is fast disappearing as society changes. Indeed, the elders found in these panels tend to be those persons appointed by the district commissioner, as allowed for in the second part of the definition. The district officer, the chief elder, tends to be a fairly young person. The whole process was intended to be simple, cheap, fair and democratic. However, this has not been the case, for four reasons: the limited jurisdiction of the elders' panel; corruption among the panel; unclear legal provisions; and people's lack of knowledge regarding the workings of the panels. In consequence a majority of cases slated for determination by elders' panels returned to the resident magistrates' courts, with litigants hiring lawyers.

From the 1990s land disputes became numerous in every location, with parties refusing to accept the elders' verdicts. The rise in the numbers of these cases is attributable to many developments, notably population pressure, land degradation, poor agricultural yields, unreliable rainfall, the HIV/AIDS pandemic, and the structural adjustment measures. Of all these causal factors the structural adjustment programmes (SAPs), initiated in Africa in the early 1980s, deserves a brief explanation. Through the programmes and their instruments, developing countries were expected to harness the benefits of globalization by pursuing policies that 'open' their economies to global competition, foreign investment and technology. In a much wider context, adjustment packages included: devaluation of overvalued currencies, an increase in artificially low food prices and interest rates, a closer alignment of domestic prices with world prices, an emphasis on tradables or exportables, and the gradual withdrawal of restrictions on competition from abroad (trade liberalization), privatization (of parastatals or large-scale government monopolies), a decrease in government spending, wage and hiring freezes, reduction in employment in the public sector or in the minimum wage, the removal of food and input subsidies, and an across-the-board reduction in budget deficits as the way to invigorate stagnating economies (Okuro 2002b). These policies have been formulated and advocated by the Bretton Woods institutions since the 1980s. The programmes involve the disbursement of financial support in tranches in the form of SAPs or sector adjustment loans, typically on concessional terms, which are conditional upon policy reform. Trade reforms are absolutely central to SAPs due to the prevailing powerful economic arguments in favour of free trade. In Kenya the demand for trade reforms was accompanied by political reforms.

The introduction of structural adjustment programmes in Kenya, with their imposition of strict austerity measures, served to worsen the situation regarding land and land reforms in Kombewa. As indicated earlier, since the colonial period the people of Kombewa have migrated to urban areas to gain employment, yet the SAPs were marked by a freeze on real employment and widespread retrenchment for those already employed. The casualties of the SAPs turned to farming and non-agricultural activities to survive. Land came under intense pressure for domestic food production. Those who initially had little interest in land saw its acquisition as a priority. New land disputes emerged as most people saw land as the only readily available resource to lay their hands on. Land infertility, resulting from overproduction, also became an issue. Those who had money started buying and renting land for food production, while those without sought help from relatives to acquire land. Migrant labourers, who hitherto had tended not to consider land an important resource, and even absentee landowners started laying claims to land and seeking its adjudication and registration. Those who had many male children and were holding family lands for younger brothers demanded exclusive possession of the whole piece of land. Others who wanted to enter informal-sector activities also required title deeds as collateral for credit. The women, who hitherto were culturally forbidden to exercise a direct claim on land, also joined in the fray, particularly widows who demanded their share of the land for the production of food for the family's subsistence.

The introduction of cost-sharing in public education and health services were added burdens on parents, indeed on the entire population, that had never been experienced before. Low-cost public schools, for example, expected parents to pay tuition fees, and contribute to building funds, development funds and the like. This amounted to about US$30 and US$400 per child per year for primary and secondary schools, respectively. University education costs about US$2,000 per student per year. This is too expensive for many parents (Munguri et al. 2002: 15). SAPs, therefore, are responsible for the poverty, unemployment and socio-economic inequalities experienced in many parts of Kenya today. It is in this regard that Moyo (2000: 1) remarked that the political and economic reforms on the continent since the mid-1980s have been accompanied by massive rural social dislocations, further poverty, growing insecurity over land and natural resources, disputed property rights, and numerous violent conflicts over the control of resources and of the state. Neoliberal economic policy reforms, imposed from above in the context of 'choiceless democracy', have added to the erosion of the basic social and political rights of Africans.

As population pressure on land continues to mount and soil fertility declines, more and more labour has been forced off the land to ensure household survival, further undermining agricultural production. The eventual result of this process is typically the sale of part of the homestead land to meet some immediate family crisis (e.g. severe illness, particularly HIV/AIDS; school fees; food for consumption). Those who succeed in purchasing this land eventually differentiate rural society into landed and landless groups, further complicating claims over land. These land buyers sometimes pay in instalments, hoping that the economic situation will improve to enable them pay in full. When the situation fails to get any better, the buyers end up unable to pay. Such cases tend to end up as land disputes in urgent need of arbitration by an independent and reliable land tribunal or court of law.

In response to the crisis, in 1990 the government of Kenya re-examined the issue of the rising number of land cases and duly created the Land Dispute Tribunal Act No. 18 of 1990. This Act gained the president's assent on 14 January 1991. It maintained the definition of an elder. As with the other acts creating the previous elders panels, this Act limited the jurisdiction of the magistrates' courts in certain cases relating to land in rural areas. It required that land cases in court be sent back to the land tribunals for mediation. The Act made provision for appeals by creating the Lands Dispute Appeal Committee, appointed by the provincial commissioner (PC) and consisting of a chairman appointed by the PC and no fewer than five people appointed by the minister. The Act stated that the minister may make rules prescribing the procedure of the tribunal in particular; the form in which any decision, order or determination of the tribunal shall be given; the evidence that may be admitted in proceeding before a tribunal and the taking of such evidence.

It is in this way that Kombewa Division Land Tribunal (KDLT) was created in 1999. I was able to interview all eight members of the tribunal. The Tribunal was initiated for several reasons, including the fact that the government was becoming concerned by the rising number of land cases being heard in court, leading many people to hire lawyers at great expense. The government realized that the elders in the village possessed valuable knowledge on land and disputes. A meeting of district land adjudication officers invited elders of sound reputation to put their names forward for eventual appointment to the tribunal. Six people were duly appointed: Odari Wanjango, chairman and retired police officer; John Oyungu, retired prison officer; Joseph Oyucho, retired teacher; Lazarus Nyathi, retired assistant chief; John Agik, retired Ministry of Works employee; Justas Ayal, retired officer from the provincial administration; the district officer; and the chief in the area where the KDLT had jurisdiction.

Before a case is forwarded to the KDLT, the litigant must exhaust the procedure of first taking his or her case to the village elders, then to the sub-location elders, and lastly to the location elders for arbitration. Only where he or she remains dissatisfied can the case be forwarded to the KDLT. Such a person must be issued with a letter by the chief introducing him or her to the members of the KDLT committee. He or she must pay the equivalent of US$4 as sitting allowance for the elders. A provision also exists in which a person may just approach the district officer to put his/her claim. The tribunal writes to the chief for further explanation before the case can be put forward for discussion. Three-quarters of the members constitute a quorum. The tribunal discusses the issues with all the parties present and may be required to visit the land under arbitration and make certain observations before determining the case. The verdict is normally typed up by the district officer's secretary and handed over to both parties. In the case of a boundary dispute, the tribunal members must implement their verdict by visiting the disputed land and then redraw the boundary with the help of the assistant chief. If the parties are not satisfied with the verdict of the tribunal, the complainant is given a letter (on payment of the equivalent of US$25) to refer the case to the appeals committee at a date and time agreed upon. The appeals committee comprises three elders from different areas. Its judgment is final. The tribunal may have over a hundred cases pending. It hears a maximum of two cases per day, and sits only twice a month.

Land Disputes before the KDLT

The KDLT hears cases of a varied nature. Let us briefly consider the main types.

Disputes related to the issue of land transfer   Such disputes arise when a person claims that he/she is the owner of a piece of land on the basis of sale by the original registered owner. In other words, the claimant asserts that the registered owner has transferred the land to him. The dispute arises because the registered owner denies that he ever transferred his land to the claimant. If such a transaction was done without involving the land control board, it has no standing in law.

Disputes involving absent landowners, particularly male migrant labourers   Such disputes arise when the parents of a migrant sold his land to a willing buyer due to economic pressure such as school fees or sickness. Such transactions are normally not formalized in the land office due to ignorance of the law. The parties usually sign an agreement in the presence of the chief and other village elders. Disputes have been reported to the KDLT in which the migrant is willing to pay back the buyer the full amount he paid for the land. The person who bought the land refuses the money, claiming that he has developed the land, say for more twelve years, and that the land is therefore his.

In hard economic times, people may hold the land legally but be unable to afford to cultivate it   Such persons normally seek assistance from those who own a plough but lack adequate land for cultivation. The owner of the land will advance his land to the person to plough and they will then divide the income. If the person with the plough has money, he will approach the land office with *kitu kidogo* – a bribe – and claim he has bought the land; however, the identification number of the registered landowner and the land number will have been illegally acquired. Many such disputes are dealt with in the KDLT office in Kombewa.

Disputes concerning land purchase and payment by instalments Such disputes arise when the person who has bought the land decides to pay by instalments. During the payment period a disagreement arises between the purchaser and the registered landowner, who decides to return the money to the buyer. Disputes arise when the legal landowner decides to return less money in view of the fact that the person who bought the land had been cultivating it.

Illegal land exchange disputes Such disputes arise when two or three registered landowners exchange the land among themselves to ease cultivation. One of the parties may decide to formally buy the exchanged land. Later the son of the person who agreed to sell insists he has the right to build a homestead on the land. Disputes of this kind are normally forwarded to the tribunal for arbitration.

Disputes involving tenants (jodak) These disputes involve those who have been given land within a particular clan, even though they are not members of it. With the expansion of the clan or the family that gave out the land, they may ask the tenants to leave and seek land where they have customarily entitlement. The tribunal rarely listens to such cases, transferring them to the district land board.

Disputes regarding succession or inheritance Such cases arise when the legally registered owner of the land dies without having made a written will. Those who belong to his family may make conflicting land claims about how much land they are entitled to. A unique situation has arisen over land entitlement of children born as a result of widow inheritance. For cultural reasons, the person inheriting the widow may decide to donate some of the land to her sons, particularly those he has fathered. After some time (usually after the inheritor has died) the children of the inheritor claim that such agreement was made without their consent and put in a claim to the land.

Cases involving the content of the land sold Such disputes normally arise when the person who has sold the land claims that the person who bought it did not buy features on the land such as trees and anthills. This is of particular relevance because anthills and trees are very important in Kombewa during the construction of a house (the anthill provides the mud necessary for the walls; most land is sandy). The person who sold the land may insist on their claim over the anthill and tree; the buyer rejects this. Such disputes are also passed to the tribunal.

These, then, are examples of disputes that have been reported to the KDLT in the last two years.

Challenges Facing the Kombewa Division
Land Tribunal

The involvement of members of the provincial administration in land issues continues to work against the aims of the land tribunals everywhere in Kenya. The provincial administration in Kenya includes provincial commissioners, district commissioners, district officers, chiefs and their assistants. All are civil servants, well schooled in state bureaucracy and directed by the office of the president. They have been continuously involved in the affairs of the former ruling party, the Kenya African National Union (KANU). They have the knowledge and contacts to obtain permits for and organize party meetings throughout the country and are skilful at isolating dissent. They may also have been instrumental in mobilizing ruling party support in the country (Adar and Munyae 2001). Since the ruling party has used land for the purposes of maintaining political patronage relations and securing political loyalty (Kanyinga 1997), it is not surprising that the tribunals equally became centres for isolating non-party support. This explains why from the 1980s President Daniel Moi repeatedly insisted that the courts should not interfere in land matters (see Amnesty International 1997). That is, the tribunals were not there to serve the people but to rather to aid the political establishment in mobilizing support. It becomes clear why politicians allied to KANU and the provincial administration have on many occasions interfered with the decisions of the tribunals.

Finally, the government, under intense pressure from the political opposition, admitted that the District Land Control Boards were being misused and should be reformed. The Members of Parliament had observed to the minister of lands and settlement that to be appointed to the tribunal or the Land Board, one 'must be a KANU sycophant'. The Kisumu Town East MP also informed the house that the tribunals were dominated by retired chiefs 'who are deadwood' (*Daily Nation*, 2 November 2000).

The second challenge facing the land tribunals in Kombewa concerns corruption. It is not only encountered in the tribunals in Kombewa but impacts on the very social and economic foundation of the country. Corruption is everywhere in Kenya. The chairman of the KDLT admitted to me that there are times when the members of the tribunal disagree, particularly when the parties concerned have bribed one of them. My respondents confirmed this, adding that the tribunal sometimes charges excessive fees for transport to observe the land under arbitration (even though it is not always necessary). The chairman indicated that, since members are not entitled to any salary or allowance, the litigants must always meet the cost of each meeting. Should a meeting be postponed, the costs rise as elders normally demand that the parties pay for their transport. It is in this process that manipulation or influence creeps in, particularly when one of the parties is financially well-off. In some cases, tribunal members have been accused of harassing parties, requesting that they summarize their submission, and hence leaving out vital information which might have helped determine the case.

Third, the members of tribunals lack an adequate knowledge of basic law. The tribunals comprising village elders were created to settle land disputes on the understanding that they were knowledgeable about local issues. Some of the local issues involving kinship and land inheritance, it was felt, would best be handled by the elders, who understood the issues well. But now this is proving unworkable as land disputes are becoming complex. With increased population and urban-to-rural migration, the demand for and cost of land have increased. Some fraudulent land transactions lead to disputes that the elders cannot resolve. Cases of mistrust among family members have increased, and in some instances rich members seek their goal without due regard for kinship ties. The central provincial commissioner Zachary Ogongo, for instance, observed that 'members of the tribunal should be knowledgeable on customary law. However, this is inadequate in handling emerging land disputes which required vast knowledge of law and fraud' (Kinyungu 2000).

Fourth, the tribunals have been under intense pressure from the Law Society of Kenya, which contends that they cannot handle land disputes and are thus a waste of resources and time since most of the cases they handle end up in court. The Law Society blames the land tribunals for the many cases before the local courts awaiting arbitration.

Finally, there are other minor criticisms, For example, the tribunals seem unable to ensure that the parties concerned are all present. Where one party is absent, the tribunal normally postpones the hearing. In some situations, violence arises when the tribunals implement their decisions. It has always been necessary for a tribunal to hire at least two police officers. They, too, must receive an allowance.

Solutions?

The most important reform to the system, suggested to me by the members of the tribunal, would be a government allowance to meet transport and food costs during the sessions. The appointment of elders to the tribunals should be democratic. It is the villagers who know whether an elder is impartial, incorruptible and of a reliable moral standing. This is not to argue that the state should remove itself from land disputes at the local level, but it is necessary to avoid any conflict of interests, not least because historically the state has always favoured KANU sycophants. Appointment as an elder on the tribunal should not follow from the fact that one is a retired government civil servant. The participation of church elders, serving or retired, put forward by their members is a necessity. Their presence will ensure the participation of other members of civil society with an interest in land. Youth and women also need to be included in the tribunals, as they too have a claim on the land. They should not be treated as minors on land matters.

The tribunal should have an independent office at the divisional or even the local level, where files and documents can be kept. This will avoid reliance on the good will of the secretary of the district officer. Since land is a very important issue, and a critical economic resource, such an office should be fully operational like any other public office. Each generation has fresh claims on land and will require registration as owners. Within these offices, the state (and other interested members) should offer to the elders simple but necessary instruction on the laws relating to land and concomitant fraud.

Conclusion

The centrality of land to economic development and social welfare is unquestionable. Land has been used from time immemorial to promote economic growth and human development. More than half of the world's population live on and earn their living from tilling the land. Further, the centrality of land to African economic development has been tied to the significance of land resources within cultural and traditional practices. The importance of the land question in African societies is bound to grow, given that it is embedded in a dynamic and broad socio-political context. It also has a bearing on the pattern of social relations in society. How land is held, and specifically how access to land is regulated and determined, are important dimensions within the organization of economics and politics of a particular form of social organization (Kanyinga 1998).

The land reform programme initiated during the colonial period, together with the economic reforms initiated by the World Bank and the International Monetary Fund, have added new dimensions to the land question in Africa, and in Kenya in particular. The reform of land tenure has generated new types of dispute over land ownership, while economic liberalization, with its emphasis on the private sector and the concomitant weakening of the state, has on the other hand opened up new and intensifying contestations over the right to land. This is particularly so because economic reform has not halted the deepening spread of poverty and has not provided a basis for supporting meaningful livelihoods for rural people. The reforms have thus opened up space for a dynamic process of change, which has led in turn to the re-emergence of the land question on a broad front. As part of the process, the state has rushed to establish policies, laws and legal systems for land ownership and arbitration that can meet the claim for legitimacy without losing control of the process. As indicated, the establishment of land tribunals as presently constituted is not enough. The tribunals must reflect economic, political, cultural, social and power-related issues if they are to operate efficiently and enjoy a wider legitimacy. Further, local realities of strengthening legitimacy must be the guiding principle in the appointment of tribunal elders. At the end of the day, it is they who possess the knowledge and judgement on land matters at the local level.

Notes

1. Land tenure refers to the manner in which individuals or groups in a society hold or have access to land, including the conditions under which such land is held. Land may, for instance, be held by a superior authority – for example, the Crown under English Law – or communally, as in most pre-colonial societies.

2. In the case of the pre-colonial communities in Kenya, there has been a deliberate policy of referring to land ownership as communal, traditional or customary. However, in the context of this chapter, and particularly in Kombewa, the land tenure system recognizes that there existed systems of interlocking, overlapping, seasonally varying and usufructuary rights over land.

3. This was after the report of the Committee on Agricultural Credit for Africa, then known as the Ingham Report, of 1950 in Kenya. The recommendations of the committee were not radically different from the Swynnerton Plan of 1954.

4. There exist multiplicity and complexity in the land law system in Kenya: for example, the Registration of Documents Act, the Registration of Title Act and the Land Title Act, among others.

5. There can be no finality of individual titles as individuals in each generation lay claims to land.

Bibliography

Adar, G.K., and I.M. Munyae (2001) 'Human Rights Abuse in Kenya under Daniel Arap Moi 1978–2001', *African Studies Quarterly*, vol. 5, no. 1: 1; http://web.africa.ufl.edu/asq/v5ia1.htm.

Amnesty International (1997) *Report on Violation of Human Rights in Kenya*, London: Amnesty International.

Berry, S. (1992) 'Hegemony on a Shoestring: Colonial Rule and Access to Land', *Africa*, vol. 62, no. 3: 327–55.

Bruce, J.W., and S.E. Migot-Adholla (eds) (1994) *Searching for Land Tenure Security in Africa*, Dubuque: World Bank, Kedhall/Hut Publishing Company.

Bruce, J.W. (1993) 'Do Indigenous Tenure Systems Constrain Agricultural Development?', in T.J. Basset and D.E. Crummey (eds), *Land in African Agrarian Systems*, Madison: University of Wisconsin Press.

Cornia, G. (1994) 'Neglected Issues in the Decline of Africa's Agriculture: Land Tenure, Land Distribution and RD Constraints', in G.A. Cornia and G.K. Helleinger (eds), *From Adjustment to Development in Africa*, New York: St Martin's Press.

Gocking, R. (1994) 'Indirect Rule in the Gold Coast: Competition for Office and the Invention of Tradition', *Canadian Journal of African Studies* 28: 421–46.

Havnevik, K.J. (1997) 'The Land Question in Sub-Saharan Africa', *IRD Currents* 15.

Hazell, P.B.R. (1992) 'The Appropriate Role of Agricultural Insurance in Developing Countries', *Journal of International Development*, vol. 4, no. 6: 567–81.

Kanyinga, K. (2000) *Re-distribution from Above: The Politics of Land Rights and Squatting in Coastal Kenya*, Research Report no. 115, Uppsala: Nordiska Afrikainstitutet.

Kanyinga, K. (1998) 'Struggle of Access to Land: The Squatter Question in Coastal Kenya', *CDR Working Papers*, vol. 98, no. 7, June.

Kanyinga, K. (1997) 'The Land Question and Politics of Tenure Reforms in Kenya', *IRD Currents* 15.

Kibwana, K. (1993) 'Land Tenure', in W.R. Ochieng (ed.), *Themes in Kenyan History*, Nairobi: East African Educational Publishers.

Kinyungu, C. (2000) 'Land Tribunals under Criticism over Ruling', *Daily Nation*, 2 November.

Moyo, S. (2000) 'Peasant Organizations and Rural Civil Society in Africa: An Introduction', in S. Moyo et al. (eds), *Peasant Organizations and the Democratic Process in Africa*, Dakar: CODESRIA.

Munguri, K., E.K. Kabui, M. Isoilo and E. Kamaara (2002) 'The Implication of Economic Reforms on Gender Relations: The Case of Poor Households in Kisumu Slums', in *Gender, Economic Integration, Governance and Methods of Contraception*, Dakar AAWORD Book Services.

Okoth-Ogendo H.W.O. (1976) 'African Land Tenure Reform', in J. Heyer (ed.), *Agricultural Development in Kenya*, Nairobi: Oxford University Press.

Okoth-Ogendo H.W.O. (1986) 'The Perils of Land Tenure Reform: The Case of Kenya', in J.W. Arntzen, L.D. Ngcongco and S.D. Turner (eds), *Land Policy and Agriculture in Eastern and Southern Africa*, Tokyo: United Nations University.

Okoth-Ogendo H.W.O. (2003) 'Notes for Constitutional Conference on Land and Property', Chapter 14 of the Report and 11 of the Draft Bill.

Okuro, S.O. (2002a) 'The Impact of Colonial Policies and Practices on Female-Headed Households in Kenya. The Case of Kombewa Division', M.A. thesis, Kenyatta University, Kenya.

Okuro, S.O. (2002b) 'The Impact of Globalization on Smuggling: The Case of Women Smugglers across the Kenya–Uganda Boundary', paper presented at the CODESRIA Gender Institute.

Orvis, S. (1993) 'The Kenyan Agrarian Debate: A Reappraisal', *African Studies Review*, vol. 36, no. 3, December.

Place, F., and P. Hazed (1992) 'Productivity Effects of Indigenous Land Tenure Systems in Sub-Saharan Africa', *American Journal of Agricultural Economics*, vol. 75, no. 1.

Plateau, J.P. (1996) 'The Evolutionary Theory of Land Rights as Applied to Sub-Saharan Africa: A Critical Assessment', *Development and Change* 27: 29–86.

Ranger, T.O. (1999) *Voices from the Rocks: Nature, Culture and History in Matopos Hills of Zimbabwe*, Oxford: James Curry.

Shipton, P. (1988) 'The Kenya Land Tenure Reform: Misunderstanding in the Public Creation of Private Property', in R.E. Downs and S.P. Reyna (eds), *Land and Society in Contemporary Africa*, Hanover NH: University of New England Press.

Swynnerton, J. (1954) *A Plan to Intensify the Development of African Agriculture in Kenya*, Colony and Protectorate of Kenya, Government Printers.

Wanjala, S.C. (1990) *Land Law Disputes in Kenya*, Nairobi: Oxford University Press.

World Bank (1998) *Sub-Saharan Africa: From Crisis to Sustainable Growth*, Washington DC: World Bank.

8

Protecting Refugees in the Era of Globalization: The Challenge of Africa in the New Millennium

Ekuru Aukot

When the international legal regime celebrated the fiftieth anniversary of the 1951 Convention Relating to the Status of Refugees, Africa had little reason to join in. Its contribution in that period was the manufacturing of refugees for the rest of the world. Refugees have remained one of Africa's most chronic problems. But that is just one side of the story. The new millennium does indeed pose grave challenges to Africa. Recent elections in Western Europe suggest that the rest of the world no longer wants refugees from Africa. Yet Africa is still needed in the global village for the advancement of humanity. This chapter offers a discussion on the flip side of that coin using the concept of refugee protection. There can be little talk of a true 'global village' if the politics of refugee protection in Africa is not addressed.

The impact of globalization is often felt negatively by a developing country, defined as 'one that has insufficient access to capital to facilitate development'.[1] Globalization does not create equal chances to trade in the world markets. The effect of globalization on a poor country without resources to feed its own citizens is to weaken the system of refugee protection to the point of near-collapse. Sometimes these poor countries have resources that could only be exploited by global forces, for instance transnational corporations (TNCs). Thus globalization may also have positive effects, such as the right to international security, movement across borders and the right to international trade across them. But only if this trade is fair!

The 'Depreciating' Refugee Protection Regime

Refugee law falls under international humanitarian law, international human rights law, international criminal law and United Nations law.[2] In particular, refugee protection at the initial stages was based on legal principles enunciated by the 1951 Convention relating to the Status of Refugees (51 Convention),[3] and its 1967 Protocol, also relating to the Status of Refugees.[4] The 51 Convention applies the term 'refugee' to any person who,

> owing to a well founded-fear of being persecuted for reasons of race, religion, nationality, membership of a particular social group or political opinion, is outside the country of his nationality and is unable, or owing to such fear, is unwilling to avail himself of the protection of that country.[5]

The above definition of a refugee was premised upon 'a well-founded fear of persecution', which was tied to the five traditional grounds of race, religion, nationality, membership of a social group, and political opinion. As discussed below, a different view can be proffered. However, still on the legal instruments, a more globalized protection of the refugee is rooted in the 1948 Universal Declaration of Human Rights (UDHR).[6] However, at a later stage and owing to differences in circumstances and the diversity of refugee problems, regional arrangements emerged. Africa came up with the Organization of African Unity 1969 Convention on the Specific Aspects of Refugee Problems in Africa (OAU Convention).[7] Other regional treaties include, *inter alia*, the 1984 Cartagena Declaration on Refugees,[8] and the Cairo Declaration on the Protection of Refugees and Displaced Persons in the Arab World of 19 September 1992.[9]

In Africa the OAU Convention recognized the right of people to flee situations of 'generalized violence', and as a departure from the rather restrictive definition of the 51 Convention it effectively expanded the definition of a refugee.[10] This found support from other countries where 'the threat to a country posed by influxes of economic migrants should not serve as an excuse for refusing asylum'.[11] This comment echoed the principle of *non-refoulement*, which prevents Member States to the Conventions from forcefully returning a refugee to the frontiers of a country where the person's life would be in danger.[12] This in the context of Africa is where the challenges of refugee protection began.[13] The en masse flight of people has, *inter alia*, one critical implication. Resources must be availed by the receiving state for the various functions, which include feeding the thousands of refugees; conducting refugee status determination (RSD); the provision of shelter, water, medication, education, jobs; and administration of refugee affairs generally.

According to the legal norms, thus, refugees became legal entities whose rights and protection enjoyed the support of law. Over the years, and particularly with the advent of the twenty-first century, those legal mechanisms for the protection of the refugee have become outmoded. This problem culminated in numerous debates about the rewriting, revitalizing, reconceptualizing of the international legal regime. The debate was spearheaded by the receiving and resettlement countries of the West, which felt that the legal regime allowed the flooding of their countries by economic and illegal emigrants masquerading as refugees, hence straining their resources.[14]

International law was no longer the generally effective instrument for ordering the world; instead other phenomena dominated. Due to shrinking boundaries, people now found free movement an alternative to their suffering. The resources that would enable the enforcement of the Conventions were in danger from globalization. At the height of globalization, and in the presence of the legal regime, Africa produced more refugees than any other continent.[15] Africa in the twentieth century led the world in atrocities, in defying international order based on legal notions and human rights. At the same time as the geographical boundaries were shrinking, and coupled with Africa's internal problems, these crises paved the way for globalizing forces to take root on the continent's soil, and effectively the legal protection of refugees took second place. However, this was not solely the work of African political despots, as is explained below. Nevertheless, in the present century, the international order revolves around globalization. And this is the biggest challenge for Africa today.

What is Globalization?

Globalization is today one of the world's most powerful processes. It is something of an enigma that is difficult to define; yet it can be felt. Giddens refers to it as being 'largely a myth ... or is at most a continuation of long-established trends'.[16] The term 'globalization' is constantly used by many in different versions, hence its economic, cultural,[17] social and political strands. Malcolm Waters defines global-ization as 'a social process in which the constraints of geography on social and cultural arrangements recede and in which people become increasingly aware that they are receding'.[18]

For the purpose of this article, I adopt the economic under-standing of globalization, which is 'widely seen in the developing world as merely the latest stage in the exploitation of the third world by the west – a project by which the rich countries gain at the expense of the poor',[19] hence the anti-globalization movement that has arisen.[20] Because of the views on inequality associated with globalization, particularly from the Third World, perceptions of globalization have become bitter and resentful of the other world. These views normally have in mind economic globalization, and within that free trade.[21]

It is also argued that globalization is replacing capitalism, although it actually encompasses it; this affirms theories propounded by Marx and Lenin that the 'world is becoming unified not by choice but because of the domination of a single way of producing commodities, the capitalist mode of production'.[22] Giddens further explains, 'It is wrong to think of globalisation as just concerning the big systems, like the world financial order.'[23] He suggests that there is more to it because 'globalization isn't only about what is "out there", remote and far away from the individual. It is an "in here" phenomenon too, influencing intimate and personal aspects of our lives.'[24] In that case it becomes almost fashionable to use the term when thinking of or attempting to find solutions to world problems, especially where economic globalization affects the developing world more. Fukuyama defines globalization as a 'centrifugal force, pushing towards unification of the world, at the expense of national sovereignty ... the development of a homogeneous state where all human needs are satisfied, and activity is primarily economic'.[25] Hence a resignation to the idea that the impact of globalization is a 'signal of death of the nation-states'.[26]

On the other hand, globalization has been defined as 'the contem-porary tendency for persons, corporations and institutions to expand out of the confines of a nation ... towards participation in and identification with world community'.[27] It is on that premiss that I raise the question here that if such a world community and identity exist and I agree they do, does it not follow that the problems that affect the world community should be solved collectively, because otherwise globalization can only breed dire consequences for the underprivileged world?

We are therefore warned that one of the consequences of globalization is an increase in economic disparity between the rich and the poor so that, in the words of Ulrich Beck, 'the globality of risk does not ... mean a global equality of risk'.[28] Over the last decade poverty has intensified. The UN declares that more than 2,400 million people live without sanitation, 1,200 million people have no safe drinking water. Similar numbers have inadequate housing, health and education services; more than 1,500 million are undernourished, not because there is no food, or due to drought, but because of the increasing marginalization and exclusion of the poor.[29]

In the light of such statistics, it would be surprising *not* to witness forced migration on a scale reflective of our global society today. This is principally because globalization as a form of 'free market ideology has increased the sum of human misery'.[30]

The South–North Divide[31]

The paradox of the 'global village' is that the world is divided into blocs – North–South, developing–developed, and so on. In the case of Africa, a question needs to be asked: does the continent want to be part of the global village? Let us suppose that there is indeed a global village, and that the village has a chief. Let us imagine further that one villager has a problem with another and it is brought before the village elders. If upon determination an individual is found guilty, then customarily he will be dealt with appropriately. But today's globalized village does not reflect such a peaceful coexistence, because it encourages transgression with impunity, fuelling conflict among the villagers (read: countries).

True to the above analogy, the US war on terrorism is, for example, calling upon all the 'global village elders' (read: presidents, prime ministers, military rulers as well as dictators) to unite over a problem now facing the 'village' (read: the USA). So, although Africa is endemically overwhelmed by its own versions of terrorism, it is today needed simply because the US government has decided to call the world to order on its own terms.

The South–North divide is one important aspect of globalization, a fact that cannot be ignored. For example, the effects of global

warming, as recently became clear in Europe, are a real cause for
concern, with profound implications for the world, including the
South. Yet witness the collapse of talks because we cannot do without
global capital generation.[32] We will soon experience migration to the
tropics, because the polar icecaps are melting, some of the islands in
the Pacific are experiencing strong tides and water levels are rising.
Thus, although we derive benefits from globalization, arguably it is
one of the new root causes of migration. It has become the creator
of a modernity that destabilizes the tranquillity of other societies
that are not direct beneficiaries. Those that do benefit become even
more forceful in their quest for economic growth.

The effective division of the world by globalization into the North
and the South has brought dangers and consequences for the planet
we all live on, which requires protection because 'other people's
aerosol sprays have caused a carcinogenic hole in the ozone layer
above our heads', thereby endangering our lives.[33] The consequence
can be seen in the competing interests of all nations. The struggle is
captured in a metaphor that views countries as a series of mountain
climbers clawing their way up 'Mount Progress'. The strongest are
near the top while others lag behind hampered by smallness of
stature, poor equipment or lack of training. They meet blockages
on their paths and cannot easily withstand natural calamities visited
on them by landslides and climatic inclemency.[34]

The foregoing describes the process of globalization; the obstacles
refer to the many problems that afflict Africa. The refugee problem,
with its seemingly unstoppable flow, and the economic deprivation
in the continent are key reasons why it keeps on falling behind.
Other factors include SAPs, IMF/World Bank conditionalities, and
the work of TNCs. The metaphor can readily be extended:

> the climbers near the top will often throw down ropes to haul the
> others up. Frequently the ropes are not strong enough because the good
> climbers never throw down their best ropes and are always selective
> about which of those lower down will receive help.... However, most
> of the strugglers believe that by following in the footsteps of the lead
> climber they will all get there in the end. There are those who select
> an alternative route and refuse help from the lead climber but they are
> not doing nearly as well.[35]

This captures further the division over globalization, resulting in
sceptics and anti-globalizers. We begin to relate it, as a phenomenon,

to terminologies synonymous with continents – 'Europeanization and Americanization' – accompanied by incidentals which aim to 'globalize' the world. These are, *inter alia*, culture, financial markets, TNCs, political domination and industrialization. Can we also Africanize the concept? The struggle is still far from over because the hope lingers on that 'when everyone gets to the summit they will join hands in mutual congratulation because they are all in the same place'. The vision then becomes that of a 'global society', with global communication, global industry, the growth of multinational enterprises, the influence of global warming, and international action for human rights.[36] I must add to that list the phenomenon of refugees, which now seeks solutions at the global level.

Africa and Globalization

Globalization and its impact on society have been traced through three spheres of social life: the economy, the polity and culture.[37] But does globalization mean anything to Africa? It certainly meant very little to the twentieth century, when the West plundered the continent's resources. Nor were Africa's problems globalized in that century. The century saw more than 6 million of Africa's population displaced and forced to flee, their rights violated; millions lived a malnourished existence; countless numbers starved to death. It was in the same century that Africa's problems intensified through the projects of colonialism, missionary activity and slavery.[38] These projects were responsible for the persecution of peoples, hence the proliferation of new states. I am afraid this is the case in the present century. It will be the case if Africa does not play an active role in the global village politics.[39]

Considering the magnitude of the problems facing Africa, is it meaningful to refer to the world as a global village? The answer is obviously no. Nevertheless, globalization and its impact are real enough and not merely abstract policies; furthermore, the processes are not easy to regulate or control.[40] It is analogous to the spread of bush fire. Africa, it appears, does not need globalization because it cannot meaningfully relate to it. As President Olusegun Obasanjo of Nigeria recently stated:

> Our societies are overwhelmed by the strident consequences of globalisation and the phenomenon of trade liberalisation. The options open to

us have narrowed as our increasingly shrinking world imposes on our countries a choice of integration or the severe conditions of marginalisation and stagnation.[41]

Hence globalization, it further seems, is not welcome in Africa since 'the promised high living standards' are yet to be realized. In that respect Africa's problems, and specifically today the crisis of refugees, need solutions. The framework within which those solutions are sought also needs addressing. In some instances globalization may have a direct effect on refugee protection, and even be the cause of people's flight. In Africa, and Kenya in particular, although it is difficult to discern any direct link with refugees, the influence on the receiving state of globalizing forces – privatization, IMF/World Bank lending conditionalities and so on – are felt within the protection paradigm.[42] One circumstance that has affected refugees is the growth of corporate social irresponsibility, which directly occasions human rights abuses.[43] This growth is the consequence of states compromising their role as protector, which has in turn resulted in them avoiding their own responsibilities under international law. One reason for this logic is the all-pervasive influence of globalization. As a phenomenon that transcends state boundaries, globalization has led to a situation where, as Pendleton writes, 'no sovereign state, whatever its political or ideological orientation, can successfully insulate itself against foreign influences in the modern world'.[44]

Refugees in Africa today reside in an environment shaped by the era of globalization, and defined by meagre or diminishing resources. Their protection and the reasons for migration are no longer self-evident issues, but complicated and beyond the control of the traditional nation-state. Today it is globalizing forces that dictate the forms of migration and help trigger flights of people across national borders.

Globalization and its agents have a presence in Africa today. One needs only to think of Rio Tinto Zinc, Monsanto,[45] the effects of Chiquita International, and the Lomé IV Convention and the privatization of Zambia's copper mines. The TNCs manipulate not only economic resources but also the legal systems. Consider the asbestos cases in South Africa[46] and Namibia,[47] and the landmines in Angola – just two examples where many people have been forced to leave their homes.

Although many African states share the blame for the refugee problem, especially in the immediate post-colonial period, the twentieth century saw the rise of other forces that influenced the way they ran their affairs. Although 'opportunistic and venal African leaders' did little to develop their societies and to emancipate their people, they were not alone, because

> the expansion of corporate dominance has accentuated the steady descent into near economic strangulation and political chaos. Many transnational corporations (TNCs) have acted as economic predators in Africa, gobbling up national resources, distorting national economic policies, exploiting and exchanging labor relations, committing environmental despoliation, violating sovereignties, and manipulating governments and the media. In order to ensure uninterrupted access to resources, TNCs have also supported repressive African leaders, warlords, and guerrilla fighters, thus serving as catalysts for lethal conflict and impeding prospects for development and peace.[48]

We witness in Africa today how the involvement of the TNCs has 'generated fierce conflicts over resource control'.[49] Within and between states, vast numbers of internally displaced persons, refugees and stateless persons are created. Thus the success of globalization through the agency of TNCs is guaranteed in Africa by authoritarian and corrupt regimes. And the money received from the TNCs is used for the wrong reasons:

> many African leaders have used revenue to reward political pals with bogus contracts for white elephant projects that contribute nothing to development. In the late 1990s, for example, President Daniel Arap Moi of Kenya built an airport – which handles almost no traffic – in his home town of Eldoret.[50]

The huge amounts of revenue received by governments in Africa could be used to build infrastructure and make vital services available to both its nationals and aliens – health, shelter, education, employment and food, provisions that lie at the heart of refugee protection. Hence one of the greatest challenges facing Africa in the coming century is not simply globalization, but preventing its forces undermining the state machinery. State apparatuses are crippled, rendering the state incapable of fulfilling certain basic functions for nationals and aliens alike.

With TNCs fully operational in Africa, economies are endangered, having been subjected to deregulation through the activities of such global institutions as the General Agreement on Tariffs and Trade (GATT), the World Trade Organization (WTO) and the IMF. Notably, the IMF's SAPs require 'African states to freeze wages, devalue currency, remove public subsidies, and impose other austerity measures... these policies have caused considerable turmoil in Africa.'[51]

The challenge for Africa is now to reinvent itself and reaffirm its trust in statehood. Evidence of the collapse of state machinery is clear in, for example, the privatization of the Zambia copper mines; the collapse of the KCC industries in Kenya; the manner in which modes of production are dictating the ownership of land, for example in Zimbabwe;[52] and the plunder of resources in the Democratic Republic of the Congo (DRC).[53] The absence or weakness of the state suits the TNCs, which seek 'low production costs, poor working conditions, and abundant and easily exploitable resources, where profits can be maximized and repatriated without legal constraints'.[54]

This situation could not arise were it not for several factors predominant in the world today. The first is the fact that of the hundred biggest economies in the world, more than half are corporations. Second, these TNCs have enormous powers to transform the world political economy. Third, and in particular, Africa has vast resources, cheap labour, huge populations and an expanding market, all of which are crucial to the plans of the TNCs. But an even greater imperative is the presence in Africa of weak political leadership, which is corrupt and willing to be compromised.[55]

How Globalization Triggers Flight

Globalization, it has been observed, is one of five interlinked processes that have caused an upheaval in the patterns of people's lives. The others are individualization, the gender revolution, underemployment and global risk.[56] Refugee problems arising from globalization can take a number of forms. In response to economic deprivation, people look to survive by going elsewhere. For instance, it may well be that a direct consequence of changes in the banana industry in some developing countries had been to encourage economic-related migrations to the North – a situation triggered by the actions of Chiquita International.[57]

Global agencies target the weakness of the state and aim, in effect, to deplete local resources, stifle local, or 'indigenous', industry, and subvert the fragile democratic process.[58] It is the last process that, in large part, triggers forced migration, in the form of either economic refugees or enemies of the undemocratic state. A wave of refugees may result from organized demands for the activities of the TNCs, supported by the state, to be redressed. In some cases this has even prompted calls for secession, as in the oil-rich Niger delta region. It happened in Nigeria during the regimes of Ibrahim Babangida and Sani Abacha; recall the execution of Ken Saro-Wiwa and others for challenging the government and the oil companies.[59]

In Angola, the global trade in diamonds, otherwise known as 'blood diamonds' or 'conflict diamonds', sustained a twenty-year war, financing the UNITA rebels and prolonging the fighting. In spite of the atrocities that marked this war, TNCs like American Mineral Fields (AMF), Oryx and De Beers continued their activities in the region. The death toll topped 3 million.[60] Such corporations also strive to corrupt the regimes in waiting, as in the case of the late Laurent Kabila, whose war against Mobutu was financed by AMF's principal shareholder, who later secured exploration contracts worth £600 million of cobalt and £3 million of copper.[61] It is the same story in Sierra Leone, where the Revolutionary United Front (RUF), led by Foday Sankoh, financed its war from 'conflict diamonds'.[62] People are still fleeing these countries; and thousands have become refugees and internally displaced persons (IDPs), who have since become the concern of the UN.[63]

Another way in which the corporations ensure their continued stay in Africa is through the supply of arms to conflict areas. The TNCs then import their privately owned security firms to perform training. The early 1990s saw considerable growth of the corporate private security sector in Africa. A good example is the work of Executive Outcome (EO) in Sierra Leone in 1995, for which the government paid US$40 million in cash.[64]

It is notable that refugee problems tend to arise in countries where the TNCs have had a great deal of involvement in search of such resources as oil, diamonds, gold, copper and cobalt. Thus economic globalization implies economic deprivation, and forced migration has found a new cause. The situation is exacerbated by the nature of the agreements signed between the South and the North – witness the case of the Cotonou Agreement, where the ACP countries are required to uphold rules of good governance as defined by the European governments.

The role of developing countries in protecting refugees is made more difficult by the recognition process, which under the OAU Convention paved the way for the recognition of refugees en masse.[65] This seems also to apply to those who are at risk of losing their lives because of economic impoverishment. This is because there are no international legal guidelines for the assistance of economic migrants. When the organizational structure of the state is disturbed, people begin to flee in search of security. In this regard, globalization is pitted against the nation-state and its exercise of sovereignty over its citizens. In effect, international law no longer sustains the sovereign state; this triggers hostility between citizens and their state. This, in turn, causes the erosion of national sovereignty and the blurring of 'the difference between domestic and foreign affairs'.[66]

The flight of people due to effects of globalization is given various designations, especially in the West/North. In the banana case, for example, many Caribbean people sought to move to Europe. Their only hope of being allowed in was to claim asylum. In this regard, it is noteworthy that international refugee law does not forbid an asylum seeker lying if doing so will gain him an audience to explain his case. We now know the range of reasons that cause people to flee. It is not easy to gain protection if you are simply an economic migrant. Many would therefore claim refugee status. Yet their flight had originated in the activity of a TNC directed from a Western country, a proponent of globalization. So, although globalization is celebrated in terms of the exploitation of natural resources, the West considers it acceptable to tighten its asylum laws. It follows that the impact of globalization on developing countries is generally negative and has left many economically devastated.[67]

Management of the current 'global economy' is volatile, political and oppressive. It constitutes a diversion of the resources of poor economies. Globalization has created an economic imbalance. Consequently, refugees become a product of modernity;[68] they become victims of corporate 'violence'. Globalization is a cause of flight and may subsequently impede the process of refugee protection.

How Globalization Impedes Refugee Protection

As we have seen, globalization creates an economically weak environment in developing countries. And it is from this environment that people flee – from impoverishment and dictatorial regimes. This is also the environment in which refugees are received en masse. By far the world's largest number of refugees are from the poor developing countries, and particularly Africa.[69]

Global processes, we have observed, not only question the relevance of refugee laws; they are themselves causal factors – witness global warming, privatization, and globalization itself. Global processes presuppose transnational networks. Yet refugee protection is the responsibility of the receiving state, and in that respect the intra-national networks become relevant. In a nutshell, what global processes suggest is the existence of victims – those who are disadvantaged – and 'victors', who do not want to share the benefits of success or shoulder the responsibilities that go with it.

It must be concluded that, contrary to the position in public international law (which refugee law is part of), nations can no longer be regarded as sovereign states and are not so regarded by the majority of their citizens.[70] The vital issue, however, is that although their sovereignty is diminished, refugees nevertheless continue to rely on them for protection, because the nation-state is the pre-eminent guarantor of refugee rights. The effect global processes have on the nation-state is, in effect, to hinder the implementation of international refugee law within its borders. The notion of refugee protection is slowly but surely being devalued.

Globalization takes various forms. These act, in one way or another, to disable the poor states, which have no resources to compete in the current global economy.[71] In consequence they become unable to meet their obligations. Global economic governance shrinks their resources. Uganda was largely perceived for the better part of 1999–2000 as doing very well economically. We were not told that Uganda was also servicing its IMF/World Bank debt. Nevertheless, the country's refugee protection record is as poor as that of other African countries. Kenya's problems have intensified since 1997, when the IMF and the World Bank cut aid. Since then the government has been involved in endless renegotiations with the institutions for the resumption of aid. Its infrastructure collapsed, then its record of governance became an issue. How can such a country afflicted by global economic woes be expected to protect refugees? A common feature of refugee protection in developing countries is the involve-ment of the UNHCR, which conducts status determination, runs the camps, and lobbies governments to comply with the convention. The state lacks power and authority. The situation has resulted in what is termed 'donor fatigue', because even the North sees its resources diminishing.

The UNHCR has recognized that globalization is a new cause of refugee problems that is not being addressed; it knows that ignoring it further will cause irreparable harm. Its response has been to engage with the corporate world.[72] Economic globalization is seen as the core issue; for it is the economy of a country that will determine the amount of resources to be allocated to the protection of refugees and to other incidental services such as status determination and legal advice.[73]

A diminished role for the state?

It has been remarked that 'if globalization is a reality ... and if globalization genuinely takes effect, the nation-state will be its chief victim'.[74] Thus today's globalized world is speculating about the degree to which the role of the traditional nation-state will diminish, or even whether it will perish as an entity. In its place have emerged regional economies.[75] Is there any threat to the principle of protection of those within such diminished states? If nationals benefit very little from their governments in terms of service provision, what is the position of foreigners, especially refugees?[76] This, in some respects, is the reason for the xenophobia that marks the refugee issue, and that is likely to pose a threat to their physical security.

The impact of globalization on receiving states can be seen operating at two levels. The first is the general level where all countries perceive globalization as a new form of international identity; the motivation to join the fray is a matter of compliance with the prevailing economic tempo. This takes the form of industrialization, privatization and the influence of the corporate world in the internal affairs of the state. The process begins when globalizing forces are invited to the territories of compliant participating states; it ends with the state reduced to nothing but a host of global conglomerates. The conglomerates strive to find weak states, where they are lured by the promise of attractive revenue earnings from resource exploitation. Dare notes that this

> coincides with that of the TNCs, the latter's interest in maximizing profits conflicts with the welfare of the citizens. Thus, the state is caught between protecting a vital source of revenue, and defending the rights

and privileges of its citizens. Too often, the state, in order to ensure an ongoing flow of revenue, sides with the TNCs against the citizens.[77]

One example of all this is the running conflicts in the oil-producing Niger delta region between the citizens and the corporations, on the one hand, and governments, on the other. Such conflicts position the citizen as an 'enemy' of the state, following which he or she may be forced out to become a refugee. Furthermore, when such a state receives refugees from another country, it is unable to protect them.

The second level is the impact of globalization internally, where certain actors or globalizing forces have affected an element of a country's tranquillity to the degree that it threatens to trigger the flight of people or displace them. There is clearly a causal relation between the plunder of the resources of poor countries and their ability to set aside significant resources for refugees. Whatever the activity in refugee protection, be it administration, status determination or the provision of services, all require resources. In Kenya the requirement that refugees carry identity cards, a contentious issue since their introduction in 1991, is a symptom of the lack of resources, both human and economic.

As a consequence of globalization, and in particular economic globalization, the South must rely on relief aid to help the refugees, hence the talk of 'donor fatigue'. What can easily be forgotten in the equation, though, is the role of the TNCs, which primarily enrich the North. There is just a little irony in the fact that the North, and its globalization discourse, should not see fit to refer to 'donor fatigue'. While this Samaritanism on the part of the developed world continues, developing countries are forced to focus their efforts elsewhere to service their IMF/World Bank debts. The result is that the condition of the refugees deteriorates, rendering the South even less capable of fulfilling its international obligations.

The power the corporate world wields in relation to states has been acknowledged even in UN circles. There is a realization that our understanding of the traditional causes of refugeeism is outmoded. This opens up a wider debate on the need to redefine refugee law and, more specifically, to rethink what constitutes a refugee.[78] Could globalization perhaps be a positive force for refugees? To what extend can globalization itself contribute to the debate? After all, if globalization is a means of liberating the economies of the world, why can't it be harnessed to address refugee problems? Such questions are important because there is reason to doubt whether globalization will include the internationalization of refugee protection. We cannot speak confidently about internationalization of the world's problems, because the current quagmire is both the expression and a precondition of the prevailing notion of internationalization, which is international law.

'Reformulation' or Globalization of Refugee Protection?

Refugees are today a global dilemma. The magnitude of their problems has prompted proposals that a global partnership be forged for their protection.[79] However, not all countries have yet ratified the 51 Convention and therefore do not yet have in place national refugee and asylum legislation consistent with international standards and principles. Consequently, it is arguable whether the enactment of international refugee legislation is today a meaningful option.

The normative international system that deals with refugees still focuses on the source of their status.[80] Usually, the root causes referred to are the traditional ones: civil wars, military conscription and human rights violations. Global processes have now overtaken these old factors, however, and the language of the law now seems inapplicable and old-fashioned. The terminology of globalization might perhaps be employed instead to address the refugee problem.

Reformulation?

The notion of reformulation of the refugee problem as advocated by some has yet to bear fruit.[81] This is because reformulation takes us back to the same international principles that have failed to produce the desired results. For example, when Hathaway proposes that the 'period of risk' applying to states when they undertake to protect refugees should be five years, he does not take into account the long unresolved cases of the Palestinians, the Burmese and the Bhutanese in Nepal, or for that matter the Rwandan refugees, the Congolese, the Oromo, the Sudanese – and there are many more. While reformulation preoccupies the international legal community, the practical business of refugee protection and its deterioration in the developing world can, to a large extent, be explained in ways other than through the presence or absence of international law per se.

If we were to adopt the logic of cultural globalization, we would consider asylum applications on the basis of global principles such as democracy, and civil and fundamental freedoms – in the name of which applicants act when they decide to leave their countries, and which serve as the basis of our criticisms of many regimes in the South. We would thereby act on our knowledge that persecution does not necessarily take a physical form; rather it can be psychological, the product of well-founded perceptions. In *Applicants A and B v. Minister for Immigration and Ethnic Affairs*,[82] asylum was sought on the grounds that the couple's opposition to the country's birth-control policies rendered them refugees.[83] The court found that the couple did not qualify as refugees because they could not be considered members of a particular social group. Arguably the court interpreted the refugee definition narrowly. The applicants had become victims because of their belief that they had the right to more than one child, on the basis of which belief they would have been persecuted. In more globalized societies like Europe, this belief would be upheld by Article 8 of the European Convention on Human Rights relating to the right to found a family.[84]

In the above case, a Western court reached its conclusion because it did not share the cultural practices of the Chinese, notwithstanding the fact of our living in a global village. Had the court directed itself to the situation in the West, asylum would have been granted. This goes to prove that what are global processes or values are not shared by all globally. In contrast *Secretary, Department of Health and Community Services v. JWB and SMB* (Marion's case) the court held, per Brennan J, that

> [E]ach person has a unique dignity which the law respects and which it will protect. Human dignity is a value common to our municipal law and to international instruments relating to human rights. The law will protect equally the dignity of the hale and hearty and the dignity of the weak and the lame.[85]

This decision focused on Western values. The gist of the argument, it appears, is that when the values of the North and the South meet, those of the North take priority. This echoes the processes of globalization, which are self-defeating. How, then, should we reformulate refugee law? Today it seems appropriate to suggest that solutions lie in economic global cooperation rather than in international legal cooperation. This would mean, for example, empowering the receiving states of the South economically to satisfy legal provisions.

Globalization?

The interrelation of states under the concept of economic global-ization impacts on the world such that today no country can address its problems independently. Harris reiterates: 'Internal refugees are the result of the breakdown of the state system and the capacity of – or willingness of – governments to protect their citizens.'[86] This is why globalization is referred to as a new human right.[87] Elsewhere 'refugees are the product of modernity. Their plight became acute when the processes of modernity became globalized.'[88] It is explained that

> The twentieth century became the century of refugees, not because it was extraordinary in forcing people to flee, but because of the division of the globe into nation-states in which states were assigned the role of protec-tors of rights, but also that of exclusive protectors of their own citizens, including the role of gatekeeper to determine who could become new citizens. When the globe was totally divided … those fleeing persecution in one state had nowhere to go but to another state, and required the permission of the other state to enter it.[89]

Globalization therefore promotes notions of global law and of governance of the world's problems including that of refugees. And economic globalization has affected the patterns of migration. In Africa, for instance, South Africa has depended on migrants from Zimbabwe, Mozambique and Zambia. Modern trends and increases in refugee populations affect already established asylum regulations and policies that had, for example, been developed as responses to the Cold War, to colonialism, and to international and regional politics.

In contemporary times, every regime seems to be a potential refugee producer, which points towards the need to globalize refugee problems to achieve effective protection. For example, the inter-national community was criticized for its passiveness in the handling of the Rwanda genocide of 1994, whereas it united over the Kosovo crisis. It appears that the West is more concerned with those refugee problems close to home than it is with those in Africa.[90]

Linking refugees directly to globalization may appear far-fetched. Yet it is noticeable that just as the impact of globalization is evident, so has the protection ideal become globalized. Furthermore, globalization presupposes the interconnectedness of the world in all aspects, including in law. This seems to apply when refugee protection is discussed in the language of 'international protection', which ought to be universal. If the situation were to be dealt with at the national level, there would be no need for mobilization at the level of the UN. The global protection ideal appears to be the culmination of a process:

> At first, the definition applied only to refugees produced in Europe, but as the concept of the nation-state was globalized with postwar decolonization, so too was the individualistic concept of the refugee, and the 1967 protocol was passed in which the Convention definition of a refugee became universal.[91]

Globalization has made the world appear smaller over the last fifty years, as is evidenced by the role of those actors that act as a globalizing force. What globalization has done is to enhance the concept of 'de-borderization', the result of which is evident in people's desire to benefit maximally from a 'village-like-environment'. This language of one village seems tenable in that notion of economic globalization in which 'mankind was supposed to be transformed into economic animals'.[92] However, when it comes to the movement of people who are seeking either protection from economic deprivation or merely a peaceful environment in which to enjoy their rights, we see restrictions in the form of tough immigration or asylum laws. De Jong challenges this double-faced attitude

> You cannot encourage people always to take the most economically advantageous decisions, but tell them to forget about it when they conclude that emigration to another country would be the best option. If the world becomes smaller, we should be inclined at least to accept some migratory movements. Since there is nowadays hardly any possibility left of becoming a legal immigrant in any countries, countless individuals have turned to the asylum instrument or to illegal ways of immigration.[93]

In this global environment, therefore, two factors have emerged to explain the refugee problem. There are those places with the potential to cause migration pressure, for example poverty-stricken parts of Africa and Asia. Then there are those forces that actually trigger migratory movements, such as turmoil, wars, repression and the violation of human rights, unemployment, and environmental degradation.[94] These factors, coupled with globalization, represent the great challenges to African states in this new millennium.

In Africa, refugee protection has become a superficial exercise; both the legal and the physical components are merely cosmetic. First, land is granted on which refugees cannot even eke out a living. Second, the states' emphasis today is on the creation of camps, which are managed by UNHCR. The camps then rely on donor communities and agencies – all situated in the North.[95]

Refugee protection thus becomes an item on the agenda for global governance, and beyond domestic jurisdiction. Should the process of globalization per se prove unable to solve the problem of the world's refugees, it may be necessary to attempt a compromise, given the disparity that exists between developed and developing countries.

There is, arguably, justification for changing the definition of 'refugee' in line with universal human rights principles. After all, the very definition of a refugee for purposes of asylum is based on saving lives. For example, where famine poses a real threat to human life, there is a need to address it by all means available, including the contribution of the global community. It is common sense that aid cannot be administered in a situation of two warring groups, and it is imperative that those who cross the border in such circumstances be distinguishable from the players. In 1996 it was reported that 4 million Sudanese were internally displaced and 465,000 had fled the country, 40,000 of whom went to live in Kenya.[96] The Somalia catastrophe was equally devastating to humankind. The question posed is, how is it possible to stick to the definition of a refugee under such circumstances? The term 'refugee' need not be used, as it can sometimes be dehumanizing and stigmatizing; perhaps 'people in need' would serve.[97]

Current developments point towards a reformulation of refugee law. Attempts are being made to sidestep the traditional definition as the reality dawns on nation-states that they are no longer protecting 'refugees' *stricto sensu* but, rather, people in need of refuge and safety. For example, the creation of 'safe havens' in Iraq; 'zones of tranquillity' for the Afghan returnees; the 'open relief centres' for would-be Sri Lankan refugees; and the 'not so safe havens' of Srebrenica and Zepa in Bosnia and Herzegovina – all point towards this development.[98] On the other hand, states are tending to take second place within their societies and losing their function, owing to the rise of supranational structures. In response, states have resorted to selling off their assets, such as forests and public enterprises, to bodies that then enjoy greater powers than the state. This reversal of roles has profound repercussions on the populations of these countries.

Conclusion

This chapter contends that existing international refugee law is no longer adequate to protect refugees. A more powerful force is emerging, which has divided the world into blocs, and weakened or disabled the state as the primary enforcer of international refugee law. African states in particular are more vulnerable and weaker than before. Globalization is responsible for a double alienation in the life of the citizen. On the one hand it has widened the gap between the nation-state and the citizen, which has compromised their rights. On the other hand, it has forged a closer relationship between the nation-state and the dynamic of economic globalization, particularly in terms of trade, finance and investment; this serves to marginalize the citizen further. Globalization has become, in effect, a new international legal norm. This suggests that globalization could perhaps be used to address the refugee problem, not least because it is a strain on the whole globe, especially in the effort it takes to enforce the existing global legal norms. Thus reform of international law on the basis of legal 'mechanisms' is no longer viable because enforcement of that law at the domestic level is ceasing to be viable. For example, countries operating under the highly indebted poor countries (HIPCs) and poverty eradication programmes would be performing a miracle if refugees could realize their rights under international law within their domestic setting.

Globalization is not a policy but a fact of life in the twenty-first century. It affects all our lives. Perhaps it is time to engage with the idea of globalization, which has both good and bad aspects. We should work with the positive elements to tackle the pressing issues faced by the planet. Either we approach the intractable problems collectively (even though they emanate from individual sources) or we will ultimately face the consequences together; for when one part of the world breeds problems, the outcome affects all of us in one way or another.[99] For example, if America refuses to check the rate of its greenhouse gas emissions, we all reap the dire consequences; the world ceases to be a safe place to live in.

The impact of globalization begs that solutions to Africa's problems be found. The first challenge is for Africa to tame globalization by checking the power of global institutions. Do we really need to privatize almost everything? Are we not capable of managing our resources for the common good? Second, if Africa is to prosper, and be able to tame globalization, it must stop conflicts. One way of doing this is to adopt a globalized perspective on the causes of conflict and to work towards the eradication of the market in weapons, which are of course produced in the West.[100] Third, Africa must strive to organize and conclude peace talks to bring order to its people, with the aim of uniting the divided African continent. In particular Africa must address the Oromia question in Ethiopia, and resolve the conflict zones of Somalia, Sudan, Saharawi, Kaprivi, the DRC, Burundi and others.[101] Finally, the African Union should take a political lead and suggest a model whereby a country might intervene in the case of domestic conflict in a neighbouring state. This could be part of a globalized approach to the refugee problem, organized at the regional level.

Refugees are the world's problem. In recognition of this inescapable fact, proposals have been made to institute an international refugee welfare regime.[102] We are witnessing the failure of voluntary repatriation (Rwanda, DRC, Somalia), persistent wars and famines (Sudan, Eritrea–Ethiopia, DRC), and the continuing rule of military regimes (Sierra Leone, East Timor, Pakistan, Afghanistan). Domestic legislation has failed to have an effect. It is time the UNHCR's mandate too was changed to reflect these global changes.

The developing world has argued vociferously for the scrapping of debts owed to the IMF and World Bank. The weaknesses of countries' economies affect their ability to administer and comply with legal and financial requirements, whether domestic or international. In this regard, the donor community should increase its funding, either to UNHCR or through host governments. Developing countries need resources if they are to follow special procedures for refugees during status determination, establish legal structures – including the appointment of specially trained magistrates to handle refugee matters, and provision of free legal counsel to refugees – and promote local integration.

In the interim, the work of UNHCR is commendable. The emphasis, however, should be on empowering the poor states economically so they can throw their weight behind the protection of refugees. If a refugee is unwilling to avail himself of the protection of his country of origin, then he is solely the responsibility of the receiving state. It follows both protection and relief assistance to refugees in developing countries is imperative, but only at the point of influx. Considering the problems of the developing world that have been compounded by global capitalism, it is difficult for these countries to guarantee protection in accordance with international standards. Although this appears as a problem of the African states, it is in fact equally that of UNHCR and the international community at large.

African states should examine critically the wider impact of the refugees under their jurisdiction; much has changed in the fifty years since the idea of protecting refugees beyond their borders came into being. Whatever proposals for reform we put forward today, they must take into account the effects of globalization. However, given today's global economy, any attempt to address the refugee problem in a purely legalistic way is destined to fail due to the economic weakness of the present receiving states. States in general are increasingly becoming less powerful. Transnational corporations are taking over economic control. Parliamentarians in these states tend only to enact laws that serve the interests of the global agents without necessarily benefiting the electorate they represent. Refugee laws are not considered beneficial to the states, in contrast to privatization laws, where the state gains in terms of employment, revenue collection through income and investment tax, improvement of infrastructure and social amenities. Such are the effects of today's global processes: their effect on human life and, more specifically, on forced migrants is enormous.

It might be concluded that there is little to be done to relieve the situation. However, there are four actions that receiving states in Africa can take in this era of global processes. First, they must entrench good governance by taking control of all that takes place within their jurisdiction, including effectively regulating global processes.[103] At the heart of such control should be the welfare of citizens. Governments must hold responsible at all times those corporations that are responsible for the displacement of people and impose punitive measures. Second, they must refer the state of affairs to the UN so that the accountability of those corporations under international law is assured.[104] Third, TNCs should be required to reinvest in those countries. This must be monitored, as the lack of reinvestment is what weakens them economically and thereby disables them from delivering services not only to their own nationals but also to those needing their protection. Fourth, and this is a call that has long been made, the IMF and World Bank should reconsider writing off monies owed by the developing countries that host refugees. The money could, *inter alia*, be used to establish such services as health, education, water and roads, which most receiving states in Africa lack; these would not only benefit their nationals but also refugees. If these measures were undertaken, it would represent a new movement towards the ideal of an asylum state.

In this millennium, Africa will greatly strengthen its bargaining power and indeed shape matters to its advantage. All that is needed is active participation by us all. For, as Sunday Dare writes,

> From the oil fields of the Niger Delta in Nigeria, to the diamond and copper fields of Sierra Leone, Angola, and Liberia, to the rich mineral deposits of the Great Lakes region, to the mountain ranges, plains and tourist havens of the East African countries, the continent of Africa is undoubtedly blessed.[105]

Notes

1. Michael D. Pendleton, 'A New Human Right – The Right to Globalization', *Fordham ILLJ* 2052, 1999: 2068.
2. See P.J. van Krieken, *Refugee Law in Context: The Exclusion Clause*, The Hague: T.M.C. Asser Press, 1999.
3. 189 *UNTS* 150; in force on 22 April 1954.
4. 606 *UNTS* 267; in force on 4 October 1967, and it internationalized refugee protection by curing the Eurocentrism of the 51 Convention. Article 1 (2) thereof provides that, 'For the purpose of the present Protocol, the term "refugee" shall ... mean any person within the definition of Article 1 of the Convention as if the words "As a result of events occurring before 1 January 1951 and..." and the words "... a result of such events" in Article 1 A(2) were omitted'.
5. Article 1 A (2).
6. Adopted by the UN General Assembly on 10 December 1948 (UNGA resolution 217 A (III). Article 14 (1) provides that 'everyone has the right to seek and enjoy in other countries asylum from persecution'.

7. Adopted in Ethiopia, on 10 September 1969; in force on 20 June 1974 (1000 *UNTS* 46).

8. Adopted at a colloquium of Latin American states, held at Cartagena, Colombia, 19–22 November 1984. In Part III (3) The Colloquium adopted *inter alia* the conclusion that 'in view of the experience gained from the massive flows of refugees ... it is necessary to consider enlarging the concept of a refugee.... Hence the definition or concept of a refugee to be recommended for use in the region is one which, in addition to containing the elements of the 1951 Convention and the 1967 Protocol, includes among refugees persons who have fled their country because their lives, safety or freedoms have been threatened ... by other circumstances which have seriously disturbed public order.'

9. See Khadija Elmadmad, 'Asylum in the Arab World: An Analysis of Recent Arab Instruments on Human Rights and Refugees', paper presented at the 6th International Research and Advisory Panel Conference on Forced Migration, 13–16 December 1998, Jerusalem; available at www.iasfm.org.

10. Article 1 (2) applies the term refugees 'to every person who, owing to external aggression, occupation, foreign domination or events seriously disturbing public order in either part or the whole of his country of origin ... is compelled to leave his place of habitual residence in order to seek refuge in another place outside his country of origin or nationality'.

11. The comment of Ambassador Jonathan Moore, US Co-ordinator for Refugee Affairs, at the Executive Committee in 1987, cited in Guy S. Goodwin-Gill, *The Refugee in International Law*, 2nd edn, Oxford: Oxford University Press, 1996, p. 129.

12. See Article 33, 51 Convention.

13. The 69 Convention emphasises in Article II (3) that 'No person shall be subjected by a member State to measures such as rejection at the frontier, return or expulsion, which would compel him to return or remain in a territory where his life, physical integrity or liberty would be threatened for the reasons set out in Article I, paragraphs 1 and 2.'

14. See www.icva.ch, newsletters of 2000/01.

15. UNHCR, *The State of the World's Refugees: Fifty Years of Humanitarian Action*, Oxford: Oxford University Press, 2000.

16. Anthony Giddens, *The Third Way: The Renewal of Social Democracy*, Cambridge: Polity Press, 1998, p. 28.

17. See John Tomlinson, *Globalization and Culture*, Cambridge: Polity Press, 1999.

18. Malcolm Waters, *Globalization*, London: Routledge, 1995, p. 3.

19. Anthony Giddens, *Runaway World: How Globalisation is Reshaping Our Lives*, London: Profile Books, 2002, pp. xix–xx.

20. See generally Pendleton, 'A New Human Right', pp. 2055–68.

21. Giddens, *Runaway World*, p. 17.

22. Waters, *Globalization*, p. 12. See also Hernanando de Soto, *The Mystery of Capital: Why Capitalism Triumphs in the West and Fails Everywhere Else*, London: Black Swan, 2001.

23. Giddens, *Runaway World*, p. 12.

24. Ibid., p. 12.

25. Francis Fukuyama, *The End of History and the Last Man*, New York: Free Press, 1992, p. 8.

26. Ibid.

27. See Pendleton, 'A New Human Right', p. 2054, where he explains that the expansion takes the forms of trade, investment, culture, citizen affinities, law etc.

28. Ulrich Beck, *World Risk Society*, Cambridge: Polity Press, 1999, p. 6.

29. Ibid.

30. Ibid.

31. The terms 'South–North' and 'developing–developed' are used interchangeably unless otherwise stated; the 'North' is also understood as encompassing the 'West'.

32. Consider the Brussels negotiations on global warming of 2000, where John Prescott, Britain's deputy prime minister, stormed out of the conference because he could not agree with other ministers, and even less so with the USA, which was adamant that it would not reduce its greenhouse gas emissions.

33. See 'Preface' to Waters, *Globalization*.

34. Ibid., p. 19.

35. Ibid., p. 20.

36. Ibid., p. 20.

37. Ibid., p. 7.

38. See, generally, Mahmood Mandani, *Citizen and Subject: Contemporary Africa and the Legacy of Late Colonialism,* Kampala: Fountain Publishers, 1996.

39. See for instance the New Partnership for Africa's Development (NEPAD) Document, 2001.

40. Giddens, *Runaway World*.

41. Cited in James Mutethia, 'Africa and Globalization', *Nigeria Guardian*, 15 August 2000, p. 1.

42. This has paved the way for the TNCs, which in turn exploit resources in these countries. Thus globalizing forces become a source of corruption. What they give back to the state is usually minimal, in terms of employment, construction of schools for the workers' children, health care services.

43. On the discourse on human rights and human wrongs, see Nicholas Owen (ed.), *Human Rights, Human Wrongs: The Oxford Amnesty Lectures 2001*, Oxford: Oxford University Press, 2003.

44. See Pendleton, 'A New Human Right', p. 2055. See also H. Adelman,

'Modernity, Globalization, Refugees and Displacement', in A. Ager (ed.), *Refugees: Perspectives on the Experience of Forced Migration,* London: Cassell, 1999, pp. 83–110. Adelman contends that refugees are a product of modernity. Hence globalization, in my view, becomes a central theme in the discourse about the twenty-first century.

45. For example, Monsanto in Kenya monopolized the production and the supply of genetically modified (GM) seeds, effectively destroying the Kenyan farmer and in turn creating a dependency on GM crops and the West. This effectively disables the state from sustaining its agricultural resources and therefore itself.

46. See *Connelly* v. *RTZ Corporation plc* (H.L), 3 WLR 373 (1997).

47. See the House of Lords decision in *Shalk Willem Burger Lubbe* v. *Cape plc* 2 Lloyds Reports 383 (2000).

48. See Sunday Dare, 'A Continent in Crisis: Africa and Globalization', *Dollars and Sense Magazine,* July/August 2001, p. 1.

49. Ibid., p. 2.

50. Ibid.

51. Ibid.

52. See Metethia, 'Africa and Globalization', p. 3, which describes how the IMF/World Bank asked of Zimbabwe, as a condition of lending, that among other things it 'privatize state owned factories and mines' while at the same time trying to prohibit it from redistributing land to the landless blacks.

53. Although African states too were involved in the DRC, this is exactly what globalization has done to other countries, to belittle them by protecting corporate interests.

54. Dare, 'A Continent in Crisis', p. 2.

55. See Dare, 'A Continent in Crisis'.

56. Ulrich Beck, *What is Globalization?,* Polity Press: Cambridge, 1999, p. 2. See also Beck, *World Risk Society.*

57. See the implications of the decisions in the banana case for the economies of the African, Caribbean and Pacific (ACP) states. See also the Lomé IV & Lomé B Convention (GSP), www.tradetnt.com/miniti/tragtslome.htm.

58. See Dare, 'A Continent in Crisis', p. 3.

59. See Ken Wiwa, *In the Shadow of a Saint: A Son's Journey to Understand His Father's Legacy,* London: Black Swan, 2001.

60. Dare, 'A Continent in Crisis', p. 4.

61. Ibid.

62. Ibid.

63. UN Office for the Coordination of Humanitarian Affairs (OCHA), *Guiding Principles on Internal Displacement,* 1999.

64. Dare, 'A Continent in Crisis', p. 4.

65. UNHCR, *The State of the World's Refugees: Fifty Years of Humanitarian Action,* Oxford: Oxford University Press, 2000, p. 301.

66. Pendleton, 'A New Human Right', p. 2055. See also Samuel Makinda, 'Sovereignty and International Security: Challenges for the United Nations', *Global Governance*, vol. 149, no. 155, 1996.

67. The term 'developing country' is employed here for various reasons. Some 99 percent of the refugee population today is from developing countries, two-thirds from Africa. Resettlement, one durable solution for refugees is sought in the Western countries although tougher asylum laws counter it.

68. Adelman, 'Modernity, Globalization, Refugees and Displacement'.

69. Africa alone has over 12 million refugees.

70. Pendleton, 'A New Human Right', p. 2094.

71. This inequality found expression in the riots in Seattle and Genoa against the WTO, and subsequent demonstrations against the World Bank and IMF.

72. See Philip Rudge, 'Corporate Social Responsibility and Refugee Protection', Oxford seminar at QEH, November 2000. See also UNHCR's Global Appeal report at www.unhcr.ch.

73. De Jong, 'The Legal Framework: The Convention Relating to the Status of Refugees and the Development of the Law Half a Century Later', *IJRL*, vol. 10, no. 4, 1998: 688–99. He notes that in the Netherlands the process is so expensive that it has forced the government to increase taxes, producing an outcry from taxpayers.

74. Waters, *Globalization*, p. 27.

75. See Kenichi Ohmae, *The End of the Nation State: The Rise of Regional Economies*, London: HarperCollins, 1995.

76. See, for instance, the detailed discussion of this issue in Ekuru Aukot, 'It is Better to be a Refugee than a Turkana in Kakuma: Revisiting the Relationship between the Hosts and Refugees in Kenya', *Refuge*, May 2003.

77. See Dare, 'A Continent in Crisis', p. 3.

78. See Article 1 of both the 51 Convention and the OAU Convention.

79. Paragraph 20 of Agenda 3 (1) of the 'Note on International Protection'; www.unhcr.ch.

80. Adelman, 'Modernity, Globalization, Refugees and Displacement', p. 97.

81. See James C. Hathaway, (ed.), *Reconceiving International Refugee Law*, The Hague: Martinus Nijhoff, 1997.

82. 142 ALR 331 (1997).

83. Article 1 (2), 51 Convention.

84. See 1950 European Convention on Human Rights and Fundamental Freedoms, *ETS*, No. 5; in force 3 September 1953.

85. Marion's case, 175 CLR 218 (1992), at 266.

86. See Nigel Harris, *The New Untouchables: Immigration and the New World Order,* London: I.B. Tauris, 1995, p. 119.

87. Pendleton, 'A New Human Right'.

88. Adelman, 'Modernity, Globalization, Refugees and Displacement', p. 83.

89. Ibid., p. 90.

90. See Philip Gourveritch, *We Wish to Inform You that Tomorrow We Will Be Killed With Our Families: Stories from Rwanda*, London: Picador, 1999.

91. Adelman, 'Modernity, Globalization, Refugees and Displacement', p. 93.

92. See C. De Jong, 'The Legal Framework: The Convention Relating to the Status of Refugees and the Development of Law Half a Century Later, *IJRL*, vol. 10, no. 4, 1998: 688–99, 691.

93. Ibid., p. 691. Consider the case of the fifty-eight Chinese who suffocated, trapped in the back of a lorry, while illegally attempting to enter Britain. See 'Deaths Highlight Contradiction at the Heart of Geneva Convention: Refugees in Britain Special Report', *Guardian*, 20 June 2000.

94. De Jong, 'The Legal Framework', p. 694.

95. The camps are discussed in Ekuru Aukot, 'Is UNHCR Still Humanitarian? Implications of Refugee Camps in a Developing Country', working paper.

96. US Committee for Refugees, *World Refugee Survey*, 1996.

97. See L. Malkki, *Purity and Exile: Violence, Memory and National Cosmology among Hutu Refugees in Tanzania*, Chicago: University of Chicago Press, 1995.

98. For details, see A. Arulanantham, 'Restructured Safe Havens: A Proposal for the Reform of the Refugee Protection Regime', *Human Rights Quarterly: A Comparative and International Journal of the Social Sciences, Humanities, and Law*, vol. 22, no. 1, February 2000.

99. Beck, in *World Risk Society*, warns of the 'boomerang effect'. He reports how a team of scientists discovered high concentrations of DDT in the blood of penguins in Antarctica. The world cannot be considered safe. Another example is the rise of global warming faced by all on the globe and not just Africa, Europe or Asia. Britain experienced severe flooding in 2000 and the finger pointed to global warming. In 2001, it was the turn of Germany, Prague and most parts of central Europe to be affected by serious flooding. This is bound to trigger action.

100. See Ekuru Aukot, 'Arrest the Gun Market, and the Bullet Factory: The Quest for Solutions by Victims of Refugeeism in Africa', working paper.

101. In a study conducted by the Center for International Development and conflict management, University of Maryland, it was found that out of the 33 countries in the world with high risk of instability, 20 are in Africa.

102. Adelman, 'Modernity, Globalization, Refugees and Displacement'.

103. One cause of refugeeism is, of course, bad government. Many of the reasons for flight listed in the convention result from the actions of

undemocratic regimes. See, for example, UNHCR's country-of-origin information, www.unhcr.ch.

104. Some TNCs have independently shown goodwill. For example, Ericsson aided the evacuation of refugees from Kosovo by providing mobiles to ease communication and coordination when telephone services were destroyed.

105. See Dare, 'A Continent in Crisis'. See also de Soto, *The Mystery of Capital*.

About the Contributors

Ekuru Aukot is a doctoral candidate in law at the University of Warwick, and a co-founding director of the Northern Frontier Districts Centre for Human Rights and Research (NFD–CHR). His articles have been published in *Refuge, Recht in Afrika/Law in Africa, East African Journal on Human Rights and Democracy,* and *University of Nairobi Law Journal.* His current research focuses on the localization of international refugee law.

Elísio Macamo is the Chair of Development Sociology at the University of Bayreuth, and a guest lecturer in the Faculty of Letters and Social Sciences at Eduardo Mondlane University, Maputo. He is author of *A leitura sociólogica – Um manual introdutório* (Imprensa Universitária, 2004) and coeditor, with Lars Clausen and Elke Geenen, of *Entsetzliche soziale Prozesse. Theoretische und empirische Annährungen* (Lit Verlag, 2003); and, with Yehuda Elkana, Ivan Krastev and Shalini Randeria, of *Unraveling Ties: From Social Cohesion to New Practices of Connectedness* (Campus, 2002). His current research is on local perceptions of disaster in Mozambique.

Inês Macamo Raimundo is a lecturer in social geography at the Faculty of Letters and Social Sciences of Eduardo Mondlane University. She co-edited, with Manuel Araújo, *A evolução da história da geografia* (Imprensa Universitária, 2002). Her current research focuses on the dynamics of internal migration in Mozambique.

Francis Njubi Nesbitt is Assistant Professor of Africana Studies at San Diego State University. He is the author of *Race for Sanctions: African Americans against Apartheid, 1946–1994* (Indiana University Press, 2004). His articles have been published in journals such as *African Issues*, *Critical Arts: Journal of South–North Cultural Studies*, *Africa World Review* and *Mots Pluriels*.

Jalani A. Niaah is at the Institute of Caribbean Studies, University of the West Indies, Mona.

Samwel Ong'wen Okuro is assistant lecturer in the Department of History, Maseno University, Kenya, where he also teaches economic history. Currently, he is a Ph.D. candidate at Maseno University studying HIV/Aids and land rights. He is also a committee member of the Historical Association of Kenya. He has publications in internationally refereed journals.

Alda Romão Saúte lectures in history at the Faculty of History at the Pedagogic University of Maputo. Her research interests include missions, education, democracy and governance, and sexual and reproductive health. She is author of *A Escola de Habilitação de Professores Indígenas 'José Cabral', Manhiça-Alvor (1926–1974)* (2004), as well as articles published in *Portuguese Studies Review* and *Afrobarometer Working Paper*. Her doctoral dissertation, 'The African–Mission Encounter and Education in Mozambique: The Anglican Mission of Santo Agostinho – Maciene, 1926/8–1974', is published as an ebook by Promédia (2004).

Cassandra R. Veney is an assistant professor in the departments of Women's Studies and African and African-American Studies at the Pennsylvania State University. She is coeditor of *Women in Scholarly Publishing* (Africa World Press, 2001) and *Leisure in Urban Africa* (Africa World Press, 2003). Her research focuses on refugees in East Africa, human rights issues, and Africa's relations with Asia and the United States. She has published journal articles and book chapters on refugees and the internally displaced in Kenya and Tanzania.

Index